C0-APQ-235

Life
as a

Mountain Man's Wife

Fae-th Davidson

A journal of tales gathered to
share and celebrate together
the creative majesty of
Almighty God
that shines through His gift of
often comical,
sometimes confounding,
sometimes sentimental
but never boring
Life
to this
Mountain Man and Wife

www.Davidson-Publishing.com
info@Davidson-Publishing.com

Life as a Mountain Man's Wife
©2015 Davidson Publishing
All rights reserved

1st Printing
June 18, 2015
ISBN 978-0-9655322-3-5

Biblical Scripture references are quoted from the following:
Complete Jewish Bible (CJB)
©1998 Translated by David H. Stern
Messianic Jewish Publishers

Messianic Jewish Shared Heritage Bible (MJSHB)
©2012 The Messianic Jewish Family Bible Project
Destiny Image Publishers, Inc.

NIV Archaeological Study Bible (NIV)
©2005 The Zondervan Corporation
Scripture is taken from the
Holy Bible, New International Version of the
International Bible Society by permission to Zondervan

Uses of the Hebrew name, *Yeshua*, are in reference to
Yeshua HaMashiach (Jesus the Messiah).

Uses of the Hebrew name *Adonai* are in reference to
God as Lord of our lives.

All photos were taken by the herein referenced
Mountain Man and Wife
unless credit is given to another source.

Where The Tales Are

in **Life as a Mountain Man's Wife**

It's All About Him	1
What A Ride!	9
Way Up There	11
"Sir, I Promise I'll Do Her No Wrong"	17
Prophetic Marriage Preparations	21
"Yep! I Will!"	27
West Meets South	29
Education & Revelation	35
Skunk Cookies	39
"Father, Thank You For My Wife"	43
Light Table Illuminations	45
Full Circles	47
Sa-where?	51
"Don't Open the Freezer"	55
That Bible Totin' Trapper	57
Captured Coon's Life Lesson	61
A Way Out	63
Most Excellent Festus	67

The Sacrificial Rabbit 71

Whatever Suits Him 73

They Call Me "Cookie" 77

"Not What I Expected" 81

Pullin' Horses Offa Shoes 85

"I Feel Like A Fish" 89

"I'll Be Darned" 93

Praise, Pelts and...PRIORITIES 95

Cute Little Sophia 99

Bridger's Salvation 101

Frozen Pedal To The Metal Of The Freezer 107

Farewell Most Excellent Festus 111

Alive In the Outback 115

Mountain Man Hot Air 123

The Renegade Crew Of Delta Air Lines 125

Wintertime Porcupine 131

The Al & The Owl In The Fireplace 135

The Catacomb Tomb Of Mephitidae Mephitis 139

Oh My Darlin' Clementine 145

Bridger Goes To Rendezvous 149

Chirp Bark 153

Shall We Gather At The River 155

The Ghost Of Carbon Peak 159

Fire On The Mountain 163

Beaver Slide 169

Trapper's Rules of Order   173

PR Predicaments   179

Lace For The Game Wardens   183

Emergency!   185

A Sunday Of Unrest   189

Bats, Bovines, Birdies & Brownies   191

Bridger's 70th Birthday   194

Mountain Man and Wife *Journey To The Land*   195
  Journey To The Land Overview   197
  Mountain Man and Wife In *Egypt*   200
    Oh My Goshen!   201
    Back In The Saddle Again   205
    Modern Day Mountain Man Moses   207
  Mountain Man and Wife In *Jordan*   210
    Back In A More Familiar Saddle 211
    Peering Into The Land   213
  Mountain Man and Wife In *Eretz Y'israel*   215
    Into The Land   217
    Most Excellent Festus' House   219
    Mountain Man On Military Maneuvers 221
    Up To The Mountain Of The Lord 225
    What's In A Name   227
    On The Road On Our Own In The Land 229
    Mountain Man Watchman   233
    Bassets In The Land   237
    Land Mines Would Ruin The Land's Ruins 239
    Trapper's "Steps"   241
    Dancing, Fishing, Faith & Gratitude 245
      on Kinneret
    Painting With A Jewish Carpenter 247
    Prolific Profound Protection In The Land 249
    Sodom Shofar Sounding   253
    The Pathfinder's Pathfinder   257
    Mountain Man Who Kids The Kids 259
    Wildlife Management In The Land 261
    Half A Shekel For Schaffer   263

Mountain Man and Wife Back Into Our   269
  Rocky Mountain Life

Hebraic and Other Heritage Roots   271

The Whole Time   275

Afterwords

Encouragement To Tell The Tales
The Adventure of Simple Patience by Trapper Davidson
Faithful Friend At My Feet
Fae-th In My Pen Name
Learned Lessons & Literary License
The Tales & Tails Continue
L'Chaim! – To Life!

Maps

Crested Butte, Colorado	5
Middle East	196
Egypt	200
Jordan	210
Israel	215

Cover Artwork

Journal Cover

Photographed from the original leather journal cover handmade by the author – will be on display at book signings, speaking engagements and other events.

Mountain Man and Wife Line Drawing
by Laine Dobson
www.lainedobson.com

We first met Laine as a trapper when he was 16 years old growing up in Monte Vista, Colorado. We were immediately impressed with what a fine young man he was and then soon discovered his artistic talent. His emphasis is on watercolors that feature his trademark of incorporating a Scripture reference hidden somewhere in every painting.

We enjoyed encouraging Laine as he earned his Art degree from Western State University in Gunnison, Colorado where he met his future wife, Tamara. We then had the pleasure of attending their wedding in Gunnison. At the time of the publication of this book he is 31 and they have a young daughter and son.

So, in keeping with our many patterns of *Full Circles* as you'll discover in one of the upcoming stories, it was a perfect addition to the design of this book to commission Laine to draw a *Mountain Man and Wife* for the cover. He used the photo in *What A Ride!* as a pose of us in addition to his own recollection of our individual appearances.

Life
as a

Mountain
Man's
Wife

The Day We Became Trapper & Fae
June 18, 1994

It's All About Him

Did ya think the Him here was referring to my husband the Mountain Man as the title implies? Well, nope.

Instead, it's up there to draw attention to the Him who gave us these *Mountain Man and Wife* stories in the first place – Almighty God – the Creator of all and so the TRUE creator of these tales. I've been recording them for years so it is time to publish a journal of them.

The date of June 18, 2015 was chosen for the publication of this journal because of its significance as the 21st anniversary of the marriage of this *Mountain Man and Wife* in Crested Butte, Colorado. Since 21 is recognized as a date of maturity in life, we believe that the ride we are sharing together has reached a certain level of maturity in both humorous and serious things.

One of those maturity progressions has been away from the *it's all about me* perspective on life. What has helped us get there is my husband's blessed and genuine desire to ask other people about themselves first before sharing about himself or our lives. Throughout our marriage he has been continually teaching me by example how intriguing this practice is, what a blessing being authentic about it is to others and then, by golly, we too wind up being blessed by finding out the most interesting things about people and their lives!

Sometimes we get weary in situations or involved in endeavors that cause us to focus on ourselves first and that's just, well – *Life*. But nowadays even those times are often because we need to put some part of our own house in order so that we can be more together in our interactions with others – whether people or animals.

So, because of our genuine desire to move forward in life in this practice of others first, it was initially with a *Mountain* of trepidation that I gave consideration to what is now the title of this book –

Life as a Mountain Man's Wife

However, since I believe it was TRULY the Lord who kept bringing this title to mind, I've stuck with His lead. That's partly because He continues to shower us with such an abundance of comical and sentimental material that we both feel it is His calling for me to share it with you for His glory and your enjoyment.

Honestly – these stories ARE NOT about me or my Mountain Man husband with the intention of exalting either one of us. In fact, although use of the word "I" is unavoidable in this setting, multiple editing reads have been done to take the word out whenever it seemed possible. If some were missed that are not absolutely necessary, those are most assuredly unintentional oversights.

Instead, these stories ARE about both of us with the intention of answering God's call as a creative way to exalt HIM – the Him who put two *profoundly mismatched* people together on purpose and then the multiple, comical, sentimental and challenging ways He has given us to operate in the bold commitment we made to our marriage – for Life – plus the story-producing experiences we have encountered while jointly operating our wildlife management services business. While doing that we look to Him for ways to encourage each other in a marriage growing daily more and more based on His leading – an amazing, nowadays mostly joyful, never-ending process of maturing that is sure to involve the rest of our days as Mountain Man and Wife.

We constantly experience His unbounded creativity in ways you are about to discover. These stories are NOT TALL TALES although there may be moments when you will wonder how such a development in them could have transpired. Instead they are TRUE TALES, each and every one of them, and you have my written word and Fae-thful promise that these things have all absolutely happened and have not been conjured up from fiction to embellish the truth. Besides, with such realities in our lives why in the world would we imagine any need to embellish them???!!!

These stories TRULY are not worth telling without including Almighty God's part in them – either implied or by His outright display of Himself in the tales. If you did not already know it, God has an outrageous sense of humor which you will find in abundant display on the pages to come. As if to emphasize

that fact, the physical composition of Basset Hounds plus His placing of them so prominently as companions in this Life as a Mountain Man's Wife is one such exhibition of the precious and loving comedy that God finds in His creation. And then there are the many other critters – both domestic and wild.

2

We imagine that you folks reading these stories have your own twists and turns in life – both expected and unexpected.

You do have those – right?

By drawing you into these stories this *Mountain Man and Wife* hope to elicit some good laughs, draw out some sentimental sighs of "Awww" here and there or maybe even cause you to shed a few mushy tears.

In the process you could easily discover ideas of creative ways to view and deal with your own life's moments – even the difficult ones – as adventurous possibilities rather than inconvenient drudgeries.

Perspective truly is monumental

Sometimes we all need to step back and reflect on various situations and get that different, mountaintop vantage point perspective on them in order to find resolution or find a more positive way to handle whatever it is that is going on. This book is meant to encourage that approach to life. We'll be needing to remember to continue doing that along with you.

Where Many of the Stories Have Happened

Most of our animal related stories have taken place in the Crested Butte/Gunnison area on the Western Slope of Colorado.

Winter approach to the Town of Crested Butte as we were coming home one very snowy day

Fall view from above Town of Mount Crested Butte
Photo taken on author's Hot Air Balloon flight five days prior to departure on our
Journey To The Land
Our home at the time was the last house on the far right in the middle of the picture.

Getting to Crested Butte
©1998-2004 VisitCrestedButte.com
All rights reserved

Some of the tales have happened during times when our business and personal travels have taken us out of Crested Butte and even out ofthe Gunnison Valley – like the time we took the photo featured a couple of pages back of Rudi Reservoir over near Aspen while we were there for a critter job someone had contracted with us to handle.

And then there's Israel. But, as you'll soon read, we'll get there.

Some of these stories were not necessarily funny at the time they occurred, although the majority of them were even then and now we have learned how to spot them right off as they happen. My husband has frequently said to others sharing a particularly memorable animal situation in the course of our business, "You better be careful what you say right now. My wife writes stories about this kinda stuff."

Thankfully the Lord has given us His perspective on such moments and He gave me the ability and desire to write about them with humor and a sentimental heart – both of which are extremely valuable coping mechanisms that my Mountain Man husband and I heartily encourage you to embrace as you read here.

You'll find some mangled grammar here – some incomplete sentences, made-up words, prepositions at the ends of sentences or thoughts, conversational style and more. Please simply enjoy it all with us and do your best to avoid letting some literary license concern you.

I know it's not proper grammar in those places. My writing training is extensive and excellent so I KNOW BETTER than some of this writing and do not wish to commit journalistic heresy without some sort of acknowledgement of proper writing techniques.

But, it's done that way for effect, definitely on purpose and not because I forgot the fine teaching of my youth.

Please see *Learned Lessons & Literary License* at the back of the book regarding the outstanding resources of that training and why I feel okay about breaking some traditional rules about that. But then, breaking traditional rules about life is part of what this *Life as a Mountain Man's Wife* is all about so at least my writing is consistent with our lifestyle.

Speaking of training, here's some from my Mountain Man that we think will enhance the meaning of the purpose for journaling the stories that you are about to read:

Mountain Man Tinder Box

The brass box keeps the enclosed char cloth dry.

A tipi-type pile of very small dry twigs is prepared and ready for the char cloth to be added to them.

Then the Mountain Man holds the char cloth in one hand and the brass encased magnifying glass part of the Tinder Box in the other so that the rays of the sun are magnified onto the char cloth until a spark ignites.

Next he *nourishes* the embers by *gently* blowing on the char cloth because *blowing too hard will blow out the beginning fire.*

Once going, the burning char cloth is *gently* placed with the pile of twigs.

After the twigs ignite, small dry sticks are placed on top of the twigs. The size of the sticks should increase as the fire grows larger.

In this fire starting and in these pages, the Mountain Man life lesson is this...

It takes patience in the preparation
to start anything worthwhile in Life.

Many of you are customers who have asked us if you or your animal situations are featured in here.

Well, you're just going to have to read the book to find out!

While trying to finish this collection Trapper, other folks and I have all continued to recall more stories from our *Mountain Man and Wife* times together plus I'm sure Trapper, the Lord, the animals and other people will continue to provide much new fodder for future stories.

So there is a fair amount of potential for a sequel book of *Mountain Man and Wife* tales to be forthcoming.

Time and circumstances will tell. I'm counting on you family, friends and customers out there to remind us of any stores not in here that you recall. You know who you are and what you've experienced connected to our tales.

To all – those of you we already know, those of you we have not yet met and those of you we may never meet – I'm also relatively certain that many of these stories will ring some sort of similar bell in your own lives.

So this will be a place to commiserate and laugh and know that if you in the past, present or future find that you're in any of these same kinda predicaments, you're not the only one! If no such bell goes off for you, please just sit back and laugh or cry – whichever strikes your fancy.

We have seen God's hand over and over operating in this approach to the life through which He is leading us. You'll see what I mean as you read on.

So many times He has prepared us for something forthcoming but we had no idea at the time that it was preparation for anything. Other times it has been more obvious what His plan was.

It is up to all of us to faithfully choose to follow the plan as He reveals each part of it. When that happens then the most wonderful things happen!
...I have presented you with life and death, the blessing and the curse. Therefore, choose life, so that you will live, you and your descendants, loving Adonai your God, paying attention to what he says and clinging to him – for that is the purpose of your life!
– Deuteronomy 30:19-20 (CJB)

And so the purpose of this book is for the purposes He has for it.

The stories are not in chronological order of when they took place but instead are placed where they are by their topic and the way the narrative flows best to the next story.

Most of the photos turned out pretty good in here. A few are not the best but that's okay – didn't know they were going to be published at the time many of them were taken.

You won't find a lot of names of the participants of these stories in order to focus on the situation at hand. A few are there for various reasons.

To all of you who have been parts of these stories – thanks for your part in these *Mountain Man and Wife* memories! We hope you find yourselves in here.

So, herein we'll be taking a gander at the tales of

Life as a Mountain Man's Wife

as char cloth in the *Mountain Man Tinder Box* which we hope will ignite a blazing fire of gratitude for the infinite creativity and *Shekinah* glory of the Master Storyteller since He is the true author, initiator and perfector of not only our faith but also these stories.

...focusing on Yeshua, the initiator and perfector of faith.
– Hebrews 12:2 (MJSHB)

May the flames of that fire be gently, comically and sentimentally nourished into inspiration in the hearts and minds of all who read here to seek Him for His plan for *Life* because His is the best plan of all – even if it seems at first that it makes no sense.

On our 15th Wedding Anniversary – June 18, 2009 – I gave Trapper this sign that I had been saving for him that says:

The Best Story
IS THE ONE WE WRITE TOGETHER

You'll soon find out how significant sign is in our stories. So this gift was given as a sign of the gratitude I feel toward God and my Mountain Man for their collaboration TOGETHER to encourage the writing of them and the day when the publication of this journal would happen.

That day has finally arrived.

So yippee! Let's head down that trail TOGETHER...*What A Ride!*

What A Ride!

I never expected to be a trapper's wife. The notion had never ever crossed my mind. Becoming a *Mountain Man's Wife* had entered my thoughts – but more in the modern day sense. There is even a written record of that thought in a poem I wrote in third person for an event on June 1, 1997:

> *Here's another chuckle we'd like to share –*
> *Just before she met Trapper, Fae had a plan.*
> *She made a list to God of her desires –*
> *Of the attributes she desired in a man.*
>
> *Now on that list she'd put "Mountain Man"*
> *She MEANT someone who'd enjoy the mountains a lot.*
> *God answered her request with such magnificent jest*
> *'Cause oh my goodness, look what she got!*

Two days into
our marriage

When I met my Mountain Man trapper I didn't even know trappers still existed. I met him at a church dinner on October 31,1992 and everybody there was callin' this fella "Trapper". Somehow we got to talkin' and a friendship with Trapper, Al Davidson, started.

My goodness – did it ever! A year and a half later we were married! For *Life*! Me *as a Mountain Man's Wife*! Not only that but we have lived it right in the middle of the Rocky Mountains and that too thrills my Mountain Man loving heart – a dream of mountain living since I was 12 years old.

When we married I did not fully comprehend what I had committed myself to (does anyone?). I am certain of a few things – that I will continue to find that out for the rest of our lives together plus it's gonna continue to be a life full of surprises, smells...and messes (right ladies who are married to outdoorsmen?...and tons more comical adventures.

The first time I went along on the trap line with my new trapper friend was in June of 1993. We were on horseback at the base of *The Castles* in the West Elk Wilderness near Gunnison, Colorado.

I did not know it was a test.

Fall time view of *The Castles*

Trapper had captured two beaver that day. They had dammed up the rancher's irrigation ditch and water was not properly moving into his pasture. Being considerate of my potential sensibilities, Trapper skillfully put each beaver head first into each of his saddle bags on the back of his horse and courteously put his duster (cowboy raincoat) over them for my benefit.

Naturally Trapper was the one who knew the trail so it was his job to lead us out. It was a rocky trail and, little by little, the duster shifted on the back of his horse such that these rather sizable beaver hind paws began to emerge out from under the duster. That hand coming up out of the water at the end of the *Deliverance* movie comes to mind – to give you some visual idea of what I was seeing. Trapper is a proficient observer and so, on horseback in front of me, he saw exactly what was happening out of the corner of his eye but didn't mention it (in true Trapper style) and, unbeknownst to me, made an important decision as we rode along for eight miles amongst the aspens and back to the trailhead. The way he puts it, "I decided right then and there that I was gonna ask this gal to marry me 'cause she didn't go squeamish on me."

I had no idea this was headed for marriage. I was just out there for a beautiful horseback ride in the Rocky Mountains with a new friend. I blissfully rode along behind, not even remotely imagining that *marriage* was going through this Mountain Man's mind!

Later I took this photo of Trapper on Rose – his mare that I had tried to unshoe (see *Pullin' Horses Offa Shoes*) and that he allowed me to ride this day while he rode Blue – his mustang that you'll meet in *They Call Me "Cookie"*.

And so *Life as a Mountain Man's Wife* was conceived, at the moment so far only in Trapper's imagination – what has turned out to be a life-long ride which began at a place *Way Up There*.

10

Way Up There

At 38 years old a lot of complications in my life over the last few years had taken away my latter 20s plus most of my 30s as well as what I figured was any real option of having a home, husband and family of my own. I had not made time for that, was regretting the multitude of choices that had caused that predicament, now was profoundly ready for all of it, had no idea how it was going to happen but – for the first time in my life – was thoroughly convinced that God had a plan to see to these rather sizeable desires which I also believe He had led me to desire at this particular time.

By 1992 I had spent the previous 20 years of my life "a might confused" as the Mountain Men are known to say. Since age 18 I had been running from traditional church making a grand mess of my life in the process – especially during the previous 12 years in Boulder, Colorado.

On March 9, 1992 I experienced an unanticipated awakening to the Lord while on the phone with my life-long friend, Kim (Thompson) Arnold. I was in a basement apartment in Boulder and she was in her married-life home in Athens, Georgia where we had grown up together and been friends since Kindergarten.

As a result, about a month later God led me to back up the horse and return to my roots (see *Hebraic and Other Heritage Roots* toward the end of this book) because He knew that was best before taking me to my future life. So with both apprehension and anticipation, I drove from Colorado to my hometown of Athens where extremely valuable time and experiences went into nurturing me in my new-found relationship with the Lord as well as reconciling various things with family and friends there.

Although at first it had seemed like going 1500 miles in the wrong direction since my desire by then was to live on the Western Slope of Colorado, it was absolutely the right thing to do for a multitude of reasons and I will remain grateful for the rest of my life that the Lord led me to such a place of obedience in doing it.

Six months later, on October 26, 1992 the day came for me to return to Colorado. I had already said goodbye to my family and was having a farewell lunch with Kim in downtown Athens when out of my mouth came a most unexpected statement: "By Sunday I'll be in my new church home." We both knew it was the first time in my life I had expressed a desire for a church home on my own volition (although I was raised in the church in Athens, Georgia) and also that I had no idea where I was going when I drove away that day – other than that it was located in the western half of Colorado where I knew absolutely no one.

In confirmation of the faith in which I was finally walking – well driving, as it turned out – as I came into Denver at sundown 2 days later I prayed out loud, "Father, I know you have SOMEONE and A PLACE for me Way Up There" and pointed to the top of the Continental Divide meaning the other side of all of those mountain tops up there – what is called the Western Slope.

I left Denver before sun-up the next morning and wound up in Montrose over in Western Colorado that night. The next morning I opened up the big Rand McNally map book to the Colorado page and asked my Navigator, "Where am I going?"

My eyes fell on Crested Butte. That seemed preposterous to me. Although I had never been there before, I knew of it as a ski town which meant to me an expensive cost of living and a transient ski bum mentality. How in God's name (respectfully spoken) was I going to find a REAL and stable life in a ski area???

Made no sense.

But, since I sensed without a doubt that the Holy Spirit was so clearly leading me by the nose throughout this whole expedition of finding a home, I obediently headed for...Crested Butte. At the Gunnison intersection ready to turn off of Highway 50 and onto Highway 135 for the 28 mile trek to Crested Butte, I asked (to be honest – more like argued) again, "Are you sure it's not Gunnison? At least it's a regular town!" All I got back was an emphatic pounding of "CRESTED BUTTE...CRESTED BUTTE...CRESTED BUTTE."

Okay...drove to Crested Butte, turned to my dog as we drove past the Historic District sign at the entrance to town and professed as a total act of faith, "Tabor, we're home". Even while saying it I was thinking, "How's this gonna work???" One thing I knew – or thought I knew – from my years of living in Colorado: a ski resort town is no place to find a real and stable life.

After a quick turn around town to somewhat scope it out and a stop for lunch at Paradise Cafe on Elk Avenue, I finally felt what I had been waiting to feel about "I'll know when I get there" but I just couldn't see my way clear to how this was gonna work...still made no sense. So I drove back down to Gunnison for the night.

The next morning was October 31, 1992. The Lord emphatically enticed me to drive back up Highway 135 to Crested Butte and find Oh-Be-Joyful Church. Obedience in the midst of mystery was becoming a theme in my life.

I was down to $16.00 in my pocket and nothing else in the bank – truly proof positive that this search for my new life was operating solely on faith in the Lord's leading and provision.

I quickly found the church – Crested Butte is not very big. It was a little bluish gray house with darker blue trim...didn't look like a church at all and that was pretty darn attractive to me in my non-denominational frame of mind. But then I looked closer at the letters on the Maroon Avenue side of the church... "Oh-Be-Joyful BAPTIST Church" it proclaimed. What??? For some unknown reason I looked at the area phone book I had picked up – don't know why since I was already there in the parking lot. Anyway, there it was listed under SOUTHERN Baptist Churches. What in the world was a SOUTHERN Baptist church doing in the middle of the WESTERN Rocky Mountains???!!!

In a fit of backsliding and negative stereotyping, I put my hand on the gearshift to back out. Ya know how we tell our dogs to "STAY" when we want them to stay put. Well, it was like that when I sensed God outright COMMANDING me to "STAY" just like I would my dog sitting there on the front seat. I was to take my hand offa that gearshift.

One vehicle was parked on my left. Again obedience reigned and I went looking for the owner of that vehicle. No one was inside downstairs so I climbed the west end exterior stairs. Inside, lo and behold, there was the pastor – Jim Kunes. As the Lord had arranged on this particular Saturday with snow already on the ground, my recollection is that Jim was involved with trying to finish building his house before winter set in more and so he had run into town to the church for just a few minutes to pick up something there. I told him my story of the last 6 months and afterwards he did two vital things.

First he picked up the phone and called a couple of single gals to arrange safe shelter – their couch in the living room in an old house that still to this day has a sign out front: "The Last Homely House".

His next action would turn out to be a life changer...for a bunch more folks besides just me: "It's Halloween and we're having a dinner here tonight at 6:30. You could come, meet the families of the church and see whatcha think. Besides, it's a free meal." I had told him of my precious few dollars left so he knew just how much I needed a free meal at that point. I gratefully accepted and headed out to find "The Last Homely House" in Crested Butte.

On the way down Elk Avenue I happened to spot a pay phone on the outside wall of the Post Office. Had that phone not come into view right then, one of the richest moments of the next 24 hours would not have happened quite the same way. This is a 2015 photo of that same Post Office. There are still a couple of small holes on the outside wall where the phones were.

The previous day I had been encouraged by three separate sources to call a certain couple, Al and Laura Van Dyke, who I was told had just moved into a house at Danni Ranch a few miles south of Crested Butte. I sensed in my heart that I was supposed to call them RIGHT NOW on that pay phone. Oddly enough, especially considering my financial condition which I was guarding so closely, it didn't occur to me to wait until the church dinner that night as a possible time to meet them. I obediently yet reluctantly pulled out a very precious quarter, dropped it into that pay phone and dialed the number. I had no idea what to say to them.

Al Van Dyke answered the phone. At the time I was very shy about talking about the Lord after all of those years of rejecting His church. So I avoided that subject. "The Lord told me to call you" is the one thing that would have made sense to Al but I didn't know that yet. Instead I babbled away at him feeling completely ridiculous and incoherent. I said something about horses, needing a job (bear in mind that I was talking to an outfitter on the LAST day of elk hunting season but I didn't consider that) and wanting to meet him and his wife sometime. I hung up the phone wondering what that was all for, wearily leaned my forehead up against the Post Office wall and hoped I would NEVER meet this couple – the husband of which I had just unmercifully embarrassed myself to on the phone.

At 6:30 I showed up at the church for the dinner. When I walked in the pastor introduced me by name, Fae Epting, and shared that I was new in town. Standing right in front of me was this bearded fella who piped up with, "Didn't I talk to you on the phone today?" For all to see my faced turned so beet red that I could feel the heat as it rose upwards upon my face. Yep – Al Van Dyke. In total embarrassment I said, "You're probably still scratching your head over that one" to which I received a perplexed nod from him.

And there, standing right next to Al Van Dyke, was this other fella who worked for him as an outfitter guide whose name was also named Al – Al Davidson – but everyone called him "Trapper."

Somehow Trapper and I got to talkin' – an occurrence which I later found out surprised everyone else there 'cause it seems Trapper was not known for talking to a stranger so easily. We didn't know what was happening to us yet but one of the gals there sure did. She went home and wrote in her journal that night: "Trapper's found the gal for him."

14

In 1999 the church building was about to be moved down the highway to make room for a new building. On the day of the last service I asked someone take a photo of me where Trapper and I had sat on October 31, 1992, eaten our lasagna and shared our introductory conversation. Trapper could not be there that day in 1999 but I sure am glad the Lord made sure he was there the night we met in 1992.

Turns out too that when Al Van Dyke had hung up the phone from that incoherent telephone interlude with me that afternoon, he'd turned to his hand (none other than ol' Trapper) and had said, "I just had the strangest conversation with some gal on the phone."

So at that very moment, red face and all, I met my prayed-for future husband and my prayed-for church all at one time...only 5 days after proclaiming to Kim in Athens, Georgia: "By Sunday I'll be in my new church home" even though I didn't know where it was going to be, and only 3 days after praying out loud while driving into Denver, "Father, I know you've got SOMEONE and a place for me *Way Up There*." I'll never forget looking up into the mountains when I said that and oh how the Lord must have smiled at those expressions of faith that He had gifted me with enough to express them. Only he knew what was coming so very soon. I surely did not expect it all to be a package deal!

Little did we know then that the man I had babbled to on the phone would be the Best Man in our wedding about a year and a half later.

Most of the rest of the Van Dyke family were also in our wedding party. His wife sang and played her guitar plus their girls were two of our four flower girls simply because they asked me during the summer of 1993 if they could be flower girls in my wedding one day. This was months before Trapper and I knew we were going to marry the next summer. I guess they could see it coming too. Children can be so observant sometimes...that is — good at reading sign...don't ya think?

Our adorable flower girls in their pinafore dresses, straw hats and boots are: Hayden Van Dyke (7) and Cheyanne Van Dyke (6) from Crested Butte plus Grace Arnold (5 - Brooks & Kim Arnold's youngest daughter) and my niece, Abbye Epting (8 - my brother's daughter) from Georgia.

Through these events then and the continuing experiences coming up, you'll discover the truer meaning of...

15

Delight yourself in the LORD and he will give you the desires of your heart.
— Psalm 37:4 (NIV)

In that March 9, 1992 moment on the phone with Kim I became so delighted in the Lord — more like enthralled with Him — that He brought the desires of my heart to me because, by golly, since He was the one who gave me those desires in the first place, He was bound and determined to fulfill them!

As for the *Way Up There* desire I expressed to God while coming into Denver on October 28, 1992 — the altitude of Crested Butte itself is *Way Up There...*8,885 feet. But, even more than that, at the time of the writing of most of this book we were living a few miles above town where the altitude is almost 10,000 feet. When God answers us He is known to answer in a big *Way (Up There)* and with the most intriguing attention to the details of our prayers.

It also turns out that just about a week before I arrived in Crested Butte, while I was preparing to leave Georgia, Trapper had sat on a log with the pastor of the church where we would soon meet and had told him that at 35 years old he was tired of being single and wanted to meet someone to share his life with. He says it was the first time in his life he had seriously expressed that desire and that the Lord had given him that desire after considering himself a confirmed bachelor prior to that day. We figured out that he gave us those desires at about the same time — something that has continued to happen quite often in our marriage ever since.

Just as I had not imagined that the answer to my prayers would be such a package deal so beautifully delivered to me by the Lord in only a few days — even during the same week — Trapper had never imagined that his expressing the desire to marry would result in him meeting his future wife so soon either. On top of that, Trapper's plan was to leave Crested Butte in three days to winter in Kansas. He had accepted an outfitter job in Montana for the next summer meaning that he would not have returned to Crested Butte.

Do ya think God appreciates it when we speak out loud our desires as an act of faith toward Him? Well I surely do and herein we have proof about that too! But Almighty God was doing some of what He does best and there was more going on. Trapper had been in rejection of the church in general for the same exact 20 years on the calendar that I had and had just come around to the notion of a relationship with the Lord being what it's really about. That adds up to Trapper's revelation on the subject being within only a few months before mine on the phone with Kim.

So the Lord was so knowingly weaving our lives toward a moment of crossing our paths — preparing me to meet my Mountain Man and Trapper for the day when he would write, *"Sir, I Promise I'll Do Her No Wrong".*

16

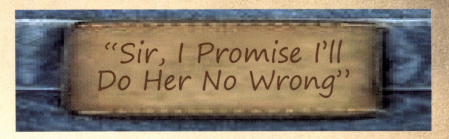

"Sir, I Promise I'll Do Her No Wrong"

There is a certain Old West romance about the Mountain Man heritage. So what better way to bring in the romance than to share about my Mountain Man's proposal of marriage.

Trapper used to spend summer through hunting season outfitting in Colorado and then would winter in Kansas trapping every year – until he married me. In fact, he delayed his departure from Crested Butte a few days until six days after we met and then left for Kansas to observe this annual rite.

He stayed in contact all that winter and then, in May of 1993, returned to Colorado. I did not know then that he had been offered a job in Seeley Lake, Montana and was not planning to return to Colorado in 1993 . But, return he did since God had plans other than what Trapper had thought his plans were.

For a good portion of that summer I still thought we were just friends. Bear in mind that I was unaware of his horseback revelation involving a marriage proposal that you found out about in *What A Ride!* As we've said about that summer ever since: "We were dating but just didn't know it!"

One day, just after things suddenly turned romantic with one brief kiss on the night of July 31, we were trudging up a dirt road toward a beaver pond above this fella's ranch. Out of the clear blue sky Trapper came out with: "I'll do anything in the world for you [I hadn't asked for that...yet] except for one thing: don't ever ask me not to trap." I hadn't considered it. I figured that if everyone around us was callin' this guy "Trapper" then that was a sizeable part of who he was. At this point in life I knew I'd better like it or leave it but trying to change what was his chosen name would be inadvisable if not impossible.

Ol' Trapper was planning. But he had to get that one thing straight. Guess he was just getting his affairs in order. It was something akin to: "Okay. We have that understanding on the table. Now we can move on." Mountain Men can be so down to earth, don't ya think?

Now get out the hankies, ladies (and even you gents too) 'cause here comes maybe the doggondest marriage proposal tale you have ever heard.

On August 1 of that summer of 1993, Trapper said to me, "I've got plans in six to eight weeks. Don't ask what they are." And you can bet I didn't.

At the time we knew that my Dad down in Athens, Georgia had pancreatic cancer and the doctors had told him he had until the first of the year to live. We had already planned to go there in early November after Trapper was done with hunting season as a horseback outfitter guide so Trapper could meet my family. We were going to spend some time there with them – especially with my Dad before he died. The plan was then to start driving West again, drop Trapper off in Kansas and I was going to continue on to Crested Butte before my job resumed at Thanksgiving when ski season opened.

What I NOW know is that Trapper's "plans in six to eight weeks" were to formally ask my Dad – old fashioned like – for my hand in marriage in person when we went down to Georgia. But, those plans changed – and rather suddenly, too.

On September 28 we were visiting friends in Glenwood Springs, Colorado. That night I got the call that Dad had only 24-48 hours to live. My family had a ticket on the next flight to Atlanta waiting for me at the Denver airport three hours away. I could see Interstate 70 that would take me to Denver the next morning out the window while we were eating dinner. All I could think about was getting to Athens in time and could not concentrate on what to do about leaving my car in Denver for an indefinite amount of time. So I told Trapper and our friends there, "I can't think about the car. Could you guys please figure that out?" and left it in their hands.

As Trapper and I were saying goodbye at 6:30 the next morning, he held out what turned out to be some yellow legal pad pieces of paper – folded to about two inches square. As he handed it to me he said, "Read it to your Dad if you get the chance. If you don't then read it to your family. But you can't read it first." I promised and off I drove, east on I-70 to Denver.

On the flight I was a jumble of emotions. First I would be thinking about my Dad. Then I would look down and see that thick little yellow square of paper peeking out at me from my open-top purse. And no, I DIDN'T READ IT! I had PROMISED!

All of a sudden I threw my hands up over my face and thought, "I'm not going to make it!" Then, being the eternal optimist I am, I mentally chastised myself, "Cut it out. They said 24-48 hours and it hasn't even been 24 yet!" I asked the woman across the aisle what time it was: "12:30 Colorado time", she said. That would be 2:30 Georgia time. My brother-in-law, Roger, met me at the gate in the Atlanta airport. We hugged and I started out into the concourse anxious to get to the car and head for Athens 70 miles away. He stopped me and said, "Sis, he didn't make it." I dropped everything right there in the middle of the concourse and we hugged and cried together. He had been married to my oldest sister for 31 years and dearly loved our Dad.

As we wandered to the underground tram that would take us to the parking area exit door, I asked him, "Roger, what time did he die?" I didn't tell him why I was asking. Roger happened to know the exact time because he had looked at a clock as he was walking out the door to come to the airport and my sister had called him with the inevitable news: "2:30" said Roger. Of course it was 2:30. In a way, I was there after all.

As we were waiting for the tram Roger said, "Sis, I have to tell you something your Dad did when I saw him on Sunday [three days before he died]. He kept his sense of humor to the very end. He was sitting in his La-Z-Boy chair and patted his tummy where the tumor was and said, "We haven't named it yet." Some bittersweet humor in a bittersweet moment.

When we arrived in Athens my two sisters (Jean and Angie) and my brother (also named Al) met me at the back door of our life-long home with a group hug. They could see us coming up the driveway and felt badly for me that I didn't make it in time. The rest of the day was a blur. Then finally, at about 2:00 am, my three siblings, a close cousin and I had finished writing Dad's obituary for the Athens newspaper. We were pretty wiped out and emotional but apologetically I said, "I know we're all tired but there's something I've got to read to all of you before we're surrounded by people tomorrow" and told them about Trapper's instructions.

As you've already figured out, that yellow paper was Trapper's proposal of marriage – addressed to my Dad. It started off with:
"Mr. Epting – Sure wish I could meet you in the great state of Georgia."

Among other things he'd written that I read to them between sobs was, "You know I'm just a cowboy trapper...I work hard, am an honest God-fearing man. Seems like I waited for ever for the right gal. Well, Sir, I've found her, and *Sir, I promise I'll do her no wrong.* So I'd like to ask for her hand in marriage. Fae will you marry me?" and then signed it:

In these almost 22 years since this was written my Mountain Man has taught me much about how to read sign. Thanks to Trapper's training, it is a very precious thing to me, especially since now I know my Mountain Man so much better than I did then, to be able to see his thought process in THIS sign. Here's my interpretation:

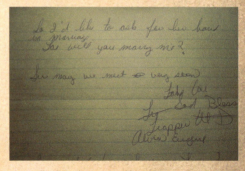

He struck through "Tra" to write "Trapper". Then he started to write Al Davidson but thought the last name too formal. So then he struck through "Al D" but then was inspired to write "Alvin Eugene" because he knew that my Dad's full name was Eugene Albert and he was trying to honor the irony of their similar names.

The whole table was sobbing by then and my tears were causing the blue ink on that yellow paper in my hands to run a bit.

How symbolic is that???...an old fashioned plea written on yellow legal paper to an Old South attorney who was 86 years old with 54 years of law practice history using hundreds of pads of that same type of yellow legal paper. I saw my Dad writing on them many times in my childhood. Trapper had no idea how symbolic that was. It was simply all he could find in the room where he was staying at the friends' house in Glenwood Springs. We keep these precious yellow legal pad paper pages in plastic sheet protectors nowadays.

Trapper won the hearts of my family right there. My cousin there at the table, Lee Epting, was the first to pipe up: "When do we get to meet this guy? He did it right!" Trapper had still found a way to propose the old fashioned way. Leave it to a Mountain Man to come up with some ingenious way to beat the elements. I called Trapper the next morning and accepted his proposal. Trapper flew into Atlanta the next night.

We inherited that family dining room table where we were all sitting when I read Trapper's proposal to my family. It's a drop leaf table that had all of the four leaves in it when it was set up to handle the size of our family plus others joining us for meals in Athens, Georgia. But we mostly keep it at this size until we have dinner company and then we too pull out the leaves.

Sometimes we'll tell folks sitting there with us, "Trapper proposed at this very table...but He wasn't there." We then share the story of how he did it.

Just as the way we became engaged was a bit unusual, so were the various ways God wove experiences into my childhood which we comically now know were *Prophetic Marriage Preparations.*

Prophetic Marriage Preparations

Unbeknownest to me, the Lord had been preparing me for marriage to my Mountain Man, well...all of my life! You'll soon see proof that His project of this was already well under way when I was only one year and seven months old. We'll get there.

My family says that back then I loved the song from the *Davy Crockett* TV series popular in 1955. So I went around singing *The Ballad of Davy Crockett* all the time – except I was singing "Daby, Daby Cockit!" – pronouncing the first name as something that rhymed with the real name – "day-bee" – and then foreshadowing-like saying the last name as what you do with a gun..."cock it".

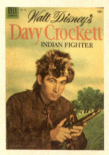

In the months just before our wedding in 1994 my siblings were cleaning out our life-long home in Athens, Georgia before I could get there. When one of them came across the old record of *The Ballad of Davy Crockett* they put it aside to give to me when I got there. Years later when I finally got around to going through keepsakes my Mother had saved for me in a metal box under my childhood bed, lo and behold, inside it were a Davy Crockett comic book and

jigsaw puzzle waiting to remind me of my fascination with Daby Cockit! I love the symbolism that my Mountain Man husband was sitting there watching when I found those items in the box.

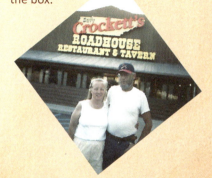

Trapper liked this history of mine so much that when we stumbled across the *Davy Crockett Roadhouse* in Tullahoma, Tennessee during a 2002 return trip to Georgia, we just had to go there. Whoever we snagged to take this photo for us decided to get creative about it.

Look what else surfaced in the 1994 clean out of our Athens home----------->

AUG • 55 •

Like I said, my family definitely associated me with this Davy character and I know of several others who have similar childhood memories. It was a big thing at the time – called the "Crockett Craze".

Apparently my future Mountain Man husband would one day have plenty to teach me about proper gun handling! Good thing somebody didn't "cock it" before I did this --->

At some of you may recall, Fess Parker played the role of Davy Crockett in the Disney TV series and was also Daniel Boone in the 1960s TV series by that famous character's name. A few years ago a friend brought us a gift of a bottle of Fess Parker wine. Until that time we didn't know Fess Parker had even established a winery out in California. Our friend just knew Trapper was a trapper similar to Davy Crockett and Daniel Boone so he thought we would enjoy knowing about the wine for that reason. Little did he know my own childhood connection with Fess Parker's character portrayals. So, after finding out about that, it wasn't long before we went online and became members of the Fess Parker Wine Club (www.fessparker.com). Although the winery offers fine bottles of Chardonnay, Shiraz, Merlot, Pinot Noir, Cabernet Sauvignon and more, we have a great time giving bottles of their *Frontier Red* table wine to friends, family and customers of our wildlife management business because of the photo on the label of Fess Parker as Daniel Boone in his coonskin cap. We have been known to embellish the bottle a bit to match Trapper's occupation – hanging coon tails from the top of it attached with velcro.

For seven years, from 2005 to 2012, I was secretary of the church in Crested Butte where we had met and married years before. During that time we gave coon tail adorned bottles of Fess Parker *Frontier Red* wine to friends for gifts one year. Our pastor's wife took their bottle home after we gave it to her one Sunday morning and apparently didn't get around to telling her husband where it came from before she had to leave for work the next morning.

He came into the church office the next morning and, without even saying hello, said, "Fae, there's a coon tail hanging out of my wine rack. Would you happen to know anything about that?" Now what in the world do you suppose gave him the idea that I would?

Other foreshadowings were prolific in my young life. One of the most prophetic pre-proposal preparations was...Skunkie.

From the time we were little girls, I had the blessed good fortune to share the grandparents of my life-long friend, Jody (Wilson) Boling, of whom I am a whole 19 days older so we've known each all of HER life. As my unofficially adopted grandparents, to us their names were Barber (which we pronounced "Baba") and Nana of Athens, Georgia. When we were five years old Barber was in the hospital for some reason. My Mother took me with her to pick up some nice, respectable flowers to take to him in the hospital. And then I spotted this cute critter on the shelf with some real flowers stapled onto its paw:

As children in our family we were simply not allowed to pitch temper tantrums. Seriously – NOT ALLOWED. But I wanted that skunk to go to "Baba" in the hospital and so, well – let's just say I took a firm position on the matter with my Mother – but we mustn't call it the temper tantrum that it really was. Contrary to what her reaction would normally have been to such a demand, she relented and purchased the skunk. As I write this I'm thinking that maybe she liked the idea herself so she gave in. However it happened, the stuffed skunk went to Barber in the hospital who was told it was from Sissy and he named it, "Skunkie". It appears I learned of fur trading early in life because from that day forward a skunk tradin' tradition began between Barber and me.

After he recovered from his hospital visit, as soon as I came down with chicken pox Skunkie came to stay with me to help me get well. Then, when Barber got sick with who-knows-what, I took Skunkie to visit him until I got the measles and Skunkie came back to me and...on it went for the rest of his life...which was quite some time because he lived to be 102! It even continued through my college years and until I was 26 years old, three years of which I lived in a house right across the street from Barber and Nana while attending the University of Georgia in my hometown.

To My dear Sissy from Barber, Xmas 1961

Handwritten on the bottom of the photo – "To my dear Sissy from Barber, Xmas 1961"

But Barber was so amazingly healthy all of his life that I had to take advantage of the news of the slightest hint of a cold to find an excuse to take Skunkie to help him get well. Over the years he lovingly put many a new red ribbon around Skunkie's neck whenever the previous one became shredded from all of the back and forth.

24

To others in Athens, this man was Dr. Robert C. Wilson – the Father of Modern Pharmacy in Georgia, former Dean of the College of Pharmacy there and the man the Pharmacy School building was named after in 1978 on his 100th birthday.

To me and my life-long friend (Jody Wilson Boling) and our families, he was her real grandfather, my adopted grandfather and our special friend together.

Here's Skunkie's appearance at my hospital room in 1976 – personally delivered by 98 year old Barber while I was there for surgery on my jaw when I was 22.

When the time came for me to venture out into the world after UGA graduation, it was decided that Skunkie should reside at their house. In September of 1980, just a few months after I had moved to Boulder, Colorado as a young adult, the word came that Barber's beloved Nana had gone to be with the Lord. I flew back to Georgia to see him and the family and attend the funeral. His exuberant Southern gentleman greeting to me was unforgettable.

I remember very gingerly sitting on his lap while mostly hanging onto the back of his wingback chair since I figured a 102 year old knee did not need a person sitting on it. We talked about life for a long time that day. He told me then that he wanted to go be with Nana so I knew it wouldn't be long for his turn. So we said our goodbyes in our hearts that day too. After several days there, I returned to Colorado.

A little over eight months later the word came that Barber had been granted his heart's desire and most definitely both he and Nana were together in the eternal presence of the Lord. For some reason I cannot remember, I was not able to return to Athens for his service. That precious visit with him in September was my final in-person memory of my adopted grandfather.

Lots of friends of the family in Athens knew about the Skunkie tradition. The story goes that one of Barber and Nana's great grandchildren was also enamored with Skunkie and coveted it.

True to Southern tradition during a time of mourning, when Barber died various women were helping out at the house while folks came by to pay the family their respects – helping with food, greeting people at the door, keeping track of who gave which flowers, answering the phone and more.

I am so very grateful to one of those women. She just happened to see Skunkie go out the door under the arm of that great grandchild who had seen the opportunity to kidnap Skunkie and was headed for south Georgia with it. Because she was one who knew the significance of this particular stuffed animal, she retrieved Skunkie from a very unhappy little boy.

She knew my Mother was at that moment on the way to the house to help out. She personally held onto Skunkie for safe keeping until my Mother arrived, went straight to her, handed over Skunkie, told her what had almost happened and said, "We KNOW who this belongs to." So Skunkie was rescued from south Georgia oblivion and kept safe for me until I could come home and retrieve Skunkie myself.

So, even today, Skunkie has an honored place in my adult home. Skunkie is even in view a few feet away as I write this.

In 1999 when I originally wrote up the Skunk Cookies story and then the *"Father, Thank You for my Wife"* story right after that (they're both coming up here very soon), it occurred to me the irony of the prominence of skunks in my childhood and how we could not have known that Skunkie would be partial preparation for marriage to my Mountain Man.

Our Father has such comical ways of running a thread of symbolism in our lives. I wonder if there's anyone else out there whose symbolic thread has such a connection with skunks...of all things! Maybe that's why I've come to be okay with the smell of them, unlike most folks. Or maybe it's a survival mechanism to be okay with the smell since it happens in our marriage from time to time. But I'm grateful that others don't care for the smell because that fact has provided us with some substantial income – and laughter – as you'll soon discover.

Skunks were not the only critter I needed to find out more about to prepare for marriage. Before meeting Trapper, when I was still single in 1990, it was an odd thing that I suddenly got all interested in the Mountain Man Rendezvous era of the 1820s - 1840s and, because I was in the travel business at the time, I even met with some guys who participated in Mountain Man Rendezvous reenactments to talk about taking "pilgrims" to the Rendezvous camps in the summers. That never did come to fruition back then. I even wondered at the time what that exercise was all about and now cannot recall what got me started on that. I mostly didn't have a clue about the mysterious ways of God in even the seemingly smallest of moments in life at that time.

Anyway, because of that interest, a friend invited me to go to the IMAX theater in Denver to see a movie called: "BEAVER!" Little did I know all this was preparation for the life waiting for me just a few years later. Many have been the moments that I have reflected on the information gleaned from that movie after I married an actual beaver trapper! Of course my Mountain Man has taught me quite a bit more throughout our marriage but at least I had a head start from the movie.

Through these things, little by little, even when it was very little, the Lord was preparing me for the life that began in earnest at the moment when Trapper proclaimed..."*Yep! I Will!*"

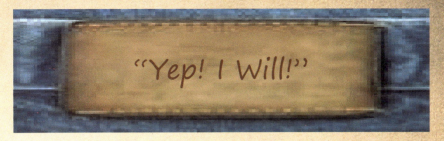

"Yep! I Will!"

Six weeks after we were married, Trapper told our church congregation, "now three things in life are most important to me: God, my wife and trapping. He quickly added, "But not necessarily in that order. At least God's always first." We now have 21 years of marriage into our packbaskets. I'll leave you wondering if I ever come out on top of the lineup.

As you can imagine (and probably relate to in your own life), your spouse's occupation creeps into all aspects of life together...from the very first day on. Our wedding was entertaining. Trapper was a clown all day. We have proof as it was well documented on video by our photographers who truly captured the day on film.

Since we had met at this little church in Crested Butte, Colorado and several members of the congregation had been so involved in getting us together, that's where we married on June 18, 1994.

The pastor of that church who married us, Jim, put some personality into the ceremony. He talked about what a joy it was to him to be involved in this marriage and recalled the day the previous summer when we all rode three hours each way on horseback up to the base of *The Castles* in the West Elk Wilderness just to get to the one particular beaver pond where Trapper wanted to be baptized. I remember that gorgeous Colorado blue sky summer ride clearly...and watching the rainbow trout nibbling at the two fellas' toes in the COLD water.

The Saddle Soap moment of our wedding

And then there was the moment in the wedding ceremony when Trapper TRIED his best to slip the wedding band on my left hand ring finger but it wouldn't go on.

"Get the saddle soap!" declared Jim to the congregation.

It finally went on my finger and the ceremony could continue. It's all on the video.

27

The moment came for us to profess our vows to one another before God and about 200 people there and we had previously agreed to Jim's suggestion of saying "I Will" instead of "I Do". As the video camera zoomed in on Trapper's face, you can almost see the wheels of determination and ingenuity spinning in his eyes as he came out with a cowboy style, drawn out...

"Yehhhppp! I Will" and busted up the whole place, including the bride who could hardly answer my own vow back for laughing and Jim, the officiating pastor, who could only respond to Trapper with, "God bless you." It was NOT just another "I Do" kind of ceremony. And thus we became Trapper and Fae...*Mountain Man and Wife*.

We had an AL-together good time at our wedding. Al was the name of the groom. Al was also the name of our best man. Al was ALSO the name of my brother who gave me away since my Dad had died nine months before our wedding. And so, we had Three Als at the Al-tar!" We didn't do that on purpose. We didn't even realize it until we noticed it one day during the wedding planning after all participants had agreed to their roles. Now you can see why calling one of them Trapper is a blessing.

Three Als At The Al-tar
Al Davidson with Al Van Dyke standing up with him waiting for Al Epting to bring the bride to the Al-tar

There are lots of blessings in this *Life as a Mountain Man's Wife*. I used to have to remind myself of that each time my hand slipped off a door knob caked with beaver grease until we found a way to resolve that dilemma. But, that's another story. Our marriage represented a cultural merger and to some folks it came to be known as *West Meets South*.

28

West Meets South

Our whole wedding weekend was loaded with activities because we knew that many people coming in from Georgia, Kansas and elsewhere were turning the trip into their summer vacations. In addition to the local activities of horseback riding, river rafting, mountain biking, hiking trails and more in which many of our wedding attendees enthusiastically participated, our planned wedding-related events included a mountain meadow picnic for the Bridal Luncheon the day before the wedding, a ranch Rehearsal Rendezvous BBQ the night before, the wedding outside behind the church since it was too small to hold 200 people and then the reception at another ranch. The out of town guests were invited to all events since they'd all traveled so far.

After we returned from our honeymoon I was talking on the phone with my Matron of Honor, Kim Arnold, who was now back in Athens, Georgia. She said, "Thank you for your planning for everything. We've never been to so many outside events in one weekend in our lives. But...you forgot one thing at the Rehearsal Dinner BBQ...toilet paper!" My mental picture of everybody running behind the trees, especially the Southern gals all dressed up, well – darn. I truly tried to think of everything but that one got by me. I guess they managed to figure it out.

One of the extraordinary aspects of our wedding weekend was the significant involvement of my cousin, Lee Epting, owner of Lee Epting Catering and Epting Events in Athens. At the time of our engagement in Athens nine months before our wedding (see *"Sir, I Promise I'll Do Her No Wrong"*), Lee informed us, "We're coming and we're bringing the cake!" He had remembered my comment to him that "whenever I finally get married, I want one of Cecilia's cakes." These are the cakes Lee and his catering business have served at wedding receptions and various other events all over the Southeastern states for many years – and still going strong at the time of the publication of this book.

And so it transpired that Lee and his family catered our wedding reception in Crested Butte, Colorado. True to his word, he and his wife, Bobbie, plus their two sons, Daniel and Ashley, brought our wedding cake on the plane from Atlanta to Denver and then drove it four hours or so to Crested Butte. They had carefully packed the sections in three graduated sized boxes, loaded them into the overhead bins on the airplane and then stood guard to make sure no one disrupted them up there.

They also brought a container of icing to glue the sections together and I had a bucket of flowers waiting for Lee to cascade down the side of the cake. Look what he creatively did for a table for that cake atop an old rusty 55 gallon drum at the ranch!

For the wedding reception luncheon, Lee had given me an enormous shopping list. Our friends, Tom and Desse Anthony and their son, Clay, took that list to Sam's Club in Denver, filled their Suburban and delivered it all to the kitchen Lee commandeered in Crested Butte.

Those of you who know Lee know his creative catering genius. He and his family managed to turn a Western ranch into a Southern wedding spread – symbolic of the merger taking place in our marriage – a Western Mountain Man and Southern raised wife. A great time was had by all there too. Among the reports we received from Crested Butte locals were:

"I've never had so much fun at a wedding!"
"Great food!"
"The South sure has a lot of wedding traditions."
Well, yep...all true statements.

Our Bride and Groom First Dance was while our band sang the country western song *I Swear* by John Michael Montgomery which was also Trapper's choice for one of the songs during our wedding ceremony earlier. Although we had practiced a few times before our wedding day, we had not mastered being able to dance together very well. We were on two different beats and had not yet overcome that. We happily have a video record of this dance – or whatever it was – and nowadays find it to be comically symbolic of much we would persevere through in our just-beginning marriage of two such utterly different people from two such utterly different worlds. We were trying

to do this dance on rocky uneven ranch ground plus the fact that from time to time Trapper would step on the bottom of the petticoat under my wedding gown and I would come to a screeching halt. On top of that, we were a bit self-conscious since our wedding guests were watching us sort this out.

As a bachelor Mountain Man in Colorado and farm kid raised in Kansas, Trapper had somehow missed out on an education in wedding traditions. Imagine that! And I was so busy with planning and preparations that it didn't occur to me that I needed to provide that education in advance of our wedding weekend.

For years I had traveled to the weddings of many of the people now attending ours. For 18 years since college I had written and delivered both funny and sentimental toasts at the Rehearsal Dinners of those couples.

For years I had been returning to Colorado on an airplane wondering when it was ever going to be my turn to be the recipient of those toasts, what the groom sitting there beside me was going to be like and what his family and friends were going to have to say about him on that night.

After all those years of anticipation...Hallelujah! The hour was *finally* nigh.

We were all assembled the night before the wedding at the Rehearsal Dinner Rendezvous BBQ – not your traditional formal event with a head table. Instead all 80 of us were gathered around a big campfire with logs for folks to sit there.

It dawned on me that the sun was setting and I knew for a fact that folks had toasts they needed to be able to read. I asked around but no one wanted to step up and get the ball rolling.

"Aha!," I pondered. "I know the perfect person who will know what to do."

One quick word to cousin Lee resulted in his spoon banging on a blue enamel pot lid and his announcement to all that it was time for the toasts to commence.

I went to our appointed log seat, sat down and began enjoying the toasts. But there was one problem – no groom! After all those years of waiting, there I was all ALONE. Nothing had changed. I was crushed. Where in campfire blazes was Trapper???

Then I heard laughter so loud from behind those trees over there that none of the rest of us could even hear the toasts. It was Trapper and his buddy, Jerry, completely oblivious to what was going on around the campfire.

Soon Trapper wandered by behind me and wondered what was going on. I was mortified that an education on the Rehearsal Dinner tradition had not only been overlooked but was even necessary at all! To me it was representative of our different worlds and it terrified me! This was unquestionably a Mountain Man bride's version of cold feet and was also one of those not-so-funny-at-the-time moments I referred to at the beginning of this book of tales.

I hated it but couldn't shake it. Even I knew that part of my tension was due to sheer exhaustion from all of the planning and preparations now coming to fruition. But, after Trapper sat down there with me I felt better and we began laughing at the toasts although the sun had set by then and some of them had to be read from down there by the golden light of the campfire.

As the party was winding down later, I was sitting on a different log in front of that same campfire. The guys had already hauled Trapper off and I was bemoaning my dismay to a friend. "We're too different," I cried with tears pouring down my face. I knew that my commitment the next day was to be for the rest of our lives – as *Mountain Man and Wife* – and at that tuckered out moment I wasn't sure I was up to it. Lee overheard that, took compassion on me, turned to his wife and said, "Take her home and put her to bed." Wise man. He'd seen his share of panicked brides and grooms in all of his years of catering weddings.

I awakened the next morning refreshed and excited and ready to finally say, "I Will" in a few hours.

A few other wedding traditions caught Trapper by surprise that were more comical since I was getting more used to the joy of watching his antics while he learned them.

One happened immediately after arrival at our ranch wedding reception. Brides Matron Jody Boling had apparently tuned into Trapper's gap in wedding training by then, came up to us and said, "Trapper, you've got to get that garter off of Fae's leg right now."

I was turned toward a conversation with someone else when I felt all of this ruckus accompanied by Trapper's hands lifting up my wedding gown from the bottom.
"What are you doing?"
"Jody told me to get the garter."
I looked at Jody's ornery, knowing grin and sized up the situation.

I also figured she was getting me back for trying to convince her that she was going to have to ride Trapper's big mule, Jasper, down the aisle when I asked her to be in our wedding. At first I don't think she knew I was kidding.

We both have our ornery sides.

"Not yet — later," I said to Trapper. I wondered how many other things I hadn't realized I needed to tell Trapper about weddings in advance and what further sport Jody had in mind to make of that lack of education. Too late now. I could see that it was going to be an interesting day in ways I'd never anticipated.

That later time arrived for Trapper to peel the garter made of my grandmother's crochet offa me. When he did that he dutifully and immediately threw it just as he believed Jody had instructed him to do earlier — perhaps even thinking that maybe he was getting the hang of these wedding traditions. The thing was, the instructor must have been in the same predicament as I — not realizing that expanded wedding tradition detail was required in Trapper's case. The garter-throwing instructor apparently failed to mention WHERE Trapper was to throw it. So, he thew it off to the south but all of the single guys he was to throw it to were waiting, unknown to him... to the north. As the crowd quickly reacted with further instructions Trapper scampered off, retrieved it and re-dispatched it where it was gathered in by my second cousin, Ashley Epting. Happily for the years of chuckles it has provided to us and to others — it's all on the video.

With great joy this celebration dance with my Epting cousin, Lee, was yet another highlight to the event he and his family had so much to do with creating. It was because of them that our *West Meets South* wedding was such a success. Once the party was over it was time for us to make our marriage a success.

It seems we refer to our wedding quite often in life. Maybe it's because it was so representative of the ingathering of two very different ways of life from two very different parts of the country and how that all came together for such a marvelous occasion.

Lo and behold, over the years of our marriage Trapper has embraced the wedding traditions I was used to and we have since been to a fair share of Rehearsal Dinners and the rest of various wedding weekends together.

But he first began learning about such things in earnest around his own Rehearsal Dinner BBQ campfire — an appropriate place for a Mountain Man to acquire such an education, don't ya think?

Turns out that the sign Brooks and Kim Arnold had on the front door of their home for the engagement party that they and Jody Boling gave us in Athens two months before our wedding was now more fitting than we all yet knew but were soon to begin learning ourselves--------------->

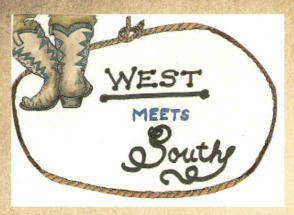

Kim Arnold sent the card below with this photo of their family taken the day of our wedding. They way she put it, "A Rootin' Tootin' time was had by ALL!" – one way we knew everyone had such a good time – even without appropriately placed rolls of toilet paper. All of the Arnold girls were in the wedding so we gave her husband, Brooks, a Stetson hat to thank him for his perseverance. They even used this photo for their Christmas card that year.

Two years after our wedding we attended a Mountain Man Rendezvous in Dahlonega, Georgia. So this time West went South instead of South coming West. Lee brought his nephews from Athens to

see us up there and Jody Boling found this whole event quite amusing. Was she really trying to scalp me, her life-long friend? What she really did do was kidnap me and take me to her home in Cumming for a night in a real bed and a tub bath. Old friends know what each other's needs are and I was grateful for a night in modern comfort.

Our learning curves spiked dramatically right outta the gate and have continued in this *Life As A Mountain Man's Wife* – loaded with all sorts of comically obvious and obviously unanticipated *Education & Revelation*.

Education & Revelation

We had been married a little over two years when Trapper was unexpectedly elected as President of the Colorado Trappers Association. Then, two months later an anti-trapping law was voted into the Colorado Constitution through a ballot initiative called Amendment 14.

Okay. I'll admit it. I grew up a city gal. Not a BIG city. Athens, Georgia was still relatively small when I grew up in it. But, I had NO background in trapping. I had A LITTLE background in horses and such – VERY LITTLE and only very recently just prior to meeting Trapper. But, I had chosen to leave Georgia and take off to the mountains of Colorado 12 years before I met him. So, I had already made the break out of the city – somewhat – but had been stuck in a city on the Front Range of Colorado for most of those 12 years. Guess I had to take it one step at a time. Then, in 1992, I finally ventured over to the Western Slope where I knew no one and met Trapper immediately, as you read about in *Way Up There*. It was about time.

Two years after we married, in 1996, Trapper was elected as the President of the Colorado Trappers Association. Two weeks after that we found ourselves over in Grand Junction at a meeting of the Colorado Wildlife Commissioners. All the players were there to make speeches to the Commissioners regarding what we thought their stance should be on Amendment 14 in the upcoming election. I had gone along as simply a supportive wife. That's all. No intention of speaking myself whatsoever. As I watched all of the speechifying, I grew increasingly frustrated. Finally I turned to Trapper and asked if it would be all right if I spoke too. "Go for it!" was his enthusiastic response.

I scribbled down some notes and wound up being the last speaker. I felt like a fish out of water – more like a two-year-old beaver booted out of the colony's lodge – and seriously wondered if I'd said anything of value. When the meeting was done, the Director of the Colorado Department of Agriculture who we had not yet met came over, shook Trapper's hand and told him he appreciated what he'd had to say. He then turned to me, shook my hand and said, "And I especially appreciated what YOU had to say." I had truly wondered if I had come off as a ditzy blonde and la la land wife. Yet here was this professional agricultural man who validated my words. I was stunned and even wondered if he was serious.

Trapper had been asking me to write a Letter to the Editor of one of our area newspapers "from a woman's point of view". So, with the above mentioned encouragement, I decided to expand the meeting remarks already written into just such a Letter to the Editor of the *Gunnison Country Times*.

I remembered that when I was scribbling those notes at the Commissioners meeting, at the last second I had changed the word "ignorance" to "lack of education" before making that little speech. My thinking was that the people who had put this initiative on the ballot were sitting there and that calling them "ignorant" was using fightin' words and not my intention at all.

I didn't think a fight would have accomplished anything and would have been terribly disruptive to the proceedings so I changed the wording to "lack of education" because I truly knew whereof I was speaking on that – my own ignorance/lack of education about the issue of trapping. I also knew from the excellent vocabulary training I had received back in high school and college that "lack of education" was the truer meaning of the word "ignorant" and that the word was not initially intended to have the negative connotation it does now.

After all, we ALL have a lack of education about SOMETHING.

Wouldn't you know it...that's the very line the *Gunnison Country Times* editor pulled out of my letter for the title in the paper: "Education Leads To Support Of Trapping". The full letter is re-printed on the next page. It could easily provide some helpful insight to those who, like myself at one time, do not feel okay about trapping.

Here's part of what it said: "Four years ago, when I met the man who is now my husband, I had a dilemma. I didn't know what to think of trapping. My first inclination was to be against it due to the emotional aspects of the issue as I saw it then. But now I know that viewpoint was due to my lack of education. When a proposal of marriage began to appear to be a possibility, I had a decision to make. In order to figure out if I could marry this man, I had to make a concerted effort to become educated about trapping. I had very little in my background to help me."

Just for fun, I sent a copy of this Letter to the Editor to my life-long friend, Jody Boling, in Cumming, Georgia. A few days later I answered the phone to her incredulous voice that didn't introduce herself but instead immediately said, " 'Very little'??? What was the 'very little' part?"

She KNEW my life. She is the same life-long friend with whom I had shared grandparents in Athens and we agreed on the phone that there probably was not one shred of girlhood knowledge in it that had come to my aid to help me to understand my husband's chosen profession. I must have decided to put "very little" into the Letter to the Editor because I knew there must be something that had prepared me for my unanticipated and unusual married life. It was not until later that the remembrances shared in *Prophetic Preparations For Marriage* came to mind.

Letters

Education leads to support of trapping

To the Editor:

I am the wife of Al Davidson, the current president of the Colorado Trappers Association.

I lived on the Front Range for many years. Were I still there, living the urban lifestyle I was then, I probably - in my own lack of education - would have voted for Amendment 14 now.

After moving to the Western Slope, my eyes have been opened. Once out here I began to discover what life is really like with regard to ranching, predators, trapping, wildlife, etc.

Four years ago, when I met the man who is now my husband, I had a dilemma. I didn't know what to think of trapping. My first inclination was to be against it due to the emotional aspects of the issue as I saw it then. But now I know that that viewpoint was due to my lack of education. When a proposal of marriage began to appear to be a possibility, I had a decision to make. In order to figure out if I could marry this man, I had to make a concerted effort to become educated about trapping. I had very little in my background to help me.

The knowledge about it I received was enough to convince me that this marriage could take place and now I have a great deal more knowledge and involvement in the trapping world. Additionally, after meeting many of the trappers in Colorado over the past few years and discovering what good solid citizens most of them are plus the professional approach the majority of them take toward their trapping profession, I fully agree with many others that trappers are not at all the "bad guys" they've been made out to be. They are most certainly not the criminals Amendment 14 tries to make them out to be.

This is what has helped me the most with being OK about trapping: I discovered with amazement that the people who respect these animals the most are the individuals who trap them. They study them - their habitat, their lifestyles, their ways of repopulating and raising their young, their feeding habits and more. They respect the intricacies of nature which these animals operate in. As much as they are fascinated by and respectful of them, they must remain realistic about them when damage or disease is evident.

So, the urban gal who once knew nothing about trapping has come to understand that there is a need and a place for trapping - especially when it comes to helping ranchers and farmers against coyotes, raccoons and foxes, helping urban citizens with skunk and raccoon problems, and more.

To those of you, Front Rangers or elsewhere in Colorado, who find yourselves in my previous shoes due to having no particular reason to know the realities of trapping and are unsure of how to vote or who to believe, I urge you to vote no on Amendment 14. The emotional appeal by the animal rights folks may sound enticing. But it just doesn't tell the whole story. I wish all of you could have had the opportunity to learn about this as I have. But since that isn't feasible right now, I ask you to please, please just take my word for it and keep animals out of the Colorado Constitution and in the hands of those who are trained to handle wildlife. I very respectfully ask that when you vote, please respect the rights of those who need trapping, even if this is not something you happen to be knowledgeable about.

Fae Davidson

When we met at the altar

we did not know that our meeting of the minds

was going to include so many smelly meetings – lots of 'em – of all sorts.

Ever since writing that Letter to the Editor my education has greatly expanded on this trapping thing. You'll be finding out more particulars on that – laughs included – in upcoming stories. One of the most classic and beloved of them is about the day we discovered – and delivered – *Skunk Cookies.*

Skunk Cookies

You can probably easily imagine that skunks have been the source of a number of humorous events in our marriage.

During the winter of 1995-1996 Trapper and I lived 28 miles south of Crested Butte in Gunnison, Colorado and worked for Delta Air Lines at the Gunnison airport. A set of circumstances had led Delta to hire a local ground crew for that winter instead of bringing in a crew of regular Delta employees.

I became the Station Manager and Trapper worked with the guys out on the ramp guiding the planes in and out, loading and unloading baggage, cleaning the plane, sky capping...you name it and these guys did it. It's a small airport.

About four times a week we worked a big 757 that could carry 180 passengers non-stop from Atlanta to Gunnison and back. There was this one particular pilot from Atlanta who became our friend. One day he said to me, "Fae, I sure would like some homemade chocolate chip cookies." I told him, "I make better peanut butter cookies." Thus began yet another tradin' tradition in my life – one that went on for the rest of that winter. I'd bring peanut butter cookies, he'd share them with the crew on the way back to Atlanta, and then he'd bring Trapper and me a bottle of wine the next time he flew in. Little did we know when that tradin' tradition began that it too would become associated with skunks.

The next winter Delta brought in a regular crew. Our status as an irregular crew, more like *The Renegade Crew of Delta Air Lines*, is another story.

Anyway, the next winter I worked as a security screener at the same Gunnison airport and Trapper worked elsewhere plus continued trapping.

Finally one day I saw our pilot friend from the last winter come out of the cockpit and down the steps of the plane. I went out onto the ramp and said hello. He told his co-pilot and the Assistant Airport Manager standing there, "She makes the best peanut butter cookies in the world!" and then asked, "How's Trapper doing?" I asked when he would be flying in next and told him that Trapper and I would bring him some peanut butter cookies that were already in our freezer.

The appointed day arrived and it was time to get out the peanut butter cookie tins from the freezer in the garage. But a couple of events had happened in that garage the day before. The freezer had gone out but, being as this was Gunnison, Colorado with, at the time, three feet of seemingly permafrost on the ground and often was designated as the coldest spot in the nation all that winter, we weren't too worried about the freezer contents.

However, the second event the day before was even more critical. My skunk trapper had brought a skunk he'd captured into that same garage. So, just to be on the safe side, I opened up one of the peanut butter cookie tins, smelled the contents and determined the cookies were fine. Into a Ziploc bag went all the cookies from that tin. Then I thought, "I'd better add some more 'cause he always shares them with the crew." As it was time to leave for the airport, I hurriedly opened the other tin, threw a few cookies from it in the bag, zipped the Ziploc and out the door we went.

At the airport we had a fun time visiting with our pilot friend and a co-pilot we hadn't met before. The topic of discussion?...skunk trapping. As I recall, that's about ALL we talked about. The co-pilot seemed especially fascinated with my husband's line of work.

Came time for them to do their pre-flight check and so it was time for us to leave. I handed the pilot the Ziploc full of cookies, we said our goodbyes and Trapper and I went back home five minutes from the airport.

As we walked in the back door and into the kitchen, I saw the cookie tin still sitting on the kitchen counter. The notion of a peanut butter cookie seemed like a pretty good idea to me too. I took one, popped it into my mouth and...UGH!...skunk! That second cookie tin was older and the lid did not fasten as tight as was obviously necessary so it promptly went into the trash. Right then I heard that Delta Air Lines 757 fly overhead.

"Oh no!" I bemoaned to myself as Trapper walked in the back door. I told him what I was tasting and said, "I know what's going to happen! They're going to level off at 30,000 feet in a little while, pull out that bag of cookies in the cockpit, pass them out to the flight attendants like before...the whole plane will be skunked! For three hours! They'll think it's a setup. All we talked about with them was SKUNK TRAPPING!"

I couldn't get that plane off my mind the rest of the day and until we went to bed – being as I had skunk breath to constantly bringing it and the individuals on that plane to mind. YUK!

My practical Mountain Man's grin-faced reaction? "I wouldn't be expectin' a bottle of wine when they fly back in next Thursday."

The next day I told my boss at airport security what I'd done. He was laughing so hard he could hardly say, "Fae, I don't think you better come to work on Thursday." I told him that I guess I'd better face the music. Besides, Trapper and I were both too curious to know what had happened on that plane.

Thursday arrived and the plane landed. Here came the pilot with that same co-pilot down the steps. What was that in the co-pilot's hands? It was a Kentucky Fried Chicken box. Together they walked straight to me, handed me the box and said, "here's some friend skunk for you." Trapper was right – no wine was forthcoming.

I had to know: "What happened when you opened the bag?"

The co-pilot said that after they had leveled off he was the one who opened the Ziploc. He got a big whiff of the cookies, stuck the bag under the pilot's nose and said, "You KNOW what her husband does for a living, don't you?" Happily they quickly sealed up the bag and the contents did NOT filter out into the plane. Those guys are trained to take care of their passengers and on that particular day, whether those passengers knew it or not, they were well taken care of in a way they never knew.

The airport folks I worked with also got a big charge out of this little episode. As the pilots handed me the box of so-called friend skunk one woman there at security said, "they must've had a time gettin' that 757 up to the KFC drive-thru window!" Thank goodness it was really chicken after all which we heartily enjoyed for that night's dinner.

We replaced that dead freezer in the garage with a chest freezer designated solely for Trapper's use. I made do for the moment with the freezer in the kitchen above our refrigerator and just didn't make any more items needing storage for awhile – especially no peanut butter cookies stored in any old cookie tins!

In December of 2010 I had the pleasure of reading this story during a women's fireside storytelling time. I made a big batch of peanut butter cookies from that same recipe and the cookie tin of them was going around the circle of women with each lady taking a cookie. After finishing reading the story I looked around the room and saw a number of those cookies discarded on the paper plates of a few of the ladies. I suppose imagining skunk taste on those cookies was just too much for a few of the women. But the woman whose house it was where this storytelling time took place asked for the recipe. She gave it to her husband and now every time I see either one of them they talk about the latest batch he's made and how everyone they serve them to loves them.

Anyhow, even with such mishaps as delivering skunk cookies to unsuspecting airline pilots and crews, my Mountain Man Trapper can continue to say..."*Father, Thank You For My Wife*".

"Father, Thank You For My Wife"

In early March of 1996 we received a call from a woman who was having skunk problems at the cabin resort she owned just west of where we were living at the time – Gunnison, Colorado. My goodness! Did she ever have a problem!

In just a couple of weeks Trapper caught 14 skunks out from under those cabins with plenty more to go. We felt so sorry for her that we gave her a quantity discount! Even so, it was still pretty downright good income for us.

One evening Trapper was saying the blessing at our dinner table. In a Trapper-style effort to thank God for blessing our income, he came out with... "Father, thank you for my wife...and ALL the skunks you've provided." I busted up and that was the end of the blessing. As I laughed I made some speculation about God's sense of humor. If nothing else, He knew my Mountain Man's heart and I'm sure He understood Trapper's meanin' in that prayer.

Bein' still somewhat newlyweds at that point (just under two years), I decided it best not to be offended at being dropped into the same sentence with such odiferous pests. In fact, as you can tell, I thought it kinda cute.

About a year before that, at a Valentine banquet at our church in Crested Butte (about 30 miles north of Gunnison), we were all challenged to write a poem to our spouses to sing to them to the tune of an old song called *More*.

In a moment of inspiration, this was what I scribbled down and then sang to my Mountain Man in view of those folks who had so lovingly gotten this Trapper and wife together in the first place and then had been on hand to get us hitched:
I never dreamed I'd be a trapper's wife
Dealing with beaver, bobcats and coyotes the rest of my life.
Then there are, of course, the smelly skunks
But I love my gen-u-ine Mountain Man, what luck!

No wonder Trapper (whose name is often shortened to "Trap" by our friends around here) was inspired at the dinner table later to put skunks and me in the same sentence in his prayer. I planted the dadgum seed, don't ya think?

At the same Valentine Banquet a year earlier (in 1994 while we were engaged) we played a Jeopardy game for that year's entertainment. At some point this clue under the category of Local Couples came up: "This couple has found that 'traps' can catch more than beavers."

"Trapper and Fae!" both teams yelled out in unison – oops – sorta forgot the rules. Everyone there knew the answer to that one. I framed the original clue from the handmade Jeopardy game board and gave it to "Trap" at our wedding reception – a happy memory on our wall.

We also have an assortment of Mountain Man prints, antique beaver traps and pelts hanging around here and there. As a girl in Athens, Georgia, if I ever did imagine the interior decor of my home-to-be someday, I can promise you that antique traps never entered the picture. Antiques – yes . Pictures – yes. But antique TRAPS – no. You never know what real life's gonna turn out like at such a tender young age – especially if you've never even met a Mountain Man trapper before. But, I met one and married one and, well – "I love my gen-u-ine Mountain Man, what luck!"

And he honors me too. There was the day when we arrived at the site of the Colorado Trappers Association Annual Fur Auction in Limon, Colorado. I was driving and as we pulled up to the curb to park we waived hello to CTA friends who happened to be standing outside the building at that moment. Trapper hopped out and came around to my side of the truck. As I disembarked we heard the wife of that couple say, "Awww. That's the sweetest thing I've ever seen" referring to Trapper's gentlemanly gesture of opening my door for me...to which her husband added, "Yeah. And I hate you for it" since now he figured his wife would be wanting the same attention from him in the future.

Our marriage isn't perfect. But over the years we have acquired various skills that help us turn difficult moments into positive marriage builders. Also, since it took us so long to find each other, we remain grateful for each other so that we can both still say, "*Father, Thank You For My Wife*" (or "husband") and maintain that life-long commitment to our marriage that we made with our "*Yep! I Will!*" vows in 1994.

It's not that we no longer have tough moments. It's that now we know how to handle them much better. My guess is that this is an acquired skill in most marriages because no one truly knows the challenges that are going to present themselves in the married life to come – most of all someone marrying into an occupation for which they have had "very little" training like I did – and like I'll bet a bunch of you reading this have done. But the Lord has helped us along – all along – including with some early on *Light Table Illuminations*.

Light Table Illuminations

Just six weeks into our marriage Trapper went over to Boulder, Colorado for a PromiseKeepers event in Folsom Field Stadium there. That year was only the second year of the existence of PromiseKeepers. The next summer when he went again, I didn't know I could have listened to the entire weekend on the radio. But when it came around again in 1996 I planned my weekend to listen to it but I didn't let Trapper know that I was going to do that.

We had purchased the inventory of a trapping supply business the year before and it was time to do a new version of our catalog. This was before I knew how to do that on the computer so there I was that weekend – listening to the radio, cleaning the house and doing the layout of our catalog on a light table in my home office.

At a certain point in the proceedings at PromiseKeepers they did a visual with a father and son up on the stage. I'll be darned – one of my Mountain Man's favorite phrases – they had a bunch of traps up on that stage. They blindfolded the young son and did a demonstration with the father guiding his son so that his son wouldn't get caught in the traps. The spiritual lesson was clear – a son needs a father to teach him about the traps of life and then guide him through them from time to time.

As I was listening to that display on the radio I was looking at a bunch of traps myself – placing little miniatures of them with an Exacto knife onto my layout of our trapping supply catalog. The thought occurred to me, "I'll bet I'm one of only a few wives of any of those guys there in that stadium who knows what those traps are called and how they are used. And there was an exceptional probability that I was the one and only such wife doing a layout of traps and trapping supplies while listening to that broadcast.

At various moments during the weekend I dropped what I was doing and hit the floor on my knees praying relative to what was being said on the radio and possibly impacting my Mountain Man husband sitting there at the event in person. Part of my prayers was that he was truly listening at those moments.

That happened five times during the weekend. When Trapper returned home he immediately and excitedly began recounting five times something had impacted him – and in exactly the same order that I had prayed when they were happening. He was still unaware that I had listened to it on the radio.

Two of the five times were the most comical – and powerful – in our lives and marriage.

Max Lucado was speaking: "Men. Ask the Lord to tell you if there's anyone you need to forgive." I threw my Exacto knife into the trough at the front edge of the light table. CLANK! I hit the floor on my knees. I knew who that person was. It wasn't me but someone from his childhood – although in the years since then I've most definitely given my Mountain Man plenty of opportunities to need to forgive me for one thing or another.

"Tell him it's [I said the name to God]."
"Tell him it's [same name]."
I stood up and went back to work at the light table.

Max Lucado again: "Now, you men who have thought of someone you need to forgive, stand up and let the men around you lay their hands on you and pray over you for your ability to forgive whoever that is."

CLANK! – into the trough went the Exacto knife again and back to the floor on my knees went I.

"Get him to stand up!"
"Get him to stand up!" I implored to God.
I knew the guys who were with him and I trusted that they would respond – if only Trapper would respond and stand up.

Trapper's version was Mountain Man marvelous: "The Lord showed me I needed to forgive [the same person I had identified] and then...I just stood up to put on my raincoat and all the guys around me put their hands on me and started praying over me!"

That cowboy trapper duster employed on the back of the horse in the *What A Ride!* story had played an important role yet again. See how creative our Creator is???!!!

Various friends have been important to us before and during our marriage. But the folks presented to me in the Mountain Man, trapping and rural life were a whole new realm for me. It has been amazing how many times things and people have come around to merge both of our worlds through quite a few *Full Circles.*

Full Circles

As far as I know, I'd never met a trapper before I met my Mountain Man. So there was also a whole world of other such folks that I had no knowledge of before meeting him.

I remember the first time we met Craig Legleiter. We had been engaged a little over a month and it was time to drive to southeast Kansas to meet Trapper's family in Altamont. I was then to return to Colorado, leaving Trapper there to observe his annual rite of wintering in Kansas to trap for his last time before our marriage.

Trapper needed some trapping supplies like lure and other stinky stuff and had been a long-time mail order customer of a business called Craig's Trapping Supplies but he had never met Craig. So we stopped by Craig's in La Crosse, Kansas on the way to Altamont. We had a nice visit and I was amazed at the variety of items he offered although I was clueless as to how a person would use any of them yet. That education didn't take place until a year and a half later, as I'll describe in a minute.

Anyway, Trapper put a plastic bag of his supply purchases in the very back of MY Honda Accord hatchback. As we got into the car to leave my first words were, "Phew. It sure smells like SKUNK in here!" I could not have said more prophetic words of a recurring theme in my married life to come. Little did I know..."very little", but we've already established that together in a previous story.

In January of 1995 (seven months after we married), Craig sold his inventory to us because he was headin' out for a job offer in Texas. But when that job didn't pan out like he'd planned, Trapper recommended Craig to the outfitter he worked for located between Gunnison and Crested Butte.

So that's how it developed that Craig sold his business to us and then wound up coming out to work with Trapper in Colorado for that summer of 1995 as a horsepack outfitter guide and ranch hand.

Craig's close proximity while I was trying to create a catalog for *Trapper's Trap Line* (our then-new trapping supply business) turned out to be extremely valuable since I was using his catalog as a guideline for making ours. At least it was a good starting reference given my novice condition.

Because I didn't know what most of these items were yet, it was quite an ordeal for me to create a catalog of them. I usually asked Trapper first but sometimes I was confounded by a description in Craig's old catalog and was glad he was handy to ask in person. I remember one description of some tool or something that was to be used for domestic animals. In my mind that meant pets such as dogs and cats. I was baffled as to how you would use the thing for dogs or cats. To my chagrin both Trapper and Craig had a good time informing me that a whatever-that-thing-was (I've conveniently forgotten) had to do with cows, sheep...livestock. My aforementioned lack of education was showing badly, especially now regarding the implements of trapping. But they were patient and I provided them with great entertainment while I slaved over this catalog job all summer.

Craig also delighted in reminding me what had happened back in January when we were at his house in La Crosse, Kansas picking up the trapping supply business inventory. While we were there it rained and rained and rained...and rained. At one point the three of us went out to Craig's truck, chattering all the way. Craig went to the driver's side and we went to the passenger side. And then, in mid-sentence, I...DISAPPEARED. Craig says one minute we were all talking and the next he was thinking, "Where'd she GO?" They found me under the truck where I had slippery-slid in the mud feet first. No one could recall what we had been talking about before. We were all too busy laughing. The guys could hardly get me out from under there for laughing so hard. I wasn't much help to them for the same reason. We were all a muddy mess when it was over.

And then it was Craig who so graciously discovered my typo goofs in the catalog AFTER it came off the press. The one he had the most fun with me about was "teepee" (since we also included supplies for Mountain Man Rendezvous re-enactors in our catalog). He informed me that "teepee" was the uppity way to spell the traditional Indian lodge and that I should have spelled it "tipi". And you can bet I did it right in the next year's catalog!

One day when Craig was out where we lived in Colorado working with Trapper they were patching a fence at Danni Ranch that Trapper figured must be well over a hundred years old by the way it broke every time they touched it. At some point Trapper lost his cool and, in total frustration, threw the fence stretcher as far as he could across the pasture. As they told the story later, Craig was a little perturbed by Trapper's display of temper. But, they retrieved the stretcher and got back at it.

As Trapper later told it, "I'll never forget it. A few minutes later I heard a loud crash and looked up to find Craig banging the fence stretcher against a tree...OVER and OVER." Craig had also reached the end of his rope – er – fence. And so the tension of the situation eased up a bit. It seems these trapper Mountain Man guys have all the

patience in the world with their trapping tools. But that pesky fence stretcher and that %X#&! fence were too much for 'em.

A couple of years later we were again grateful to Craig along with some other folks when I wound up operating a dealer booth without Trapper there at the Kansas Fur Harvesters 25th Annual Convention in Abilene. Trapper was usually there at all of the state conventions of contemporary trappers in Colorado, Wyoming, Utah, Nebraska and Kansas that we went to while we had our trapping and Mountain Man Rendezvous supply business. But this time he had gone with several other men from Crested Butte to the PromiseKeepers rally in Washington, DC that same weekend.

So there I was in Kansas, a Georgia lawyer's daughter somehow willing to sell trapping supplies that two years before I had known nothing about while my independent, doesn't-like-crowds Mountain Man husband was willing to be crammed onto The Mall in DC with what was reported to have been a MILLION men. The things we get into for each other...Fae in my un-natural element with the crew selling trapping supplies at the 1997 Kansas Fur Harvesters Convention while Trapper was off in Washington, DC in HIS un-natural and very crowded element.

Craig and some other guys thankfully unloaded the truck, set up, helped man, take down and reload our dealer booth and generally made this whole experience go easier for me. Thank goodness they were there because I could not have answered all of those trappers' questions by myself.

When we attended the 2013 Colorado Trappers Association annual convention near Canon City over Labor Day Weekend, a fella introduced himself to us as Bruce Davidson, said he was from Pratt, Kansas and that he remembered meeting me at the 1997 Kansas Fur Harvesters convention when I was, as he put it, "handling that Trapper's Trap Line booth without your husband there".

I suppose a woman doing such a thing without her trapper husband there in that setting had made a lasting impression! The same last name of Davidson had connected us way back then and it was a fun coincidence that he cropped up again just as the writing of this book mentioning that event was starting in earnest. He was also happy to meet that trapper husband of mine who had been missing in action in 1997 – but in action in Washington.

Back in 1997 after Trapper returned from Washington, DC we discovered yet another way that God had previously been at work weaving the fabric of our future lives together without our knowledge. Trapper showed me some stationary that he had picked up at the apartment where they had stayed in Washington which belongs to a friend of ours. When I saw the address on the letterhead it sounded mighty familiar to me – 200 C Street, SE. I located a box that had come from my childhood room closet in my family's life-long home in Athens, Georgia. My digging around in it produced a letter I had written to my parents in the summer of 1974 while working with a girlfriend from Athens as a Congressional Intern in our Georgia congressman's office which had arranged an apartment for us three blocks from the congressional office building where we worked.

Sure enough, there in the upper left-hand corner of the envelope of that letter was the return address of my 1974 apartment – 200 C Street, SE.

That's right – in 1997 my husband stayed in the very same building I had lived in 23 years earlier! Out of all the places they could have stayed in Washington, DC, to us that was an amazing development and a not-so-accidental coincidence that God must have immensely enjoyed tying together for us knowing that one day we would each come to know Him more intimately before He finally put us together.

From 2004 to 2013 I did the bookkeeping for a friend's retail bed, bath and kitchen store on Elk Avenue in Crested Butte. A new young gal began working there and while we were getting to know each other I told her what my husband did for a living. She said, "My boyfriend's father is a game warden over in Carbondale near Aspen." Turns out that Trapper had met her boyfriend at under a year old and was riding in a backpack on his game warden Dad's back over in Marble, Colorado some 25 years earlier. Her boyfriend has been working for us since 2010.

So many *Full Circles* have blessed our marriage. You'll see a reference to Laine Dobson and his family in the front of the book since he did the line drawing for the cover. We have known Laine for what is now half of HIS life. Then in early 2014 we discovered that a new customer of ours is also a customer of my cousin Lee's catering business in Georgia. Most of these *Full Circles* have come around during our years in Crested Butte where we've lived the majority of our married life together. But all sorts of predicaments happened during the relatively brief time we made our home in...*Sa–where?*

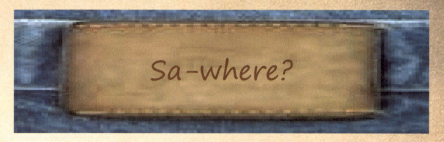

Sa-where?

For a few years we lived in a VERY small town in Colorado. It was so small folks passed through before they could figure out how to say it. There it was, as a brain teaser, on the highway signs on the way there. Saguache. Go ahead. Take your best shot at pronouncing it. Aw c'mon. Okay. I'll tell you... eventually.

We moved there in May of 1997 because real estate in the Crested Butte/ Gunnison area where we were living then (and later moved back to) was getting too pricey for us. Looking back now we know that we really never did completely leave Crested Butte because we went back to visit so often. Then, in 2004, it became obvious that we needed to move back to Crested Butte full time again instead of going back and forth so much. So, many folks never even realized we left at all because we stayed so connected there.

To tell you the truth, we'd always wondered how to say the name of that town too. Believe me, we had fun with those mail order takers. And we engaged in a lot of mail order since our commercial district consisted mostly of 1 grocery store, 1 liquor store, 1 1/2 restaurants (the half was only open for lunch), 1 branch of a bank, TWO gas stations (but one of those was at the grocery store) and a doctor's office (two doctors came one day a week each – we couldn't get sick on other days!). There was always that bewildered pause when the order taker got to the "name of city" part of the order – especially the ones who already had it on the screen.

UPS was our friend...except when we ordered stinky trapping supplies. And let's not forget the Post Office as part of the commercial district there. The two ladies who worked there then had a tough time with the smelly parcels too. They solved the problem by putting them out the back door (can you blame them?) until we could get there. But somebody always asked them, "Got a skunk around here someplace?' They loved us anyway. We gave them flowers to make amends when it was too awful. So the florist 32 miles away loved us too. The UPS driver just gratefully rang the doorbell and RAN to get away from the smell he had been hauling around in his brown delivery truck. "What has brown done for you?" as their slogan goes – a lot in our case. Bet a lot of other trappers have a similar relationship with their delivery drivers.

That area is big cattle ranching country. True to my Trapper's unobtrusive nature, when we moved there he decided to let the ranchers hear about him by word of mouth instead of going around introducing himself and his Wildlife Management services. That proved to be an extremely wise approach to life there. We were told they liked us 'cause we didn't come to change it but to just blend in and appreciate the rural landscape and slower pace. We were plum happy WITHOUT all the amenities or hustle and bustle of city life that lots of other folks have to deal with. And, there was always mail order.

With a nickname like Trapper in a town of only 600 people, it didn't take folks long to find out about us...including the county Sheriff's Office there in town. The dispatcher there told us this story:

One day in the Fall of 1998 they got a call saying, "There's a man walking into town with a sleeping bag on his back and a gun slung over his shoulder." So they sent out the Undersheriff to investigate. This was the radio transmission back to the Sheriff's Office: "Made contact with subject. It's just Trapper."

The rest of the story is that Trapper had a traditional ashwood packbasket on his back and, yes, an UNLOADED (good move) .22 caliber rifle on a shoulder strap. But he was also wearing a beaver hat which looked like LOTS of extra hair. This caused the caller, who was a friend of ours, not to recognize Trapper at a distance. For some time when we'd see our Undersheriff we'd say, "Have you saved Saguache from any more invasions of the dreaded trapper lately?" We also dished out a little ration to the caller. Sometime after that I saw him at the bank and HE brought it up for a laugh. But at least both of those fellas were on the lookout for all of us.

Now – about how to say the name of that little burg – Saguache. Here's a hint. In January 2001 we received a letter from a friend who said that he and his family were "trying to figure out if there was going to be a way to get to Sawatch (or wherever it is you guys live – Hooked On Phonics certainly worked for me!)." Although the phonetic spelling was right, the actual spelling was not.

The attempts of others at saying it were truly inspired and plentiful. For example, it's not "Sag-you-ache" (although that's sorta how it's spelled and, by the way, if you sag you WILL ache). It's not "Sausage" (although Trapper loves the biscuits and gravy I make with the stuff). It's not "Sasquatch" (didn't see any sign of Big Foot around there). And it's not "Sag-you-ahh-che" (no Ute Indians still living in tipis there) or "Sah-guchi" (no Italian shoe makers there either). As we told our friend in a letter back to him, "you're way ahead of most folks who know where it is but cannot for the life of them PRONOUNCE it!" He was right with the phonics: "Sahh-watch". Trapper's Dad and three "Sconies" (trapper friends from Wisconsin) figured it out right off. They said they "look at their "Sah-watch" to see what time it is."

We were somewhat of a curiosity to the folks who already lived in Saguache when we arrived but some wholeheartedly embraced us there.

In Saguache Trapper, in addition to his trapping, worked as a ranch hand at Coleman Ranches – the founders of Coleman Natural Beef which is now nationwide.

Just before we left Saguache, Frances Coleman paid us a high compliment when I ran into her at the Post Office: "I hate to see you two move away. You're normal!" Well yes, from Frances' ranching world point of view plus Trapper's successful education of his wife in that rural world, we WERE normal. *I'll Be Darned.*

Frances had an ornery side to her personality for which I provided her great sport. She was in the habit of delivering Trapper's paycheck to our home every two weeks. One morning I was working from home doing marketing projects for a medical clinic in Alamosa south of there. I had begun my work before Trapper left for his day of calf branding out at the Coleman's. Uh oh – I became so engrossed in being creative that I lost track of time and had not changed out of my nightgown, robe and slippers after he left.

At about 10:00 am the doorbell rang. It was Frances with the paycheck. Now the ranching world goes from before sun-up to past sun-down. It's not a lazy life and I knew Frances was not a lazy gal. I wasn't being lazy either but I didn't know if she would know that, given my appearance. I didn't want to keep her waiting so, since we were both women, I figured I needn't take the time to change. Big mistake. When I opened the front door I greeted her with, "I know what you're going to do. I just know it. As soon as you get back out to the ranch you're going to tell everybody there how you found me here." I also knew Frances and it would have been pointless to ask her not to do that.

Sure enough, according to Trapper, Frances drove straight to where they were branding calves and could not get out of her vehicle fast enough before CALLING OUT to my husband and all those cowboys out there within earshot, "Let me tell you how I just found your wife – still in her nightgown!"

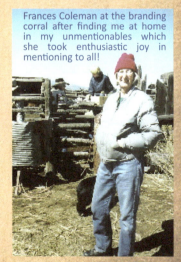

Frances Coleman at the branding corral after finding me at home in my unmentionables which she took enthusiastic joy in mentioning to all!

Lesson learned. To this day I try to get dressed earlier in the day when I'm working at home – just in case someone unexpectedly shows up. Occasionally time gets away from me like it did that day. But I always think of Frances Coleman when it happens.

That sure gets me to the closet in a hurry.

In my steady progression in rural life education, lo and behold the Colemans *invited* me out there to take these photos of a day of calf branding.

It's curious why the cowboy trapper, as he described himself to my Dad in his proposal letter, opted for a ball cap that day when all the others donned their traditional cowboy hats for the task.

Telling folks NOT to do stuff very often backfires anyway – like the day when we moved to Saguache and curiosity got the better of our friends helping with the move. Trapper should have known what they would do when he told them, "*Don't Open The Freezer*".

54

"Don't Open The Freezer"

When we moved to Saguache about 100 miles southeast of Crested Butte some guy friends hauled horse trailers and helped haul things into the house we'd purchased down there. When the time came to move our chest freezer into the garage, Trapper told the men, "Don't open the freezer." Can you believe it? He honestly believed these guys would honor his request.

Well, instead he might as well have handed them an engraved invitation to...open the freezer. Trapper and I were upstairs in the house setting that good ol' light table in place when a familiar scent wafted up to us. We looked at each other and said at the same time, "They opened the freezer." Of course they did. And they immediately received their just reward for doing so as the scent of skunk passed over them all...and up to us.

As you know, skunks have been a running theme in our marriage. And apparently we are not the only ones who have had that impression.

About a year after we moved to Saguache we invited, Jim Kunes, our pastor friend at Oh-Be-Joyful Church up in Crested Butte, to come down and preach a sermon at a little church there. So, on the appointed weekend Jim headed down the highway on Saturday afternoon to spend the night with us before offering that message at the church the next morning.

He said he pondered if he could find our house as he drove down Highway 114. Since he had helped us move in, there was a good chance he remembered how to find it. Even if he wasn't one of the freezer opening culprits the year before, he certainly suffered the consequences of that event with the rest of us which probably led him to the rationalization he entertained on this day as he drove down the road toward us: "All I have to do is get to a certain corner, stick my nose in the air, and then I'll be able to find the house."

He had no way of knowing what was happening down in Saguache at that very moment. I was in the utility room in the middle of the house switching laundry from the washer to the dryer when all of a sudden my nose started burning and my eyes started watering. I knew that Trapper was out in his fur shed skinning a skunk. He had done that many times before and had never had any significant problem with the scent bags on those skunks. He extracts and sells the essence (that's a polite way to put it). Most folks don't know this but it's sometimes used for...women's perfume! Lure makers also buy it.

Anyway, there he was out there and placed his horse syringe into the essence bag. He hit some kind of obstruction and nothing would come out. So, he chose another place to extract the scent and when he put the syringe there, out shot the essence through the first hole he'd made in the bag.

Oh my goodness, the whole neighborhood STUNK like SKUNK! That explained why I was able to be so affected by it in the middle of the house with not one window near that utility room.

Within minutes Trapper stuck his head in the side door to the house and yelled, "Put a bucket of soapy hot water out the back door." He certainly didn't have to explain why. So I prepared the bucket. Just when I opened the back door to put the bucket out there I heard our neighbor, who had apparently come over to investigate our aroma, say to Trapper, "You're wife's not gonna let you into the house." No kidding.

It wasn't long before our friend Jim showed up. When he told us what he'd been thinking on the way down the highway and then his nose test turned out to be a true compass, we told him we couldn't think of a time of pondering getting a nose full at the corner could have been more prophetic.

There was another time at that house that a skunk happened to climb up into a tarp in the woodshed and gave up the ghost. We guess he figured he might as well get it over with now rather than take his chances with Trapper around.

Soon after moving into that house in Saguache we purchased a second freezer – an upright one for my purposes that we put INSIDE in the utility room – with shelves to put all sorts of yummy things in (including peanut butter cookie tins) but NOT for Trapper's critter use.

So, at this point we began saying, "We have His and Her Freezers". When we moved back to Crested Butte both of those freezers wound up in the garage together which is rather risky business in our case – as you found out in *Skunk Cookies*. Alas, when a guy working for us brought a beaver into the garage and unwittingly put it in the upright freezer, Trapper quickly informed him that, "Oh no, that needs to go into MY chest freezer, not Fae's freezer. We DO NOT mix the contents." Now we have even purchased a second chest freezer for Trapper. My upright freezer has had its unique moments – especially one which you'll soon discover in another story – *Frozen Pedal To The Metal Of The Freezer*.

Discoveries are prolific in this *Life as a Mountain Man's Wife*. One was how much a Mountain Man from history had impacted my Mountain Man and how much Scripture matters to *That Bible Totin' Trapper*.

That Bible Totin' Trapper

When I met Al Davidson, I truly didn't know trappers still existed. So the concept of a Godly or Christian trapper was also remote. It wasn't long into our friendship before Trapper introduced me to Jedediah Smith – my Mountain Man's hero from the Fur Trade Era. They called Jedediah Smith *"That Bible Totin' Trapper."*

Jed would have appreciated that my Mountain Man trapper and I met at a little church situated smack in the middle of the Colorado Rocky Mountains where everybody just called him "Trapper". So, it was a rather appropriate moment while we were driving home during one of the primary times when I was writing up these stories that Trapper suddenly started randomly singing, "Jedediah, Jedediah, say a prayer for me" – a line from a song by a guy named Nightsinger that we saw several times at various rendezvous up in Wyoming in 1996. Jedediah clearly made a lifelong lasting impression on Trapper who, true to his heritage, is also a Bible-Totin' Trapper. At least I've happily seen him reading it a bunch – at times with a beaver pelt cover on it too!

The year after Trapper and I met would show me a side of life I knew I was desiring in some form but it came to me in a way I never had expected – by getting to know and eventually marrying a trapper. As my soon-to-be Matron of Honor put it when our engagement seemed to be imminent, "I envy you. You're going to have a life so close

to the land." No kidding! I soon found out just how close to the land we were talking about – and I am still in awe of getting to do that even though sometimes it is a little too close for comfort. And then we ventured into another Land I could never have imagined. But you'll find out more about that later.

On January 8, 1994 I wrote the following in my journal:

"My 40th birthday and the night I received Trapper's engagement ring. I realize how much I need to give up of my ways and thoughts of doing things and let Trapper's light shine – for there is so much light there if I will step back and give him a chance to shine. I have a lot to learn from him. God has given me a jewel. I am only beginning to find out the value of that jewel."

It wasn't until I re-read this the next day that I realized the play on words I had written considering that I had received a diamond engagement ring the night before. Now, 21 years later, this book turns out to be a way to give my Mountain Man "a chance to shine."

Consistent with his engagement proposal, Trapper wasn't there in person to give me my engagement ring either. He was back in Kansas all winter trapping to pay for it and my wedding band. Trapper had said, "We got engaged in Georgia, we're getting married in Colorado so I want to get the rings in Kansas" – a fine piece of symbolism of our past separate childhoods merging with our future married life. So we had picked them out in Kansas in November but I did not know until I opened the box that he had shipped the engagement ring to friends in Crested Butte for them to deliver at my 40th birthday party.

I framed that journal entry and asked a friend, Desse Anthony, to take it to our honeymoon Cabin #8 at Spring Creek Resort so that it would be waiting for us on a bedside table there.

This request gave her the opportunity to short sheet and toilet paper the bed. We never imagined she had such a mischievous streak in her! It was quite an entangling discovery at the time – her version of the age-old Shivaree, we figured. But still not something we were at all expecting from her. Another lesson learned, eh Desse?

I am STILL finding that I have much to learn from my Mountain Man – that life-long ride I mentioned earlier. We could all learn a lot from Mountain Men and their simpler, more basic approach to life. What many of them are really about is a deep respect for God's creation. It's not something easy to see right off when the world is pounding us all with the opposite message.

I am grateful to have discovered this back to basics way of life and I reverently and often thank God for extracting me from the politically correct sidetrack that was leading me down a path of deception and lies. I don't know how I got on that path for I wasn't raised to go that way.

We have a friend named David Barton who is the founder of a nationwide ministry called WallBuilders (www.WallBuilders.com) which is based on foundational scripture from Nehemiah about rebuilding the wall around Jerusalem which is symbolic of rebuilding the ruins of a nation's Godly heritage – similar to the situation in America today. Please look up this website if you do not yet know of it.

We became friends with David when he came to Crested Butte as a speaker at the Community Prayer Breakfast in the early 1990s. From time to time after that he returned to go on horsepack trips. Since Trapper was one of the guides on those occasions, we also became friends with his wife, Cheryl, their children, his parents and the staff members when he brought them with him at various times.

David tuned into Trapper's interest in "That Bible Totin' Trapper" and one day a box arrived from him with copies of two Jedediah Smith books enclosed as a surprise gift. So Trapper sent David a beaver pelt as a thank you in the tradin' tradition of the Mountain Man. In July of 2002 we were returning from my 30th high school reunion in Athens, Georgia and dropped by Aledo, Texas and the WallBuilders ministry building to say hello. In the course of visiting with David we discovered that there was Trapper's beaver pelt gift on the wall right behind David's desk.

And then there was the Bible Totin' that Trapper has done at home. In 2005 the worship leader at our church in Crested Butte concocted a most ingenious plan. One Sunday morning she asked the congregation to sing *Amazing Grace*. By pre-arrangement with Trapper, as we began singing the third verse he started walking down the aisle dressed in his Mountain Man garb and carrying a burlap bag along with his beaver fur covered Bible.

Through many dangers, toils and SNARES
I have already come;
'Tis grace that brought me safe thus far
and grace will lead me home.

Trapper then dumped out the burlap bag on the carpet at the front of the sanctuary and proceeded to share with the congregation about how often the subject of traps and snares comes up in Scripture – an amazing number of times. So *Amazing Grace* has a whole bunch of expanded meaning to us.

Because *"through many dangers, toils and snares I have already come"* is an apt description of my single life before meeting the Lord on a more personal level which was also not long before meeting my Mountain Man, I had lots of things needing emotional healing. Therefore some trapping imagery has special meaning for me which I am sometimes led to share – now being one of those times.

Since most of us have some sort of baggage in life, maybe there will also be special significance for you in the *Captured Coon's Life Lesson.*

Captured Coon's Life Lesson

Trapper has captured lots of raccoons over our years together. One of those occasions provided a special memory – and spiritual life lesson.

Experience has taught Trapper that caution is required when releasing most animals – especially raccoons. He says that if you're not careful when releasing them they are likely to try to run up your leg. For example, although Trapper knew better about where to release raccoons, one time he released one that promptly ran up onto...the back axle of our truck. The coon went running back and forth on that axle and we ran back and forth on both sides of the truck trying to coax it outta there so we could drive away without harming it. This required some time and patience but finally we had another mission accomplished.

So then he located a place on a little wooden bridge with only about a one foot drop to a creek ("crick" in the Mountain Man Trapper vernacular) below – a perfect place for raccoon releases!

There was one problem with this one particular raccoon. He appeared terrified of leaving the trap. Trapper shook the trap. I prodded the coon's behind with a stick. We did everything we could think of to coax that raccoon outta that trap. It kept clinging to the pan at the back of the trap – the thing that triggers the door to close the trap. Then, when we finally got it to head for the door and while Trapper was holding the cage over the creek, it held on for dear life at the end of the trap and just did not want to drop down into the water where it could so easily swim and get away from us. Freedom was at hand for that imprisoned critter but the coon just could not comprehend how much better it would be...on the outside...out in the inside. At some point during this process I straightened up and then observed,

"There's got to be a spiritual message here. Hmmm. This is probably exactly what God feels like when we insist on staying trapped and then hanging onto the very things that trap us. He must be saying, 'Look! There's freedom right in front of you – ready and waiting for you! It's an easy leap of faith! Just step out into it! Go for it!' "

Doesn't it seem like sometimes He has to prod and poke us to get us to take that leap of faith into everything He has waiting for us instead of staying in the things that trap us like negative behaviors, old memories of past transgressions and more...the things that keep us from meeting the full potential He has created for us? There's a perfect verse in God's Word about this:

For I know the plans I have for you," declares the LORD, "plans to prosper you and not to harm you, plans to give you hope and a future.
– Jeremiah 29:11 (NIV)

Whenever the temptation has ever occurred to me to want *A Way Out* of our marriage because of some tough moment or other, the Lord reminds me that this marriage was, thank goodness...and Him...a life sentence for which we are grateful. It took us forever to find each other, for heaven's sake, so I'm declaring right here and now and in writing that bailing from this *Life as a Mountain Man's Wife*, even as crazy as it gets sometimes, is not an option.

Of course there are those times when situations in life attempt to ensnare us. In those potential predicaments we have discovered that we can usually take a step back from the entanglement and some choices are in order because, if we will look for them, the Lord will show us how He has provided *A Way Out*.

A Way Out

If you're anything like I was when I met my Mountain Man future husband, I did not have any clue about the mechanism of a snare.

Just in case you're also wondering what a snare looks like, you'll see pictures of one in the next few pages.

Trapper has taught me a bunch about the actual confounding conTRAPtion called a snare.

Then, after he did his Sunday morning exposition of trapping imagery in Scripture, I had an idea. I asked him to make a snare for me so I could have it on hand for use in various Bible study lessons or when other opportunities cropped up to share the following spiritual message related to snares. It's interesting how often it is appropriate to share this!

To get this demonstration going, I ask for a volunteer to take off their shoes and wait for my instructions. Often times the folks I'm sharing with know the importance of animal control and related equipment in my life so it's understandable if they begin to wonder what I'm up to and then wonder what they have gotten themselves into when they see me laying a snare cable out on the floor.

I then explain to the assembled group or individual that when temptation comes at us we usually have a choice regarding our reaction...AND...our reactions to trials really are our choice because no one and nothing can MAKE us feel any certain way without our agreement – a life changing concept well worth grasping right there alone!

Some snares have a gizmo called a stop to guard against ensnaring an unintended critter.

Although I doubt if the enemy of our souls will install a stop on our behalf, God's Word tells us that the Lord provides *A Way Out* of potential snares in our path:

No temptation has seized you except what is common to man. And God is faithful; he will not let you be tempted beyond what you can bear. But when you are tempted, he will also provide a way out so that you can stand up under it.
– 1 Corinthians 10:13 (NIV)

Imagine that the loop is temptation. Although the enemy of our souls is holding the other end of that snare cable, Almighty God Himself is also at hand just beyond the enemy waiting to help us in our moments of temptation...if we'll let Him by looking to Him for the solution to the circumstance.

At first the snare's loop of temptation is loose and it is easy to step out. Sometimes we're not paying attention or are not experienced in life or mature enough in dealing with temptation. Or sometimes we're too overwhelmed by life or are so taken by surprise that we do not heed the dire warning.

> Moreover, no man knows when his hour will come: As fish are caught in a cruel net, or birds are taken in a snare, so men are trapped by evil times that fall unexpectedly upon them.
> – Ecclesiastes 9:12 (NIV)

Other times we are simply too plain stubborn to listen to reason. So then we step a little more into the snare of temptation and it goes over the top of our foot. But Almighty God is still there beyond the enemy and offering us *A Way Out*.

If we still do not heed God's loving warning we may then turn and walk away from Him and the noose of the snare of temptation begins to tighten. But it doesn't hurt that much...yet...so we STILL do not heed the warning.

Keep walking away from the Lord's solution and then some pain begins. We realize that we're ensnared and we begin to struggle.

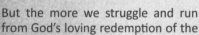
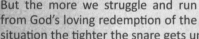

But the more we struggle and run from God's loving redemption of the situation the tighter the snare gets until we are absolutely captured by the enemy of our souls. In fact, the metal piece in the snare loop here is a Sure Lock and for sure the enemy has a lock on us – or so he thinks.

But wait!...there is...The Great Snare Releaser!

We have a Savior – Yeshua – who is standing there in front of Almighty God and looking compassionately over the snare as our Advocate. He reminds His

Father that He has paid the painful price of our giving into temptation and that He has provided *A Way Out* with His own blood. God then sees us through the redemptive sacrifice and work of His Son and allows Yeshua to step in, flip the release on the Sure Lock that's not so sure after all and we are...REDEEMED!

My eyes are ever on the LORD, for only He will release my feet from the snare.
– Psalm 25:15 (NIV)

That is, if we allow Yeshua near us to grab ahold of the not-so-Sure Lock and release us to freedom from the temptation!

We have escaped like a bird out of the fowler's snare; the snare has been broken, and we have escaped. Our help is in the name of the LORD, the Maker of heaven and earth.
– Psalm 124:7-8 (NIV)

The ensnared volunteer is usually quite happy for me to hit the Sure Lock and surely let them outta there by that time. Ankle rubbing usually accompanies the happy release and they are usually are a little more reluctant to volunteer so easily for my animal-related spiritual demonstrations in the future.

By the way, you might enjoy knowing that the person who posed for these snare photos here is the same gal who short-sheeted and toilet papered our honeymoon cabin. Some 18 years of friendship and experiences later, looks like I finally got her back and got her ensnared in the process!

All of this snaring education led at some point to ask Trapper to define lures and baits and tell me the differences between them so that I could add that to my spiritual snaring demonstration presentation. Seems to me that I should have that down after 20 plus years of knowing him and learning about his occupation. But, since Trapper has a glorious habit of coming out with insightful yet unique and concise ways of describing things, the Lord urged me to consult Trapper who came through yet again when he responded with...

"The lure gets the animal's attention and attracts them to the bait which is waiting for them in the trap or snare. The bait is what gets them to step into the snare and get captured."

I had not thought about that. I guess I thought animals just happen along, step into the snare and get stuck in it naturally. Trapper doesn't have occasion to use snares much n his chosen profession nowadays but it's still a terrific teaching visual anyway.

Another subject all of this snare stuff brings up is that of fear. Wouldn't you know it, there's also scripture that ties that into the snare imagery. When fear takes hold we have a major problem.

My husband's profession gets him into some frightful situations from time to time with bears, mountain lions and such. There is even an occasional human-caused predicament to be managed. We've even dealt with fear together in the Middle East – as you'll discover regarding our *Journey To The Land*.

When other folks are the potential source of our fear, here's what God says about the matter:.

> *Fear of man will prove to be a* **snare,** *but whoever trusts in the* **Lord** *is kept* **safe.**
>
> Proverbs 29:25

This is a sign I made and hung my Mountain Man's demo snare prominently on it. It resides beside my desk at home. Whenever I start to think things like, "I can't get everything done", "I don't know how to do that", "Why would anyone want to read what I write" and more, all I have to do is look over my shoulder at this sign, pray against that fear from you-know-where and carry on faithfully.

Speaking of being faithful, many of us have known magnificently faithful furry friends. One such critter in our lives was a white and rust color spotted red heeler...*Most Excellent Festus.*

Most Excellent Festus

One of the most definitely memorable characters of many who have come into my life because of our marriage was Festus, our red heeler cow dog.

Ol' Festus was a trappin' hound from the get-go.

Trapper was in Kansas trapping the 1993-94 winter of our engagement. I was in Crested Butte.

One day I called him in tears with the vet's news that the time was about up for my old dog, Tabor. The jaw cancer he'd had for over a year was about to take him. Tabor had been with me since he was weaned and for almost 13 years by then – most of my single life years – and Trapper felt badly for me. It was Tabor who had accompanied me in my travels that had led me to Crested Butte and my Mountain Man.

A few days later Trapper was out trapping at a farmer's place in Mound Valley, Kansas whose female dog had just birthed a litter of pups. One in the litter looked a lot like Tabor. So, when the farmer asked Trapper what he could pay him for his trapping services, Trapper said, "How 'bout letting me have that little yeller pup there?" and told the farmer the situation. The farmer was agreeable but the pup was not – wouldn't have anything to do with Trapper. But there was this other little white pup with rust-colored spots in that litter that wouldn't leave him alone – followed him everywhere except when he'd run in front of him, flip upside down on his back at Trapper's feet and get so excited that he'd...well, you know how it goes.

So, the white pup got to go trapping right away in life and loved it. Although reluctant, the farmer finally agreed to let Trapper have him. He named him Festus after the Gunsmoke deputy – Festus Haggen – who was, as Trapper recalled, a trapper when he met Marshal Dillon. I wonder how many of the rest of us (who were alive yet) picked up on THAT at the time it aired in 1964!

Yes, our Festus was truly a character. And he loved hanging out with characters. He was at his best when he got to go to a Mountain Man Rendezvous. When we travelled around to so many of them in 1996, we began noticing that he would be calm until...we turned onto a dirt road. At that point he would go berserk and then that activity would heighten the second he spotted canvas tents. He loved it so much that we gave him his own tin cup to wear on his collar which others in the camp were encouraged to fill...with water.

Festus was a friend to all at the Rendezvous. One guy there even gave him the camp name of Canvas since he was the same color and loved the sight of canvas camps so.

And Festus considered himself on guard duty once our vehicle was packed to go and then was repacked at the end of any event.

He was quite a salesman of our trade goods at the Rendezvous too.

Trapper considered him an extra pair of eyes out there – which came in handy a number of times when he chased away a variety of curious critters attempting to join their trapping expeditions uninvited. I recall one day when Festus came STRUTTING back to the truck long before Trapper could get there. I noticed Festus had a sorta special air about him. When Trapper got to the truck and before he had a chance to say anything I asked, "What happened out there? Festus is rather proud of somethin'!" He told me that Festus had just chased a bear away from where he was setting traps.

So, I'm grateful along with Trapper that Festus loved to go trapping.

Trapper found out Festus was a good fur dog early on in their acquaintance. Back in Kansas, when Festus was only about 3 months old, Trapper and his trapping partner were baffled as to how the beaver were getting in and out of this one particular giant beaver lodge. Festus, who had apparently waited long enough for the humans to figure it out, started digging at a knothole in a tree laying down near the lodge. The knot fell out and they discovered that the tree was completely hollow. Trapper says, "The beaver were using it kinda like a great big straw to travel to and from the lodge." He caught a 75 pound beaver there after Festus dug out the solution to the mystery.

Festus showed us right off how sociable he is. He also displayed his affinity for the driver's seat – rather, the floorboard.

One June Sunday afternoon a couple of weeks before our wedding, we decided to have a nice relaxing day together and take a break from all of the preparations. We loaded up Festus and Tabor (who was miraculously still with us), drove to Taylor Reservoir southeast of Crested Butte, noticed that the water was way down, saw a bunch of other vehicles out on the beach, drove onto it and promptly...sank. We shoveled and shoveled – to no avail. So much for our nice relaxing day together. Well, at least we were together but it was not very relaxing.

Eventually a group of folks in a 4WD vehicle noticed our plight and came to help. There were three people in the back seat and a couple in the front plus the driver. They pulled us out easily enough and then, while the driver was out and we were thanking him, all of a sudden their vehicle started ROARING like crazy. Festus had gone visitin', had jumped onto the driver's floorboard and was curled up on...the accelerator! We rushed over, got him out, apologized profusely and off they went.

Finally we settled down to our nice relaxing day together – higher up on the beach. About a half hour later we started laughing, "What if that thing had somehow slipped into gear? We would have helplessly watched five very wide-eyed individuals race straight into the reservoir – with Festus driving!" And there are a few Nebraska Fur Harvesters members who will recall seeing the brake lights of our trapping supply van on all night at their convention in Crete in 1996. They got a big kick out of telling us about it the next morning. We figgered Festus used the brake pedal for a pillow!

Trapper and Festus had all sorts of Mountain Man adventures together in all sorts of weather. Seems Festus led the way on some of them.

When we adopted a big cream colored lab dog who was in the Gunnison paper as lost with no home in early 1997, what better name could we have given him than yet another Gunsmoke character? We chose "Chester." Shortly after that someone offered to give us a cat named "Miss Kitty." We declined.

A few years after Festus came into our lives, Trapper was looking up something in the concordance of his Bible and came across the name Festus in there. He turned to Acts 26:25 and read it out to me where Paul addresses a Roman governor as "most excellent Festus." Our heeler immediately took to the addition to his moniker. Then, sometime after that, Trapper was standing at the door watching the dogs playing under the apple trees in our Saguache backyard while I was fixing dinner. With a pensive look on his face he mused, "Oh *Most Excellent Festus*...and his Court Jester Chester." Perfect.

Whenever beaver trapping season rolled around, Festus was ever ready with his mad dash around to the driveway in front of the house. You can almost imagine him yelping, "Oh boy, I getta go, I getta go!" as he effortlessly flew through the air and piled into the back of the truck.

Trapper and Festus had a great love and tremendous respect for one another for 15 years. You wouldn't naturally think of Trapper as a guy who would care about getting a dog a coat to contend with our snow and sometimes sub-zero winter temperatures. But I know better and you've also seen evidence of Trapper's soft heart in some of these tales. But, here's living color proof...

Festus knew his place in life, in Trapper's heart and in mine too.

He didn't have any problem taking advantage of those soft spots.

Speaking of faithful furry friends, one I only briefly saw but never formally met very likely saved my life at the cost of its life and therefore came to be called *The Sacrificial Rabbit.*

The Sacrificial Rabbit

On one fine December evening I was driving down Highway 114 from Gunnison back to Saguache where we were still living for a little while longer before returning to Crested Butte. I was tired from an all day book signing event at the Arts Center with Phoebe Cranor – whose _Ranch Life_ and _More Ranch Life_ books I had published. So, I was not at my most alert...but sure needed to be.

Just as I reached the top of Cochetopa Pass I spied a white rabbit sitting to my left on the side of the road. But then as I passed by him, all of a sudden that rabbit hopped up and hopped right UNDER my left front tire. It's not so much that I ran over him but that he ran under me and there was no escaping the inevitable result.

I was sickened by it and recall driving on thinking out loud, "Oh that's so sad. That was awful!" But then I shifted to thinking, "That just goes to show that you never know what an animal's going to do." It also reminded me that there were often lots of deer and elk on that road at night and I experienced a sense of heightened awareness about watching for them.

Within a mile I came around a curve near the bottom of the pass and there, standing right in the middle of the road, was a HUGE bull elk with a gigantic rack on his head. Because I had slowed down due to the rabbit's demise and reminder, I was easily able to avert a collision with the monstrous elk.

My focus then shifted back to that rabbit up on top of the pass and my perspective on that rabbit completely changed. I began thanking God for what He had just done in providing The Sacrificial Rabbit which had caused me to be at a level of extra caution which I just knew had kept me from hitting that elk which would have either killed or seriously injured me, the elk or the car – possibly all three.

When I reached our home in Saguache I told Trapper what had just happened and we recalled a time when a family of 10 (parents with eight children) had left our house traveling on the same road but within the hour had come limping back to us with the front end on their vehicle looking like an accordion. The 16 year old just learning to drive had not had the benefit of The Sacrificial Rabbit and had to learn this one the hard way when she hit her elk. I'm fairly certain the recollection of that incident came to mind when

I was thinking about elk prolifically wandering on that road and, thankfully, slowed down to watch out for them which frightfully paid off a short time later. My Mountain Man had seen much in his 20 plus years of dealing with elk as a horseback elk hunting guide. Being the hunter that he is, Trapper was glad for more than the obvious reasons already mentioned that I didn't bag an elk that particular way.

However we did wind up with an elk in a different and more unusual way. We had heard from our Game Wardens down in that area that they were shooting elk as pests that were giving the alfalfa and potato farmers fits by eating their crops. Having nowhere to take them, they were having to waste them. We asked our Game Warden to let us know the next time they had one like that because we would be willing to process it and put it in our freezer for winter meat. A few days later came the call that they were headed our way – would be to our house in 20 minutes. It was a Saturday in August with truly a 100 degree temperature that day. We knew that the two of us could not process it fast enough in that kind of heat and that a big risk of spoilage was on the horizon. What to do in this situation? This was one of those times when my education as a *Mountain Man's Wife* went into high gear. The one grocery store there in Saguache couldn't take it because the USDA will not let domestic meat preparation equipment be used for wild game processing. I had not known that before. I had not had a reason to know that before. We still had a situation to handle.

But then I had a bright idea. I called the owners of the liquor store there and asked if we could use their beer cooler for the elk until Monday morning. It was before liquor stores could be open on Sundays so they said this would not cause them a problem. When the Game Warden arrived with the elk in the back of his truck a few minutes later we were able to take it into our garage, quarter it, wrap it and haul it over to the liquor store cooler. On Monday some friends came down from Crested Butte and Gunnison and helped us retrieve that elk from the liquor store and finish processing it. Although it was a frenzied time all around, it was a handy way to acquire elk meat and I remain grateful to God for *The Sacrificial Rabbit* which He provided that kept me from tangling with an elk on the highway.

In April 2013 we went over to Boulder, Colorado to see friends from Israel visiting family there. Young Josiah here was intent on capturing a rabbit and Trapper gladly gave him some homemade box trap instruction plus they made a homemade sling shot together. They were both happy guys – the kid and the *Mountain Man Who Kids The Kids*. Sometimes things work out for me and my Mountain Man even if we have to be creative about it. At those times we just need to figure out *Whatever Suits Him*.

Whatever Suits Him

Have you noticed that Mountain Men are NOT a bunch who like to get all suited up? It just ain't natural to 'em. I found this out right away after our engagement.

As I mentioned in "*Sir, I Promise I'll Do Her No Wrong*", Trapper came to me and my family in Athens, Georgia in the midst of much going on. It was my Dad's funeral and we'd become engaged the night before through his yellow legal pad paper missive I'd carried to Georgia on the airplane. So, my family wanted to meet Trapper.

We were in Glenwood Springs, Colorado when I received the call that Dad had only 24-48 hours to live. There was no time to get back to the Crested Butte area where we both lived to gather the proper clothes for a funeral.

Soon after I arrived in Athens a friend pulled together some clothes for me to wear since she knew all I had with me was a blue jean skirt, a couple of Western shirts and a pair of Western boots – what I'd had with me when we went over to Glenwood Springs not knowing we'd both wind up in Georgia in a couple of days. This was not appropriate for a Southern funeral – especially for my own father.

Then, all of a sudden the next day, Trapper was on his way there too. Of course it wouldn't have made any difference if Trapper had been able to get to his wardrobe in Crested Butte because there was NO SUIT IN IT anyway!

At the time I was too new at the prospect of becoming a *Mountain Man's Wife* and, under the circumstances, rather caught up in the nostalgia of my childhood Southern traditions. I didn't yet know Trapper didn't wear suits. There in my childhood home world a suit was just standard garb for such occasions (and yes, it is for many men out here in the West too). So, one of my brothers-in-law came to the rescue. While Trapper was still in flight I guessed that he and Carter were about the same size so Carter offered a suit for Trapper to wear. Fit him pretty darn good too!

But then there was the infamous matter of...THE TIE. My Mountain Man was kinda rusty at tying the confounded thing. So my 29 year old nephew went to work on him – another true bonding experience between Trapper and my family right away. As I later wrote in a poem that included this incident:

> Her nephew had a time
> Trying to tie Trapper's tie.
> Tying a tie backwards is tough,
> No lie.

Sounds a little like Dr. Seuss, don't ya think?

So, there we were all gussied up. I'd never before seen Trapper in a suit and tie and he'd never before seen me in such fancy duds and...HEELS! To get those heels I had to take them offa the feet of one of my Dad's law firm partner's wives in the kitchen the night before. We sent her home in bedroom slippers.

I may not have been very successful at getting the shoes off of horses when Trapper and I met but I was able to disengage them from the feet of a family friend who could see I needed help. Rose, Trapper's mare, was not so accommodating – another story.

We knew it was a momentous sorta reverse fashion statement type of occasion in our lives so my nephew (the Tie Tyer) took a picture of us. But I guess the camera couldn't even believe what it was seeing 'cause the picture didn't come out! Darn. We have no photographic record that we ever dressed up like that – only witnesses. I don't know if anybody but Trapper realized at the time how unusual this would be in our lives to come – including me. But Trapper knew there was a good chance it would never happen again.

That night we were both on the phone talking to our pastor friend in Crested Butte: "Jim, we've got Trapper in a suit," I told him. Trapper chimed in, "I've still got my cowboy boots on!" Jim laughed and said, "Good. Keep your identity over there."

A few months after that the time came to plan our wedding – a combination Southern/Western event with a ranch reception in Crested Butte. By then I was a bit more tuned in to my future life and couldn't (and still can't) even imagine Trapper in a tuxedo.

Trapper wasn't the only one in our wedding party who had no business in a suit or a tuxedo. But, what to do? The solution was brand spankin' new black jeans, fine off-white Western shirts, black cowboy boots and...Bonanza style bow ties.

Perfect. Although he was on hand for the occasion we found a way to make sure the Tie Tyer's services were not required this time – probably much to his relief...and Trapper's.

The dilemma of the need for a suit just didn't come up in our first six years of marriage until May of 2000.

We received an invitation to my nephew's wedding (the Tie Tyer's brother) in Blacksburg, Virginia – plus an invitation to the Rehearsal Dinner. And there were those ominous words on the bottom right-hand corner of the Rehearsal Dinner invitation – "Coat and Tie". Funny but I had never considered those particular words "ominous" before marriage to a Mountain Man.

Now don't get me wrong. I'm okay with many of the less casual things in life and I don't mind seeing men in suits a bit – unless they're bein' too stuffy in 'em. My Southern upbringing told me this was a reasonable and appropriate request on the part of my sister and her husband who were giving this night-before-the-wedding shindig. It's just that suits don't suit my Trapper and my job is to respect his wishes too. Oh boy. What to do THIS time?

Again we found the perfect solution.

We pulled out Trapper's wedding tie, his gray dress jeans and those same black cowboy boots he'd worn in our wedding. Then he wore his black cowboy hat (made of 4X beaver felt – naturally), a nice Western shirt and...a leather vest. It was a coat...just missing the sleeves! No one said anything. By then my family had long since just accepted Trapper as, well, Trapper.

True to form, Trapper is an independent individual and not much into social traditions about things like suits, coats and ties, formal non-Mountain Man stuff like that. I'm learning to appreciate that more and more every day but it sure took some getting used to at first. Of course, so does this whole lifestyle of being a *Mountain Man's Wife* – right ladies with husbands who are very different from your upbringing???!!!

Here are the men of our generation at my nephew's wedding in Blacksburg, Virginia in May of 2000.

Every type of traditional (so to speak) men's dress suited for a wedding is represented here. It's almost as if they planned it in advance.

From left to right: a coat and tie on my brother (Al Epting), Trapper's coat with no sleeves and his Bonanza style tie from our wedding, a suit and tie on my brother-in-law (Carter Morris) and a tuxedo with a bow tie on my other brother-in-law who was also the father of the groom at this wedding (Roger Mosshart).

About those heels – I've not worn a pair since that day of my Dad's funeral. I'm happily over wearing those things for life! Various flats, tennis shoes, hiking boots and winter boots with good ice grippers on the bottom of them have become my style. It's been awhile since I've worn cowboy boots, though.

Like many women in the Rocky Mountains, we often carry a pretty pair of shoes to switch into after we can take our boots off during the winter treks from home to our destinations. And I have a Georgia friend here who knows the Southern protocol of "no white shoes after Labor Day or before Resurrection Sunday." We've joked about it every year. However, I'm not averse to wearing my WHITE winter snow boots. That suits me! And usually that's necessary at the time of Resurrection Sunday (or Passover) because usually there's still snow on the ground here.

A suit on Trapper has actually happened one other time in our marriage... on the occasion of his own Dad's funeral in Kansas in May of 2006.

It was a blue Western suit that was in his wardrobe in Kansas. We made a special effort to make sure we had a photo taken this time but, alas, I could not find it in time to put it here. Heels on me were long gone so back to...a suit on him and heels on me at the same time are not likely to ever happen again.

My future brides matrons met me in my blue jean skirt in Atlanta for lunch together before I flew back to Colorado after the combination of my Dad's funeral and the beginning of our engagement. I tried unsuccessfully to convince them all that they would be riding horses and mules down the aisle in our wedding. But they figured out I wasn't serious. Or was I?

Well, I did manage to outfit them in dress cowgirl boots. At least I've had footwear success with women even if not with horses as you'll soon discover in that upcoming story (*Pullin' Horses Offa Shoes*).

It's quite a culture shock to go from being all dressed up in the South to riding horseback in the snow of the West Elk Wilderness back in Colorado on super short notice. But that is how it happened when circumstances evolved like they did and I went overnight from being a catered cousin to finding out that *They Call Me "Cookie"*.

76

They Call Me "Cookie"

When Trapper and I met he was not only a Mountain Man trapper but had been an outfitter guide in Colorado for 20 years or so. As I've described before, we became engaged when I was in Georgia because of my Dad's death. Then I stayed there for three weeks with my family. The night before I was to fly back to Colorado I received a phone call from Trapper and his outfitter couple employers in Crested Butte.

To my surprise they asked, "Would you cook for us in hunting camp?" Their camp cook had bailed out with two days to go before packing in a first season group of elk hunters. I said, "Well I've never done anything like that but, if you think I can do it, I guess I can do it!"

Trapper met me at the Gunnison airport the next day. At the gate I went straight to him and gave him a kiss. During our little reunion there I noticed this fella standing behind Trapper who was staring at us with his mouth literally hanging open. I soon learned that his name was Mack who had arrived on an earlier flight and that he was one of the hunters on our trip. Turned out half the group for our hunt was also on that plane with me but I hadn't known it. As we laughed about it later, when Mack had seen Trapper at the airport he had thanked him for coming to the flight to meet the group. Trapper had honestly confessed, "We're really here because my fiance is on this flight." Mack, a returning hunter who Trapper had guided before, had reacted, "Sure, right Trapper." Didn't believe a word of it. He'd thought something along the lines of, "Trapper getting married - no way." Thus Mack's awe when Trapper started kissing this blond gal who came off the plane. As I recall, it was the first time Trapper had used that foreign word fiance so it's possible he wasn't too convincing – not a word that naturally rolls off a Mountain Man's supposedly confirmed bachelor tongue.

So that was how it happened that I wound up, within a 24 hour period, going straight from three weeks of catered food in Athens, Georgia to riding horseback into the West Elk Wilderness to a hunting camp with a dirt floor cook tent where I would now being the one producing cook stove catering myself – culture shock payback for all that Southern pampering and catered food with which I had just been graced. Many of you reading this know how it goes with Southern Hospitality when a family member dies – especially if your cousin is Lee Epting Catering – the same cousin who had exclaimed, "When do we get to meet this guy...he did it right!" when we got engaged.

I must say I was a bit apprehensive about being holed up for six days in some canvas tents – just me, nine guys and some horses and mules – and trying to prepare meals with only snow and coolers for a refrigerator. Although one of those fellas was my new fiance I still thought they'd be put off by having a gal in camp when they were expecting Jumbo like before. But not only were they okay with it, they ALL looked after me...like the day I cut my finger slicing apples for that night's cobbler and all nine of them were right there taping it up together. Gotta take care of the cook, ya know! They were so welcoming to me that as they rode in from their hunt in the afternoons, they'd wave and greet me with "Hi honey, we're home" as their horses came down the hill and past the back of the cook tent where I was enthusiastically waving back at them.

AND, I'm pleased to report, there were enough tents for me to have proper sleeping quarters for a still-single gal – just in case you were wondering.

There was the more serious moment in camp when one of the hunters came running up the hill and into the cook tent to warn me to prepare myself for a shot. The best horse in the remuda, Gypsy, had suffered a broken leg when she was kicked by another horse and had to be put down. It fell to Trapper to fire the shot. Gypsy was the horse he'd chosen for me a year earlier for our first ride together on Danni Ranch three days after we met. That was because she was so sure footed and gentle. I made just enough noise in the cook tent to try to cover the sound of the shot for myself but not upset the situation - to no avail because I still heard it loud and clear. I remember thinking, "Now this really IS the Wild and Woolly West – the real thing."

After the shot, adorned in my cook's apron, I met Trapper in the middle of the path. It was the first time I'd seen tears in his eyes. "That was one of the hardest things I've ever had to do" he murmured as we hugged. It was an emotional part of our engagement months of learning about each other. From these framed photos of ourselves at the time, it's obvious we had a LOT to learn about each other...

Our Respective Engagement Photos

If this doesn't display the difference in our approaches to life at the time we met, nothing does! Another "memory on the wall" as the song in our wedding ceremony described it. Trapper is riding Blue – a wild mustang that he had rescued a few years before we met. This photo was taken at the hunting camp where we went just after our engagement began.

We put the photo below of me in Trapper's hometown newspaper in Altamont, Kansas as well as in the Athens, Georgia newspaper to announce our engagement. It was the first view Trapper's family saw of me – hadn't met me yet. Did they really think this is what I all-the-time looked like? Trapper keeps this on his chest of drawers.

Trapper knew I was a novice at this hunting camp cooking regimen so, being a good fiance, he voluntarily got up at 3:00 am to get the cook stove fire going for me – a job which would normally be the cook's responsibility alone. Poor guy. At the time I had no idea what I was doing to him by accepting his generosity. He'd leave to guide his hunters around 4:30 after breakfast, then have to stay alert all day with them and then socialize around the campfire after dinner. I could take a nap after the breakfast dishes were done but Trapper didn't have that luxury. He was pretty bleary-eyed trying to keep up with being a good fiance, a good guide and a good trapper all at the same time. You see, he also fit in some time to set and check his beaver traps while out in the wilderness during hunting camp. All the while he had his trusty and GIGANTIC mule, Jasper, there to help out.

In the next year's camp (yes we did this again after marriage) one of the guides offered Trapper what he called a "marriage builder tip" that he "not continue skinning beaver right in front of the door of yours and Fae's tent."

Given various particulars of the trapping profession, that marriage builder has carried over into a lot of situations in our married life ever since. And Trapper had his own marriage builder plan. He STILL got up at 3:00 am to start the cook stove fire for me the second year – now with the task at hand of being a good husband.

That guide was the same fella who named me "Cookie". In fact, every now and then when we see him in Crested Butte he still calls me "Cookie".

Since I had never even been in a hunting camp before I wound up being the cook in one, that first time I wasn't at all sure what to expect.

I have now learned that this is a common occurrence in *Life As A Mountain Man's Wife* because many, many things have turned out to be most certainly *"Not What I Expected"*.

"Not What I Expected"

Do any of us REALLY know what we're getting into when we get married? I think all of you married readers here will heartily agree that there are many aspects of married life that we never anticipated. The rest of you – take note.

Expectations. They sure can getcha into trouble sometimes. And sometimes they give you a good laugh when you look back and see how those expectations turned out way different from what you expected. I was so immediately confounded by the Mountain Man trapper lifestyle that I could never have anticipated some of the stuff that goes on around here. But, it's great fodder for these stories. I hope you think so too.

In our pre-marital counseling our pastor cautioned us about expectations before our wedding and then again during our post-marital sessions when we could even better comprehend the wisdom in that advice. A few months into our marriage I asked our pastor during one of those sessions and in front of Trapper, "Is it normal that marriage brings out the worst in a person?" "Absolutely," Jim emphatically confirmed.

Well, some expectations I had and some I did not.

For instance, I never expected to be ALLERGIC to my husband. People joke about that but in our case and during a certain time of the year, I truly am allergic to Trapper. Little did we know before we married that I physically react rather unhappily to the smell of beaver and to the touch of beaver grease. The musky smell makes me nauseous and gives me a headache. Touching beaver grease makes the skin on my hands start to shrivel and dry up. Since Trapper was in Kansas trapping both the winter after we met and the winter during our engagement, we were not together during a trapping season prior to our wedding to discover this little malady of mine. Naturally Trapper is, above all, a BEAVER TRAPPER.

Such situations lead to creative fixes. I lived in fear of every doorknob in the house until we came up with several solutions. Trapper had to learn to wash up more after skinning. We also installed heated plumbing and an industrial sink in his shop at one house. I talked about marriage builders in a previous article – which is what we even told the plumber that this new plumbing was. I have a notion that this difficulty with the stinkiness of trapping just might be a fairly common circumstance out there – including women whose husbands or sons are hunters. Right ladies? – and you fellas wanting to make peace with your ladies? – or you single trappers and hunters who have yet to find a gal who will put up with it all?

Expectations played a role in one of the first comical moments of our engagement.

We became engaged on September 29, 1993 at the time of my Dad's death. Trapper flew from Denver to Atlanta the day after I did and met my family (plus a great deal of Athens, Georgia) during the weekend of Dad's funeral. What a way for a quiet, shy, not-big-on-crowds trapper guy from Kansas and Colorado to meet his future wife's family! But the Georgians took to him right away. In fact, one of my friend's five year old little boys was so enamored with Trapper that he kept walking up to him and gently touching him to make sure he was for real.

My Mother had been showing signs of Alzheimer's Disease for four or five years when Dad died. She had been so devoted to him for 54 years as this photo displays. Although she handled his passing quite gracefully, it was not easy for her.

So, her short term memory wasn't serving her very well anymore. After Trapper arrived at the house, he was introduced to her several times.

But bless her heart (one of the most famous Southern sayings of all time), she just couldn't remember – except to remember that this was a new face. Even so, her sense of Southern Hospitality kicked in and she was quite welcoming to whoever-he-was all weekend.

At one point when he walked in the back door like he belonged there (which he DID but she just couldn't remember who in tarnation he was), with a statement so characteristic of her she exclaimed, "Well come right on in!"

I couldn't be mad. She couldn't help it and so I patiently kept telling her his name, Al Davidson, every time she asked. At one point my Mother and I were visiting on the couch in the family room and Trapper was sitting in a chair to one side of us. He got up and left the room and she turned to me and asked: "Who IS that man?" This time I took both of her hands in mine, looked her in the eyes and calmly responded, "He's my fiance."

She considered that for a moment and then, with a perplexed look on her face and a quizzical twist of her head mused, "Not what I expected." I didn't think to ask her what she HAD expected and so I just told her: "Me either."

I didn't know it but Trapper was coming back into the room at that moment and so was just outside the door and overheard this little exchange. Trapper took it in Mountain Man stride and we've had some warm remembrances about it ever since. And we chuckle every once in awhile when we occasionally hear someone say, "Well come right on in!"

I only partly knew the answer to that question about what I expected myself anyway. What had I expected? I can tell you somewhat by repeating the verses in that poem that was also shared in *What A Ride!*

Here's another chuckle we'd like to share –
Just before she met Trapper, Fae had a plan:
She made a list to God of her desires –
Of the attributes she desired in a man.

Now on that list she'd put "Mountain Man"
She MEANT someone who'd enjoy the mountains a lot.
God answered her request with such magnificent jest
'Cause oh my goodness, look what she got!

My 80 year old Georgia Mother had no concept of a Mountain Man Trapper.

Although I knew of such from studying history and had then become friends with one, it was still somewhat of a new one on me too.

And I EXPECT a daily lesson in what that means for the rest of my life.

So far, I'm getting that education on a fairly regular basis.

I can tell you what I DID NOT expect – as stated in the lyrics made up for that song I mentioned in "*Father, Thank You For My Wife*":
"I never dreamed I'd be a trapper's wife..."

A part of the rest of the story here is that three months after my Dad died my Mom died too – on December 21, 1993.

Since our wedding was not until the next June, she didn't have a chance to get to know Trapper and find out that even though at their one and only meeting he didn't seem to her to be what she'd expected, in many ways he is. For years she had been telling me to "go to church" – that I "would meet the right man there."

After running from that for 20 years I had finally come around on the subject a year and a half or so earlier. Ironically, when I went to church I DID meet my husband there (see *Way Up There*). By golly, bless her heart (as they say prolifically and preciously in the South) – Mom was right!

Four months after my Mother's death and two months before our wedding, my siblings and I re-gathered to finish cleaning out our family home in Athens, Georgia since we had decided to sell it.

When we came to a pile of towels anywhere from 30-55 years old I expressed that I had no interest in them. My two sisters knew better. One said, "You're marrying a trapper. You WANT these old towels" and the other sister nodded her knowing agreement. Having been married for 22 and 32 years each at that point, they knew a whole lot more about what to expect in marriage than I did. We have gratefully used those towels in a multitude of ways in our 21 years of marriage ever since. Many a mess has been either prevented or cleaned up with them.

Just as those old towels have come in handy, the multitude of ways I've been able to get myself plain ol' red-faced embarrassed have been handy for entertainment for ourselves and for certain others who have made it known that they have not forgotten those moments even so many years later. Since I was so sensitive about my greenhorn-ness in the beginning, it's a good thing that I'm now able to laugh about *Pullin' Horses Offa Shoes.*

Pullin' Horses
Offa Shoes

Being red faced is a rather common condition for me. I embarrass myself quite often. However, there are a few times since meeting Trapper that stand out in my mind and DEFINITELY in the minds of several others.

You've already read the tale of the very moment Trapper and I met on Saturday, October 31, 1992 when I colorfully displayed my embarrassment in front of a sizeable number of the church congregation the moment we all met.

But in telling that tale I haven't yet shared what happened at church the day after we met. During fellowship time after the service I was standing there talking with two of my new friends, Jim (the pastor) and Trapper. With great enthusiasm I turned to the pastor and said, "Jim, after church Trapper's going to take me to the ranch to teach me how to pull horses offa shoes." Okay – it came out backwards.

Many have been the laughs since then over the mental picture of what you would have to do to pull some horse upwards right outta his or her shoes. Most picture a giant sling and maybe four whopper-sized magnets pulling on the shoes or something along those lines.

This became such a solid part of our early days with my new friends in my new home that for Trapper's groom/birthday cake at our wedding reception (yes, we married on his actual birthday) I ordered a horseshoe shaped cake with chocolate icing and an inscription in yellow letters:

"Here's to pullin' horses offa shoes!"

which someone read aloud to the reception attendees right before all 200 of us sang happy birthday to my Mountain Man Trapper.

Since we're not believers in superstition, it didn't occur to me to tell the cake baker which direction the horseshoe needed to be pointing before the words were put on. I'm glad it was like this since superstition would say that the open end needed to be up.

We also carried that theme through on the family ring bearer pillow that I had found waiting for me in my childhood bedroom in Athens, Georgia while we were cleaning out the house in April 1994 after our parents died and two months before the wedding. I figured our Mother, with her  knack for sentimental things, had put it there waiting for me to one day finally have a need to use it. But I'll bet it was not what she expected (more coming soon about that) for a horseshoe to one day be affixed to it. Yes, it was a new horseshoe – couldn't imagine putting a used one on that precious satin pillow.

Anyway, after church back on November 1, 1992 (the day after we met), Trapper did take me to Danni Ranch as promised and he did TRY to teach me how to "pull shoes" (the correct cowboy term). What a thing to do for a first date? – except that we didn't consider it an actual date. Besides, having a horse's hooves one at a time between my knees was not exactly what I would call the most graceful of first dates. It makes even more sense that we put a horseshoe on that ring bearer pillow later at our wedding, eh?

I never did accomplish getting all of the nails out of any one of those four hooves. Trapper had to finish them all. His recounting of the afternoon includes an editorial comment apparently by his horse, Rose: "She kept turning around and looking at Fae with the funniest look on her face as if to say, 'How long's this gonna take???' " Well, at least I tried.

During our conversation getting to know each other that day an especially telling moment happened when, at the same moment, we each said to the other, "You haven't been married before EITHER???" It's like we skipped the dating process right then and there. He was 35 and I was 39 and we were both sick and tired of the whole dating route. We discovered that both of us had separately accepted the fact that, if we ever did meet a person to marry, there would most likely be an ex-spouse through either death or divorce and that there was a great big possibility of children from that other marriage. We were both stunned to meet someone without all of that going on. There were various reasons in each of our lives that had caused that to happen but the one we come back to the most is that God had kept us for each other and knew the day would come when we would meet and then eventually marry. And we didn't meet at all until we were both walking with Him and by then were good and tired of all the other stuff we'd had going on to keep us from getting serious about marriage.

It's funny but the thing that could have been embarrassing – about being in our 30s and both still not married – was the one thing that was NOT embarrassing but instead was a mutual revelation that brought us more together. For my part, maybe so many other red face causing things had happened in the last 24 hours that I was past being sensitive about this one. We have a lot of trust in the fidelity of our marriage. We tell folks, "It took us so long to find each other that, well, why would we want to mess that up?" Several folks in their later in life unmarried condition have told us that we have given them hope of still finding a husband or wife.

While writing this story I asked Trapper what embarrassments of mine come to mind first. Without hesitation *Pullin' Horses Offa Shoes* was his very first recollection. "That limb going into hunting camp" was a close second.

So let's back up the horse (so to speak) to a day in October of 1993 when we were riding into hunting camp (see They Call Me "Cookie") and that dadgum limb Trapper was talking about. We were all of three weeks into our engagement but we hadn't been together those three weeks because I had stayed in Georgia after my Dad's funeral and had flown back in the day before. So I was on my best behavior now in the world of my new fiance – on horseback. This was the day I learned NOT to ride too close to a pack mule.

One of the other guides was riding lead and Trapper had protectively positioned himself in front of me leading his HUGE mule, Jasper, and another one named Pepper – both mules packed to the hilt. At one point our little caravan went under a certain tree. The packs on the backs of the mules first obscured, then pushed forward and then released a low-hanging limb that I didn't see until WAY too late – when it was coming straight at me. By the time I saw it coming there was no chance of leaning forward so I flattened my back on the back of the four-legged critter under me and let the limb pass over me. That part worked great but I lost my balance in the process and...down I went. It would have been a soft landing if not for that large rock – the only big one in the immediate area – that connected with my hip. That took the breath right outta me and rendered impossible my attempts at gracefully and quickly getting back up on my horse, hard as I tried, before Trapper and the other guide noticed I was out of commission. I heard Trapper's quizzical and worried voice from uphill, "Fae, where ARE you?" All I could see was the underside of my patiently waiting and seemingly, from that vantage point, very tall horse. I had been found out and so there was nothing to do but step up on some logs or rocks or something to get my 5'2" self (with a GIANT bruise and a groan) back atop my horse. Thankfully the hunters were coming in later and didn't see their cook down for the count.

Since I've mentioned outfitters and hunting camp in both parts of this story, let's now fast forward to the day of the December 1999 Board of Directors meeting of the Colorado Outfitters Association in Alamosa. Trapper was there with me and I was making yet another presentation to this board on behalf of Wildlife Organizations Legal Fund. Since January of 1999 my job as director of this fund had been to raise the necessary money and handle the press and public relations involved with our effort to overturn Amendment 14 voted into the Colorado Constitution in 1996 which banned the use of various trapping equipment. I already knew this outfitters group and we were becoming good friends. During my presentation someone made a silly comment to which I came back with my own sly remark. During the laughter I felt that tell-tale heat in my face again and then felt a gentle breeze to my right. The condition of my face was so evident to all in attendance that the new President of the COA was fanning me with a sheet of paper.

When I next saw him about three months later at a banquet of the Colorado Mule Deer Association in Grand Junction, I told him I already knew I was going to embarrass myself in advance and to "get your fan ready." As one of only two speakers on the agenda, I had been asked by the CMDA President to keep it lively and funny. While driving to Grand Junction that afternoon I pondered how to do that and came up with the idea of singing the little song I had made up years before that I mentioned in "*Father, Thank You For My Wife*". I am not a public singer but somehow I managed to scare up enough courage to sing it in front of 350 people I didn't know who were expectantly gazing at me from what seemed like hundreds of large round dinner tables:

> *I never dreamed I'd be a trapper's wife*
> *Dealing with beaver, bobcats and coyotes the rest of my life.*
> *Then there are, of course, the smelly skunks*
> *But I love my gen-u-ine Mountain Man, what luck!*

Since I had under-estimatedly only hoped for tolerant grins around the room at best or at least a polite chuckle or two, when to my utter amazement the whole room burst into enthusiastic applause as I finished the song I was so shocked that even though I knew my face was going to be somewhat red BEFORE I did it, the thundering applause sent my face to overload and fire engine red only maybe describes the hue. I discovered later through his tablemates that, although I couldn't see him from the podium, the Colorado Outfitters Association President was faithfully fanning away at his table. From then on the attempt to turn my face red at Colorado Outfitters Association meetings became a tradition for as long as he was President. He says it was so much fun for him because I would turn SO red.

Time and predicaments will tell if there are more red-faced moments to come in this *Life as a Mountain Man's Wife*. Trapper does his best to keep that tradition going 'cause he takes great pleasure in watching it – as well as causing it.

But Trapper has had his own share of moments that would cause most folks to turn red – from frustration if not from embarrassment – like the circumstances that resulted in him telling me, "*I Feel Like A Fish*".

"I Feel Like A Fish"

Trapper pulled a good one when he was packing to go to the Colorado Trappers Association Rendezvous on the last day of August 1997. While stretching a tarp over the truck, an errant bungee cord got hung up, suddenly broke loose and then came flying over the top of the truck and HOOKED HIM. I'll tell you where in a minute.

He wandered across the street to the home of our neighbor for help. She went to the phone in her house and made two calls – one of which was to try to reach me over at a nearby church where I was in training to help out at the school there the upcoming year. When no one answered the phone there she promptly hopped into her truck and raced over to the church. Since she didn't know where I was in the building, she ran through the sanctuary looking for me. When I heard this ruckus in the sanctuary and investigated I was greeted with, "Hurry, hurry Fae! We've called the ambulance for Trapper!" (her other phone call). I took her at her word to hurry so much that I forgot to slow down long enough to ask her what had happened. I rushed out to my car and made a mad dash for home not knowing what I was going to find there. Good thing home was only about two minutes away. I don't think I could have stood the suspense much longer.

When I got home I found Trapper serenely sitting by himself across the street from our house at a picnic table under the trees in our neighbor's front yard. And there it was: a bungee cord hanging from his JAW! He looked up at me with these innocent blue little boy eyes and calmly said, "I feel like a fish." That will always remain one of the most memorable and ridiculous moments of our marriage.

The ambulance arrived and took Trapper to the hospital in Salida (45 miles away over a small mountain pass). I followed in the car but of course they could travel faster than I could. By the time I got there Trapper was clearly making that emergency room team's day. When I walked in everybody was laughing. Due to the hospital folks' misunderstanding of something in the wording by the ambulance crew when they called into there while on the road, the emergency room folks were expecting a guy who had been airplane bungee jumping. They said they had spent the time while waiting for his arrival speculating on how in the world some nut jumping from an airplane got the darn thing hooked in his jaw! They were also expecting a big pile of bungee cord to come in attached to their prospective patient.

After extracting the hook the doctor told Trapper to remain quiet, stay clean and dry and not talk much over the next few days. "Can't do it doc," Trapper firmly told him. Coming up was one of the two weekends of the year when my quiet-natured Trapper had a command performance to talk since he'd been elected as President of the Colorado Trappers Association at this same event a year earlier and he had lots of times when he was to speak, give out awards, etc. at their annual Labor Day Rendezvous. The doctor did not want to hear that this was a family CAMPING event either.

We did it anyway, kept Trapper's wound as clean as possible considering that we were camping and things went along just fine. Trapper got others to do some of the speaking and a deep voiced fellow to do the awards presentations for him too. Making himself be heard over a crowd, considering the condition of his jaw, was just not something Trapper was interested in doing at the time.

Then, four days later while we were packing to leave the Rendezvous, Trapper was pulling a ROPE (not a bungee cord) tight over the tarp on the trailer. He pulled with all of his might and then...can you believe it?...the rope BROKE! and he punched himself full force WHERE ELSE but in his jaw at exactly the same spot where he'd hooked himself with the bungee cord a few days before. OUCH! — but that's not exactly what he blurted out for all in the camp to hear when it happened. His outburst wasn't that terribly offensive but it was LOUD. All who came arunnin' were graciously sympathetic about his outspoken expression of dismay.

He healed up pretty quickly and the laughs about it (including the ones at the insurance company) would have been all that remained except for my bright idea of a present for him. Unknown to Trapper, the nurse in the emergency room had entrusted to me the remnants of the bungee cord and hook after they were extracted from my husband's jaw. I tucked them away in my purse at the time thinking, "I've got to figure out SOMETHING to do with this."

A couple of weeks after the bungee cord event Trapper was talking to our trapper friend, Craig Legleiter, in Kansas. I was on the line with them, thank goodness, because I then got to hear this exchange between them:
"Hey Craig," said Trapper. "Ya been fishin' lately?"
"Nah," replied Craig. "Have you?"
"Yeah," baited Trapper.
"Catch anything?," said Craig as he took the bait.
"Sure did. I caught a Large Mouth Trapper!"

We both busted up while Craig was most likely sitting there in Kansas wondering what was wrong with us. So, Trapper proceeded to share the tale of his unexpected fishing expedition. That gave me an idea and I purchased a cross-section slice of a tree like they use to mount a fish...

Trapper thought it was pretty funny too and it now resides on the wall.

At our wedding three years before Trapper had asked a fella to sing *I Swear*, a song that John Michael Montgomery had made popular that year of 1994, during the ceremony. One line says, "We'll hang some memories on the wall." No kidding. Who could have predicted "Large Mouth Trapper Tackle" to be one of those – along with the antique traps, Mountain Man gear and animal pelts here and there.

I'll give you a hint about what Trapper yelled when he punched himself in the jaw that day in September of 1997. It was NOT *"I'll Be Darned"*.

"I'll Be Darned"

On that same trip to the Colorado Trappers Association Rendezvous in September of 1997, a young friend went with us. We had known him and his dad for a couple of years when they would come to our home to buy items from our trapping supply business – *Trapper's Trap Line*. I was driving our truck, Trapper was on the passenger side and our twelve year old friend was sitting between us on the bench front seat as we headed to eastern Colorado for the Labor Day Weekend camping event.

We were coming into Colorado Springs on Highway 24 when the subject of the current President of the United States came up. Our young friend told us something his grandfather had said directly to the President, to which Trapper responded, "Is your grandfather some big general or something?" Before he could respond and because we knew his last name, the light bulb came on for Trapper and me, we both looked toward him in the middle between us and said at the same time, "Is your grandfather Chuck Yeager?"

"Well, yeah," he said. We don't know how we managed to miss this detail in our two years of knowing them but, since Trapper and I had both been little kids during the beginning of the United States space program, we knew exactly who Chuck Yeager was. For those reading this who were not alive or do not know this period of American history, in 1947 he had the guts to be the first person to break the sound barrier in an airplane. We all knew who he was back in the 1950s and 60s in those early days of the first manned space flights because what he did is what opened the door to space exploration which was a huge deal at the time.

On the way home from the weekend we discussed a movie about the first astronauts, *The Right Stuff*. Our young Yeager friend described a scene that we also remembered – when the government guys were at the bar where the test pilots hung out. They were speaking derogatorily of Chuck Yeager (played by Sam Shepard) across the room there when Fred the bartender came up behind them and offered them a drink.

He then informed us that Fred was played by none other than his grandfather, the real Chuck Yeager. So, in the movie the real Chuck Yeager listened to those two guys speak of him played by somebody else. We watched our video of the movie right away after we got home and found it all to be true in the scene and when the credits rolled by.

During that ride home young Yeager also told us that his grandfather was coming to visit in a couple of months to go elk hunting and asked us if we'd like to meet him. However, Trapper was not completely convinced that he wasn't making this up simply because he had the last name of Yeager. So he didn't 100% expect it to happen and, even if it was true, he didn't count on a 12 year old to remember or be allowed to invite us over in November. We should have known better because he was a very astute kid. He also said to watch TV on October 14 a few weeks later for the celebration of the 50th Anniversary of his grandfather's Mach 1 supersonic record breaking flight that Chuck would be flying. We did that wondering if we were about to meet this man.

Chuck Yeager in the Bell X-1 cockpit – the plane he piloted to break the sound barrier
©Public Domain

He DID remember to call and invite us. When Chuck came to visit we drove over to where his family lived. As we walked up to Chuck Yeager Trapper was apparently dumbfounded that this whole thing was for real. He had that same little boy look in his eyes as when he told me "*I Feel Like A Fish*" in a previous story, offered his right hand toward Chuck Yeager and uttered as they shared a firm handshake, "I'll be darned" to which Chuck responded, "My name's not I'll be [something similar to darn], it's Chuck." You know what he really said.

Now, compare what Chuck Yeager wrote on the above photo of him in the X-1 he flew back in 1947 to the photo he gave to Trapper the day we met him. Although we don't think his successful supersonic ride had anything to do with luck, I'll be darned – it's basically the same darned inscription!

Although we have never experienced supersonic heroism in our marriage, there was a special day when we realized just how fragile life is and on that day we seriously grappled with *Praise, Pelts and...PRIORITIES.*

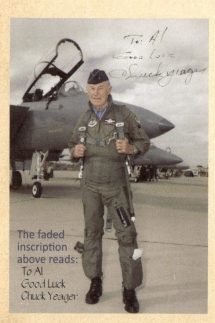

The faded inscription above reads:
To Al
Good Luck
Chuck Yeager

Praise, Pelts and...
PRIORITIES

The weather in Saguache, Colorado was crisp and clear at 4:30 the morning of February 16, 2003 when we headed out from our house there on our four hour journey to Hugo in Eastern Colorado to take Trapper's and two other guys' pelts to the Colorado Trappers Association Fur Auction. We were in two vehicles – both fully loaded with pelts.

Trapper was riding shotgun with our 38 year old nephew, Roger Mosshart (the "Tie Tyer" in *Whatever Suits Him*), driving a Buick Rendezvous he'd rented from Avis at the Denver airport so he could come visit us after he'd finished the business his company had sent him out from Georgia to do. We'd laughed the night before about how appropriately named this SUV called a "Rendezvous" was, considering the American Fur Trade era history of the 1820s-1840s and the amount of fur they'd be hauling in it the next day – especially all of the beaver pelts. And it was because of the space needed for pelts that he'd rented a larger vehicle instead of a car like he usually did then for his business trips. He'd mentioned the week before that he was glad to be getting an SUV "in case of inclement weather also." I was driving our Subaru Outback also stuffed to the gills with pelts. Between us we were hauling 67 beaver, 42 fox, 44 coyotes, 110 muskrats, 14 skunks and 5 bobcats.

We were merrily a little under two hours into our trip when we turned east onto Highway 24 toward Colorado Springs. Instantly the weather went south as we headed into the heart of South Park (historically where the original trappers often wintered) – clouds on the ground, snow and ice on the road. At some point the guys decided to pull in front of me. Great trailblazers they were – leading the way and truly, as it turned out, protecting the women-folk. We can now only speculate what would have happened to me in our smaller vehicle in a few miles instead of what happened to them in the larger SUV.

It was still dark and very blustery when we reached about seven miles east of a town named Hartsel. There was a snow plow coming toward us. I was somewhat back from the guys because I don't like to follow too closely on icy roads. At first my concentration was focused on the snow plow as it arrived to my left. Suddenly my attention was riveted up ahead as I saw two sets of tail lights – one set abruptly turning left and the other (my guys) abruptly turning right. We knew this road. There were no turns out there – just T-posts and barbed wire fences. I later remembered some headlights on my side of the road that then disappeared but I couldn't think about that at the moment.

The next thing I saw was a mangled blue Ford truck off in the snow on the left and then...one of the most horrifying sights of my life: that maroon Buick Rendezvous FACING ME off in the snow on the right-hand side of the road – with NO FRONT END LEFT. No one was moving inside. In those seconds before trying to get my seat belt off, while either steam or smoke (I wasn't sure which) was coming out of the front of the Rendezvous, I prayerfully begged, very LOUDLY: "God NO. PLEASE NO!!!!"

At that moment I then saw one of the happiest sights of my life – Roger emerging from the driver's side, apparently unhurt. We met and hugged in the snow. "You okay how's Trapper?" all in one sentence. I was almost afraid to hear the answer: "I think He's got a couple of broken ribs," said Roger as we trudged in the snow together to the passenger side.

"Hallelujah!," I thought to myself. "That means Trapper's alive to TELL Roger he's got a couple of broken ribs!" Trapper was still strapped in by his seat belt and air bags were hanging in front of him and also on the steering wheel where it had been a life-safer for Roger. Trapper could hardly breathe. He'd had the wind knocked out of him and his favorite coffee mug lay broken on the floor. Coffee was all over the place – on the airbag, in the console and gear shift mechanism and all over Trapper. Who cared? He was ALIVE! And, as it turned out, he had no broken ribs after all but was rather sore from where the air bag had caused that coffee mug to slam into him.

When Roger came back from checking on the occupants of the wrecked Ford truck and reported that all were okay, the three of us huddled in the snow together and uttered one of the most joyful prayers of our lives. We praised God for His answer to our prayer for travel mercies spoken aloud the night before at our dinner table. We'll never say THAT prayer lightly again! We thanked Him that no one had sustained serious injuries – not Trapper or Roger or the three people in the Ford truck. We were shaking not only from the close-to-zero temperature but even moreso out of total gratitude.

Blessings upon blessings began to unfold as the sun rose on this frightful scene. We soon found out who some other people there were. In a vehicle behind the Ford truck were a fella and a gal who were carpooling to their jobs as Security Officers at the Department of Corrections facility in Buena Vista. It was their testimony that saved the day. They had been watching a white

96

Chevy Tahoe that had been "driving crazy for miles." They "knew it was going to cause something." It did when it jerked out from behind that snow plow to try to pass it, causing Roger to swerve to miss it and then start sliding on the ice and into that blue Ford truck traveling behind the Tahoe. We are so very thankful to those guards for sticking around at the scene, to the point of being late for work, in order to give their statement to the Colorado State Patrol Trooper. It was their witness that caused the Trooper to blame the cause of this accident on The Phantom Chevy Tahoe that was long gone by then. Their statement completely exonerated both drivers of the two now-totaled vehicles. "Ah-hah," I realized later, "those were the headlights I saw an instant before tail lights ahead of me started going places they shouldn't be going!" No citations were issued since the departed Chevy Tahoe was the real culprit.

Now we had another dilemma – how to combine a two-vehicle load of pelts into one little Subaru Outback. I recall someone at the Colorado Trappers Association Rendezvous a few months before this commenting on how we were "another one pushing a Subaru to the limit" as we amazingly got all of our gear into it then – all the while wondering about the wisdom of deciding not to take our truck that time. Well to whoever said that, you should have seen THIS!

Avis was outstanding toward Roger. They brought another Buick Rendezvous over to Hartsel for him. Good thing. I don't know how THREE of us would have fit into the Outback with all those pelts in there. Our plans changed from going to Hugo first to getting Roger to DIA first since we decided to go with him there. We resumed our previous  positions – Trapper riding shotgun with Roger and me in the Outback behind them. Even though the replacement Rendezvous was silver (shall we say like the trappers of old, "trade silver") instead of maroon, their interior looked the same as before (minus all those pelts) and it occurred to all of us: "Did all that really happen this morning?" We left Roger at the Denver airport.

When we finally did arrive at the CTA Fur Auction site in Hugo that afternoon someone commented on the stuffed and mounted Havalina wild bore in the auction.

"Well," I said to them, "we've got a stuffed Outback out back." And you can be sure that they wanted to see that!

I honestly do not know how Trapper got all of those pelts into that Outback, even though I watched him and took pictures while he did it. I can tell you this – it was WARM in there as I drove on across the state to Denver and then Trapper joined me to go on to Hugo in the Outback. Had there been anyone injured and out there in the snow at the scene, we would have had ample means to keep EVERYBODY warm until help arrived. We were packin' a plentiful plunder of plews (Mountain Man jargon for fur pelts)! And even though it was mid-February with snow on the ground, never once did I need to turn on the heater since it was solid fur from behind my head all the way to the back of the car.

The EMT folks got quite a charge out of this pelt packing exercise. One of them was very confused because Trapper had on a Georgia Bulldogs cap that Roger had given him back when we were first engaged in 1993. The EMT at first thought that these two guys had hauled all this fur from Georgia to Colorado. "We've got PLENTY of coyotes around HERE!," the EMT told Trapper.

That night, sitting at the Trail Blazer Motel in Hugo, we talked about it all and what this had done in our marriage. We asked each other: "When things get crazy in life as they do from time to time, what one word can we say to each other and we'll know what we mean?" Trapper came up with it: "PRIORITIES". We've used it often and believe me, it brings the craziness to a screeching halt.

As we drove back through that same place on Highway 24 going home the next day – something akin to getting back on the horse instead of choosing a different route home to avoid it – we thought about the trappers of the 1800s and wondered if they ever had a Rendezvous near that spot in South Park. If they did, they never had a Rendezvous there like the one we had there!

A couple of weeks after the accident a friend who was an administrator in the medical profession said, "Can you imagine what the EMTs would have been thinking had they come up on all that FLATTENED road kill all over the place like that? They would have wondered what in the world kinda crazy accident scene this was!" It was good to laugh that hard about the whole incident. Amongst all the critters we started out with were 110 inside-out-and-flattened muskrat pelts. A box holding most of them exploded in the accident but Trapper thought he'd extracted them all out of the totaled Buick Rendezvous. But, since the count was only 107 at the Fur Auction, we figure three errant muskrats were going to be REALLY be flattened if they were still in that vehicle. I'll never forget coming up on that smashed maroon Buick Rendezvous and seeing no movement inside. In many ways we'd like to forget how we almost lost each other and someone else we love and how others we love almost lost two people they love as a son, husband, father, brother, nephew, uncle, cousin or friend. In other ways, we don't ever want to forget...PRIORITIES.

Serious times do happen in this *Life as a Mountain Man's Wife*. Oftentimes, like this time, we find humor in the seriousness. Then other times things are just plain funny – like when we met *Cute Little Sophia*.

Cute Little Sophia

Since our area is a resort town loaded with second homes belonging to folks from all over the country, many of the property managers in Crested Butte call us for their various critter circumstances in and around those homes. One Fall day in 2004 we received a call from a property manager who said that there was a raccoon in the attic of a log home about 5 miles up Red Mountain and that there were five sisters up there having a reunion who had seen it.

When we arrived to check it out, two of the sisters were waiting for us, took us out on the back deck and showed us where they had seen a critter go into a gap between two logs. They both gave us this description:

"It has a furry body, a long furry tail and...pink ears" at which time they both twirled around their index fingers on top of their heads to demonstrate the pink ears. From that we could easily determine that it was NOT a raccoon after all. For one thing, the tail didn't have black rings on it and, for another, raccoons do not have pink ears.

Before we had a chance to ask any more questions another one of the sisters appeared on the back deck there. She too gave the same description: "It has a furry body, a long furry tail and...pink ears" at which time she twirled around both of her index fingers on top of her head to demonstrate the pink ears.

In quick succession the fourth sister showed up..."It has a furry body, a long furry tail and...pink ears" at which time she twirled around both of her index fingers on top of her head to demonstrate the pink ears and then the fifth sister came out the door and said....well, after all, they are sisters who appeared to be very close and you can guess what she said while twirling around both of her index fingers on top of her head to demonstrate the ORANGE ears...no, just kidding, she said pink ears too – exactly like her four sisters. They all five agreed that they had named HER *Cute Little Sophia*.

Okay. We got the message but didn't have the heart to tell them what we were thinking. Trapper went up into the attic, saw more sign of droppings and use of insulation to build a nest but still didn't tell them what he'd seen that *Cute Little Sophia* had been up to up there. He set up his traps but because of the moniker they had given the creature, he decided to wait until he had proof positive to tell them.

First thing the next morning we received a phone call saying that they had heard the trap door slam during the night and wanted us to get back up there to check it out. They didn't want to look but then that was Trapper's job anyway. So up the mountain we drove again that afternoon.

Trapper went up into the attic while I stood in the living room with all five sisters listening to them all talk at the same time – especially about looking forward to seeing *"Cute Little Sophia"* and talking much about HER.

Pretty soon Trapper looked over the edge of the loft and down into the living room at the six of us and announced: "Ladies, we have a PACK RAT" – just as he had suspected it was all along.

Immediately the demeanor of the gathering switched from *"Cute Little Sophia"* to exclaiming – in unison in exactly the same words and in exactly the same tone, "Ugh! Yuk!" "HE" did this and "HE" did that. I was standing there in the middle of them awed by their ability to be in such unity of mind and speech. What sisterly devotion they had in their joint disdain for "HIM"!

And then Trapper made this observation: "You better be careful what you say right now, ladies. My wife there writes stories about this kinda stuff." But it was too late – their descriptions of the pink ears and the unified reaction to HIM were too classic to avoid being recorded. That comment resulted in a photo shoot outside on the front deck where the sisters took turns with Trapper in the middle of the group and each of them holding the trap with the pack rat in it – amazingly enough considering their change of heart about HIM – the pack rat, not Trapper, who already had a nickname. Trapper didn't get a "Cute Little" name from them either.

Therefore it is an absolute given that this pink-eared  and furry tailed tale be included in my first ingathering of these stories in book form. Darn – I was unable to locate any of those photos with the ladies but you can see why they thought that this critter was kinda cute before they found out what HE was.

Perhaps similar to the various creative sounds folks make to describe the condition of their vehicles to auto mechanics, we get the most comical descriptions of animal antics – in either sound, body language or facial expressions. This story is a perfect example but another is the gentleman who made a "krrrrr, krrrrr" sound to describe what seemed like a sawing activity that the pack rats were performing in the attic over his head when he was in bed.

Folks are so appreciative of Trapper's ability to resolve those animal situations. There is only one Savior and Trapper is not He, but He has provided Trapper with ample opportunities to be a hero not only to people but to animals – what he and He did in bringing about *Bridger's Salvation.*

Bridger's Salvation

I was raised by very devoted Christian parents in Athens, Georgia. Since they were born in 1907 and 1913, they were the same age as my contemporary friends' grandparents. Christianity was simply something they did as a solid and honorable way of life and they expected their four children to adhere to its principles also. End of discussion. Don't question it. Just do it. It was real to them and that was that. What more explanation could possibly be needed?

But then came my Junior High years in the hippie 60s when we were culturally TAUGHT to QUESTION EVERYTHING, High School & College in the racially volatile early 1970s and the beginning of my young adulthood in the disco dancing/women's lib late 70s. Then came the career world in the travel industry in the 1980s of my life.

That old fashioned training of my parents collided with the cultural reality I was facing which is how I became...a might CONFUSED – with lots of help from the worldly ways around me. As soon as I was out from under my parents' roof at 18 years old I tried to run away from their training. To me the church was hypocritical, patriotism was out of fashion, a man's loving commitment in a relationship to me was too much to expect or even hope for because, for various reasons, I didn't think anybody would want to offer that to my confused self plus the world had seemingly turned that word commitment into a negative term. That led to a bunch of back-turning on my upbringing in order to try to find significance in myself. How crazy that was!

Oddly enough, part of the difficulty was that I didn't do any of those rebellious things with total commitment because I just couldn't shake that old fashioned training from which I thought I wanted to run. I reverently say THANK GOD for His use of my lack of commitment to total rebellion in a positive way because I was so wrong in my head in the running and these are the very same things I stand firm in conviction FOR now – especially after marriage to my conservative, basics-believing Mountain Man husband. God knew exactly who I needed to marry as a part of His plan to straighten out my might confused head and He has used both of us to participate in doing that for each other.

So, that's why I love opportunities to encourage parents to discipline their children, teach solid values and integrity to them and pass on their convictions for Godly lives to them without apology while believing that they will bear fruit

– eventually if not right away because the enemy of our souls will keep trying to steal that fruit.

Train up a child in the way he should go and when he is old he will not turn from it.''
– Proverbs 22:6 (NIV)

I am living proof. But, because of my experience, I also encourage talking about it with them so that they can appropriate it into their hearts and so that it is alive and real and active as THEIR OWN faith – not just going through the motions for their parents.

After I asked God to give me a way to express it in a more lively fashion, the following happened and it describes how God turned my confusion around in a more visual and entertaining way:

On November 16, 2007 we were over on Ohio Creek Road northwest of Gunnison and Trapper was beaver trapping. He had our first Basset Hound, Bridger, out there with him.

Even as a puppy Bridger would go to great lengths to make sure he went wherever Trapper was going – including surprising us with his ability to jump those short little legs across a gap in the land and onto a little tuft of grass we

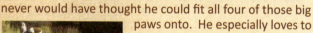

never would have thought he could fit all four of those big

paws onto. He especially loves to climb around on the beaver dams and he is a surprisingly good swimmer – even with those short little legs. He's ready and willing to go no matter what the weather is – as long as he gets to go.

He sports a cocky "What's in it for me?" attitude which we can handle and even laugh at when put forth by our dog – just not when people do too much of it. Because of Bridger someone sent us this T-Shirt.

Back to Ohio Creek.

Trapper and Bridger were down in the willows on the creek so I couldn't see what I am about to describe but later we found that the mental picture I had from what I could hear matched the circumstances exactly.

All of a sudden there was a SPLASH and a frantic PADDLE, PADDLE, PADDLE. Trapper saw that Bridger had broken through the ice. Trapper was only a few feet away from him but there was ice on top of the water between them. I couldn't see them but I could hear Trapper insistently calling out, "Bridger, come here. Bridger, Bridger come here."

But all Bridger could see to do was to try over and over to get a purchase up on the slippery ice in front of him to get to the creek bank. That notion kept him paddling AWAY from Trapper. I could hear Trapper crashing through the ice all the while calling out Bridger's name.

All the while I was on the side of the road praying out loud, "God please take care of Bridger." I could tell my husband was okay because I could hear his worried voice. If I had known then what I know now – that "Hosanna" in Hebrew means "Save us!" – I would have been crying out "Hosanna" out there on Ohio Creek Road

Bridger was completely spent and at the end of himself when Trapper finally crashed through enough ice to get to him. Bridger was going down for the last time when Trapper reached down into the icy water, plucked him out by the collar and plopped him on top of the beaver lodge there. In an instant Bridger had gone from near death to a Basset-sized mountaintop.

Soon they returned to the car – both of them sopping wet and shivering...

Talk about peace!...
and adoration of your savior!...

We know who Bridger's Savior really was that day...
with Trapper as a willing helper.

As I said at the top of this story, because of a variety of reasons and influences, from the time I was 18 until I was 38 I was a lot like Bridger – paddling away from my Savior. I look back now and recall so many times when God was calling out my name through family, friends, events and circumstances. But I ran from Him – especially from His church – for those 20 years…and made a big mess of my life in the process.

On March 9, 1992 at 7:30 am Almighty God broke through the ice, reached down and gently grabbed me by the collar to rescue me. Within a few months he plopped me at almost 10,000 feet in the parking lot of a little church in Crested Butte, Colorado where I met my husband that very same night – my first night in town. I had been spiritually near death and He took me and plopped me down in a safe place on a mountaintop.

The sentence the Holy Spirit had used through Kim Arnold on the phone that day in 1992 was, "You have a lot of great ideas about your life but God has the best idea."

Is there anyone else out there reading this book who can relate to paddling away from God in life? Is there anyone else out there who has felt the Lord gently grab you up out of the pit? Maybe there is even someone out there who is right now frantically paddling away from God too.

Just like Bridger, God was calling out my name the whole time. Just like Bridger, there were people praying for me the whole time. Maybe that's happening on behalf of your life right now and you do not even know it or that has happened on your behalf in the past.

You can believe that it's not about going to church itself – one thing that had been a stumbling block for me. It's about believing in the life and salvation provided by the Lord and out of that comes a natural desire to be surrounded in life by fellow believers in Him.

It is such a profound relief to find that we can FINALLY stop paddling away from Him, allow Him to bust through the ice in our hearts, begin to learn how to rest in Him, find identity in Him and KNOW that HE has the best idea – our best interests ALWAYS on His heart. Since March 9, 1992 I have called the relationship God freely offers to all who believe in the salvation provided by His Son, Yeshua (in Hebrew) as the biggest ADVENTURE of all. It continues today for Trapper and me and He offers it to everyone at all times.

You can climb to a mountaintop but you cannot top the adventure of walking intimately with Almighty God.

To share that adventure he gave me a life with a Mountain Man and that means I never know what to expect next – like this when I opened the door to get back in the truck one day in 2013…

...and the preposterous day that Trapper applied the *Frozen Pedal to the Metal Of The Freezer.*

Frozen Pedal To The Metal Of The Freezer

It was November 5, 2008. Being conservatives, we were quite discouraged about the Presidential Election results from the day before but were trying to move past it. So, Trapper decided to drive his ATV up to the Washington Gulch trailhead in the Gunnison National Forest about a mile from our house. A few hours later he showed up at our home on foot asking me if I would drive him back to the trailhead in our Subaru Outback and then follow him home while he drove the ATV.

The ATV accelerator throttle was sticking.

He wanted to make sure he could get home safely or at least I would be there if he had an accident or needed further help. He was also concerned that the brakes might give out because he was having to use them so much to minimize the effect of the stuck accelerator.

When we arrived at the trailhead Trapper hopped on the ATV and, very slowly, we made our way to the house with me in the Outback keeping a safe distance back from him on the ATV. I did not see the red tail lights come on a bunch so I knew he was not using the brakes a lot as anticipated. So far so good.

Trapper went straight into our driveway and had the ATV running in front of the garage door waiting while I punched the garage door opener from the Outback. I parked the car a safe distance back to give him room to work with it and then got out and started walking toward the ATV to help him push it into the garage.

BUT...he didn't look back to see that I was coming to help.

If I had known what was about to happen next I would have run to him at the ATV instead of walk. Before I could get there, Trapper, who was still seated atop the ATV, gently touched the ATV accelerator thinking he could SLOWLY drive it into the garage. After all, it had been behaving all the way home.

With horror I watched him ZOOM into the garage full speed ahead and drive...right up the front of our upright freezer on the back wall.

NOW I was running.

Trapper hopped, rather fell, off the ATV which was now perpendicular to the concrete garage floor with the tires spinning on the freezer door. It was a good thing there was an added seat on the back of the ATV with storage boxes on both sides because the ATV was now resting upright on that and so it did not flip over backwards and pin Trapper under there. He turned the ignition off just as I got there.

This was not a funny event...yet. We had a serious predicament on our hands – rather, on our freezer door. The first thing we did was make sure no gasoline was leaking onto the garage floor. Satisfied that was not going on, we knew we had to get it down ASAP – no time to call anyone to help us.

I am not a particularly strong individual. I am a GIRL, after all. But the adrenaline was pumping for both of us and we had to resolve this dilemma RIGHT NOW.

So Trapper devised a plan. After he told me what we were going to do it occurred to me to run get the camera and take a picture of this situation before we changed it. But I didn't do that for a couple of reasons:

1) If his plan did not go well, I figured that I would not want this photo;
2) No gasoline was leaking YET so the faster we got this thing down the better;
3) I was afraid that if I left he would try to do it by himself and then we might be facing number one above.

Trapper pushed the on-end ATV away from the freezer door. He then had me pull back on the handlebars with all of my adrenaline-laced might while he guided the front end down to the concrete.

We tried to do it slowly but I only had so much might and he only had so much strength. And so he dropped it...but not too hard or too far.

It was down. And we were exhausted. Adrenaline rushes take a lot out of a person.

And we thanked the Lord that nobody got hurt with no property damage done – except to our upright freezer door which bears the scars of this event to this very day. It still works and we still laugh at times when we open the door.

The ATV is still in service for us too.

Although this photo was taken about a year earlier because of the massive amount of snowfall that winter (450" over the entire winter), it is taken from about the same spot where I had parked the Subaru Outback and started running toward where Trapper had parked this same ATV just in front of the garage before heading into the freezer door on the back wall. In this photo he's AGAIN working on the ATV for some reason or other.

Anyway, returning to that November 2008 night of the trip onto the freezer door, we recapped the whole thing before going to sleep and were so very grateful that the situation had turned out okay.

But then at about 3:00 a.m. we were awakened by a big ruckus in front of the closed garage doors right underneath our bedroom. We went running downstairs to discover a bear trying to rip them open! Trapper chased him off and the next morning we discovered he had torn off the fronts on both doors but had not been successful in breaking through.

We speculated that he was either a very happy Democrat bear out celebrating the election or maybe he was a very upset Republican bear taking it out on our garage doors. Or...maybe he wanted to see the tire tracks on our freezer door.

We soon had steel garage doors. We also put up motion sensor lights all around the lower portion of the house including at the garage doors so at various times of the year we gave quite a blinking light show to the neighborhood – especially when the bears were bulking up on calories right before they went into hibernation in November.

As for fixing the ATV, while writing this up over six years after it happened, I couldn't recall what Trapper had done to fix it. I had no recollection of him driving it up onto either a trailer or into the back of our truck. That is an event I think I would have remembered because of the trepidation I would have been feeling imagining the accelerator getting stuck again and him flying either off the front end of the trailer or a repeat performance up the back of the cab of the truck. So, I asked Trapper to tell me how he resolved it.

He said he figured out that some ice had frozen on the throttle and all he had to do was spray some WD-40 on it. My goodness I wish he'd thought of that before we went out to the trailhead to get it in the first place. But, if he had, we wouldn't have such a story which I am happy to say has given us much laughter.

The first time I tried to share this story with some friends a few days after the fact I started laughing so hard I could not finish a sentence. I wasn't laughing when I started telling it that first time. But I suppose all of the stress of those moments of that ATV driving up and coming down from our freezer door in the first re-telling morphed into one of the funniest times of our marriage in my mind.

If Number One scenario had happened of course it would not have become so funny and Trapper knew I was not being flippant about his potential harm in it all. In fact, he was laughing too. However, for about a year I could not tell it without laughter.

Sometimes the potentially worst times can turn into the absolutely best times of life. We still have tire tracks on our upright freezer door plus a big dent on the left side. Every time I see it I think of that funny day.

And Trapper continues to give me material for these stories in continually creative and different ways. He's not trying to on purpose. But things just keep happening.

Our various horses, mules and dogs have also given us many adventurous, funny and sentimental moments – especially when we have had to tell them goodbye, like the day we reluctantly and tearfully survived *Farewell Most Excellent Festus.*

Farewell
Most Excellent Festus

November 17, 2008 was a bittersweet day in our marriage. The time came for us to say farewell to *Most Excellent Festus*.

We took this photo because we actually found Bridger and Festus this way just a few days before we said Farewell to Festus.

The day before, during Prayer & Testimony Time at our Sunday church service, Trapper tearfully asked for prayer as we would be "going through an Ol' Yeller Moment" the next day. Because Trapper was having trouble talking, our friend and fellow dog lover who was leading that part of the service helped out sympathetically saying, "Festus" and then I helped out (also tearfully) with, "In the scope of things some people might not think this is very important but – it is. Part of what's so hard is that Trapper got Festus for us when we were engaged so he's been here our whole marriage."

Lots of folks know that when someone asks Trapper how long we've been married he is fond of replying "the whole time" so that he has time to figure out how many years it's really been while they're still laughing. So on that Sunday after Trapper's prayer request, even though I already knew the answer, I whispered in his ear, "How long has Festus been with us?" "Fifteen years," he said. And I responded, "The whole time." He smiled through his tears.

Our vet came to our house the next morning instead of us having to go to clinical surroundings for this unhappy task. There all together on the living room floor we said goodbye to Festus. While Festus was snoring from the first shot I read over him the following Scripture:

But I have had God's help to this very day, and so I stand here and testify to small and great alike. I am saying nothing beyond what the prophets and Moses said would happen– that the Christ would suffer and, as the first to rise from the dead, would proclaim light to his own people and to the Gentiles. At this point Festus interrupted Paul's defense.

111

"You are out of your mind, Paul!" he shouted. *"Your great learning is driving you insane."*
"I am not insane, most excellent Festus," Paul replied. *"What I am saying is true and reasonable."* [emphasis added]
– Acts 26:22-25 (NIV)

I referred to this passage in a previous story, *Most Excellent Festus*, which shared some precious Festus trapping memories, how Festus picked Trapper instead of the other way around, and how a few years into our marriage Trapper had accidentally come across the above reference to Festus while he was in the concordance of his Bible one day. He had read it out to me at the time and we had begun calling our furry friend "Most Excellent Festus" ever since. So, this Scripture was not new to us but as I read it aloud in the situation of putting Festus down, it took on meaning much more profound than it ever had before...phrases like "I have had God's help to this very day" and "testify to small and great alike" (pets and people alike) and the word "suffer" (which we were trying to help Festus out with at that very moment) and Christ "as the first to rise from the dead" and then the comical-sounding exchange between Paul and Festus regarding Paul's sanity plus the ending: "What I am saying is true and reasonable."

Oh what a picture of God's unconditional love for us those dogs in our lives represent!

We thanked our vet for her compassion toward us that day. Her gentle and loving kindness to us made this very difficult Ol' Yeller Moment profoundly more bearable. She even said, "You're doing this while he still has his dignity." That touched us both – but Trapper especially deeply – a guy thing.

Trapper had received permission from the family who owns property over at the base of Carbon Peak to bury Festus at a spot that he had shown me years ago that was special to him. He and a friend went up there three days before and made the necessary preparations so that when Trapper, Bridger and I went up there to bury Festus it would all be ready and waiting.

The base of Carbon Peak is just a couple of miles off of Ohio Creek Road where exactly a year before Bridger had received his salvation (see *Bridger's Salvation*). It's an area we go to a lot – mostly for beaver trapping.

It's a place with a view of The Castles on one side, Whetstone Mountain on the other, Carbon Peak above and The Gunnison Valley below. And the Lord provided us with an astoundingly gorgeous day to do this. We shared a bottle of Fess Parker *Frontier Red* wine (some of you remember that he's the guy who played Davy Crockett, Daniel Boone and, of all crazy coincidences – the dad in Ol' Yeller) and spent a good part of the day there.

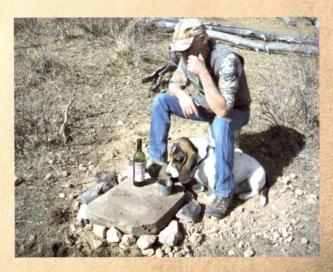

You can also see Bridger here facing Whetstone Mountain with Carbon Creek below as if he's looking for Festus down there where Festus and Trapper (and Bridger more recently) had been on so many trapping adventures together. And when Trapper put out a holler to the mountains as if calling to Festus, the echo was endless — it just kept going and going and going and returning and returning and returning for an unbelievably long while. That was astounding too.

So we sadly said a fond...
Farewell Most Excellent Festus.

Even though Trapper lost Festus as a partner that day, Bridger the Basset Hound and of course me, his wife, have been here to help handle things from time to time which is how from time to time we dealt with critters that were *Alive In The Outback.*

114

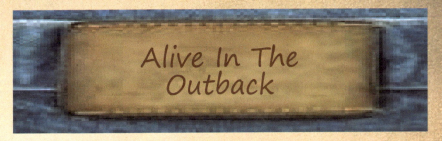

Alive In The Outback

It's not what you may be thinking...the Outback I am meaning is not in Australia. It's a Subaru Outback.

It is an amazing phenomenon. When Trapper is unable to check the traps and that necessity falls to me, it's almost guaranteed that a critter will stroll into them.

When we know in advance that Trapper is going to be gone or otherwise unable to check traps for some reason, if at all possible he will remove or trigger the traps at our various job sites so that I will not have to deal with animals getting into them. Sometimes the situation is such that we have to leave them actively set or he is unexpectedly unavailable and that means I have to go check them and deal with whatever gets in them.

We noticed that a certain pattern developed over the years: The almost sure-fire way to get various elusive critters into various traps or have someone call with an emergency animal situation was for Trapper to go out of town.

Trapper participates in a Mountain Man Rendezvous reenactment almost every year which takes place during the first week of August. The camp was only two miles from our house – up good ol' Washington Gulch road where so much has happened to good ol' Trapper (see the *Frozen Pedal to the Metal of the Freezer* tale earlier).

For two summers we had a big job going on where we were picking up several ground squirrels (chipmunks) twice daily and relocating them away from this particular customer's attempts to have an attractive garden. In fact, they would have been happy just to have ANY garden considering the massive number of furry things that were running rampant there. During the two summers we did that, in 2011 we captured 194 chipmunks, 11 marmots, 40 mice and 10 birds. In the summer of 2012 we captured 290 chipmunks, 13 marmots, 135 mice, 3 Richardson Ground Squirrels, 3 birds and a few ermine. Most of these critters were taken to happier homes away from this property, with the exception of the birds and ermine which the customer was happy to have released on their property. During the following winter those customers sold that house and our two-a-day job came to an end. We don't know what the new owner is doing about the animals other than just forgetting about having a garden and all living happily together on the property there.

Anyway, during Rendezvous time I needed to check those traps twice a day those two summers. In 2011 there was one day that was particularly ridiculous, or "addicalous" as one of my nephews used to say when he was a little boy.

At the time we didn't have a reliable separate vehicle for our business which resulted in using our Subaru Outback for our business.

That day, just as I was finishing loading the morning's critter captures at the aforementioned job, I received a cell phone call from a property manager advising me that there was a chipmunk loose in one of the houses in town where they had guests for the week. He asked for our help, which translated to me since Trapper was unavailable.

So, I hurried to finish loading which meant I didn't have time to properly rearrange for that one last trap in which I had found a chipmunk right after the call. There was one little square hole left in the back so I turned the trap on end thinking that the enclosed chipmunk would just drop down in the end of the trap on the (thankfully) rubber mat in the back of the car.

Off I went to meet the property manager at that house in town. But on the way I looked in the rear view mirror and saw the back of a chipmunk hanging on for dear life in the TOP of that trap standing on end. I had a stop sign coming up and honestly hoped that no one would come up behind me. Someone did. All I could do was hope they were laughing instead of cursing at me.

I next needed to go get the key to the house with the errant chipmunk running around in a bedroom that they had closed off. That meant I had to stop on Elk Avenue, the main street of Crested Butte, right in the middle of the business district, and go inside.

Before going into the property manager's office I was compelled to take a photo of this *addicalous* scene in the back of the Outback even though it meant I would be displaying it on Elk Avenue a few minutes longer in the process:

It turned out that the property manager was already over at the house but some of his office staff came out onto Elk Avenue and enjoyed some chuckles from that *addicalous* scene after I told them about it.

I then went on over to the house with the critter problem and the property manager and I chased that chipmunk around the room together and got 'im outta there!

I must say that Trapper would have been substantially more adept in that effort than I was but I did my best as a substitute trapper.

I set traps just in case there were more chipmunks in the room and left to go release those critters from the car.

Here's the back of the car that day.

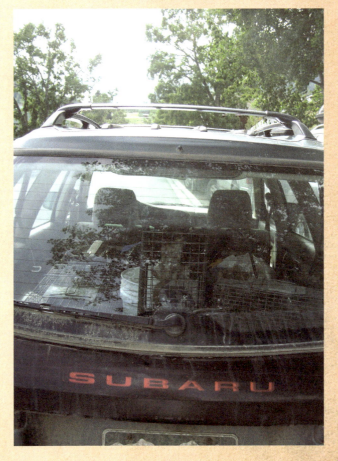

But since the glass reflection makes it difficult to imagine what the person behind me at the stop sign saw, thankfully we took one with the hatch lifted open so you can really get the idea...

117

118

A few days later I had another load in the car that included a couple of traps with marmots in them. This time I went up Washington Gulch Road where Trapper came out of Rendezvous camp to meet me and help with the releases. We opened the back of the car and started pulling out traps. But one was, uh oh, EMPTY! I told Trapper, "I KNOW there was a marmot in that trap. Where'd he go?" I very cautiously opened the door behind the driver's seat and..."whew" didn't see a marmot loose in the car. At first I thought that I was mistaken and that maybe it was just an extra empty trap that had been in the car but then said again to Trapper, "I KNOW there was a marmot in that trap. Where'd he go?" I noticed a jacket laying there in front of the end of the trap closest to my driver's seat back. I lifted the jacket and, lo and behold, there was a loose marmot staring at me for a millisecond before he went flying out of the back of the still open hatchback of the Outback and into the wild again.

Apparently he had chewed out the wire in the back of the trap while I was checking the chipmunk traps in that house in town. Came the dawn as we looked at each other that, oh my goodness, that marmot could have so easily hopped into the front seat with me while I was driving up Washington Gulch Road to meet Trapper. Mere words cannot describe what a mess that would have been. Since it didn't happen, I won't even try. If it had happened and had I survived, I would have yet another tale to tell here.

During Mountain Man Rendezvous Week in August of 2010, I received word from a customer that we had successfully captured a porcupine in a trap in her garden. Of course Trapper had tried for days before he left for Rendezvous to catch this thing but it did not have the decency to get in there in time.

Anyway, I knew that I could not lift that trap straight up with the porcupine in it and that dragging it out would have destroyed the very garden we were trying to protect from the porcupine. Trapper had prearranged for a friend to help me if I needed it and oh boy did I need it that day! He and I lifted that porcupine trap over the flowers, out of the garden and into the Outback. We then headed down-valley to check a live beaver trap – another critter that had elusively avoided getting trapped before Trapper left.

Naturally we had a live beaver in that trap on the same day as the porcupine we had brought down from the mountain garden. So our friend and I dragged that live beaver trap to the car.

We stopped so he could take this photo of me pretending that I was doing this by myself. Those of you who know me know that I'm too honest to try to perpetrate such a fib on you our readers – or my Mountain Man.

Okay. So now we had to figure out what to do with the beaver AND the porcupine – both alive and well inside their respective cage traps. Believe me, I sure was wishing we owned a truck for our business at this point! But at least we had purchased a handy rack that fit on the hitch on the back of the Outback which made this possible:

We wrapped the porcupine trap in a tarp so as not to annoy the porcupine, folks on the highway or those in town while transporting these critters.

We THEN had another bright idea – to take both the live beaver and the live porcupine to...RENDEZVOUS!

We didn't have a way to tell Trapper we were coming up there. No cell phones are allowed to be turned on while reenacting pre-1840 life. When we arrived we knew better than to drive right into camp. But soon the reenactors heard what we had in the car and came to take a look.

The decision was made to make an exception and allow us to drive the car through camp and as close as possible to the ridge overlooking the nearby river. After all, that live beaver trap plus the beaver in it weighed over 100 pounds altogether. There they took the trap out of the car and carried it to the top of the ridge and released that beaver which immediately headed down the hill to the water while the adult reenactors cheered and the children chased after the beaver.

Now this was a bunch of people reenacting the Fur TRAPPING and Fur Trade era of this country. So our little exercise of RELEASING a beaver in addition to taking a modern vehicle into camp were both unorthodox and historically backwards behavior.

But the kids and the adults all had a fascinating time with this and, all said and done, it turned out to be a very special and much discussed attraction for that year's Rendezvous.

For some reason no one was interested in us releasing a live porcupine into camp – imagine that! So Trapper and I gave him yet another ride in the back of the Subaru Outback to take him away from the camp to release him.

Then we came back and reconnected with our Trapper's wife's helper on the critter collection run earlier. He and I left the camp and I took him back to his vehicle so he could go home.

It was a blessed day for everyone – the Rendezvous camp, the beaver, the porcupine, Trapper to show folks what he does for a living, Trapper's wife who received the very necessary help I needed from our friend and he himself just because of the adventure of it all.

That's him on the far right of the group photo above – obviously not dressed for the occasion of being at the Rendezvous but then neither was I. But he was absolutely correctly dressed for the job we had at hand that day before we ever arrived at the Rendezvous.

121

After we acquired a new truck for our business use in 2012, we did not have as many animals loose in our Outback anymore but it still occasionally happened when we were using the car for a quick run somewhere instead of going home for the truck. There was this one day that I drove the Outback to town to do bookkeeping work at a store on Elk Avenue – not trapping work.

After I parked I was getting some things out of the back when I noticed a piece of carpet we had in there had a corner nibbled off. I then spied some pieces of dog food in there. "Uh oh – there's a mouse loose in here," I thought. As I walked away I had a thought – one which has reoccurred from time to time in marriage to my Mountain Man, "What if it had run across me while I was driving to town just now???!!!" After finishing my business in town I tentatively went home wondering if a mouse was going to run over me as I drove. That was a long 10 minute drive! Trapper placed some mouse snap traps and other types of our business equipment for rodents in the car. We never caught that mouse but I KNOW it was in there before. I've seen their evidence too many times in this *Life as a Mountain Man's Wife* and can now easily recognize their sign. I'm sure a lot of you know what that sign looks like.

Sometimes the sign is painfully obvious – like twice (not once, but twice) when our usually faithful Outback has had trouble starting and our mechanic has taken very long tweezers and pulled mouse nest material out from under the hood somewhere in the engine area. Rodents just love to chew on vehicle wiring for some reason. On those two occasions our mechanic, who knows well my Mountain Man's occupation, has said, "You two need to find a trapper somewhere to solve this problem for you." I'm all for surrounding our vehicles with traps of all sorts in the garage.

In April 2015 we finally traded in that Subaru Outback. It had served us so well for 13 years that we replaced it with a Subaru Forester. True to form with the way this life of ours goes , within six weeks we had a need to use the Forester to haul live beaver traps. Time will tell if we'll need to put any live animals in the Forester.

My Mountain Man has taught me well how to recognize sign even though sometimes he enjoys making things up "just to be ornery" – a concept I have never grown accustomed to and do not happily embrace. There have been moments in our marriage when I know absolutely that my Mountain Man is telling a tale – that is, spouting *Mountain Man Hot Air.*

Mountain Man
Hot Air

In the last story I mentioned our friend who was on hand to help me out when Trapper couldn't be there. But this friend's primary reason for being in town was because he was one of our resort area's hot air balloon pilots for a long time. For several years Trapper and I crewed for him. He

would come over from Montrose about two hours away and spend the night in our guest room. We would all three leave by 5:30 am to go set up the balloon in a cul-de-sac high up in a Mount Crested Butte subdivision. He would then go pick up that day's customers for the balloon flight. After lift-off Trapper and I were the chase team driving the pilot's truck and trailer all over Mount Crested Butte. We were good ones for this job since we knew the roads all over the mountain because of our many customers who have experienced animal situations in their homes sprinkled all over the ski area there. When they finally landed we would get there, help pack up the balloon and basket and share a Balloonist Blessing ceremony on the ground with the customers.

It was also a good thing that we knew the mountain and its roads so well because I am awful at backing up a trailer – one part of this *Life as a Mountain Man's Wife* in which I have not been victorious. I was therefore very careful while driving to not get myself on a street that didn't have a way to stay going forward – either by means of a cul-de-sac to turn around in or a through street. Great big parking lots were also my friends. Our balloon pilot friend knew of my limitations in this regard so he did his best, to the extent of the control he had over the situation, to pilot the balloon to places that would accommodate my limitations. Trapper over in the passenger seat needed to be ready to jump out and go help them in a hurry sometimes. He had the strength to do that while I exercised my brain to try not to get into a dead end predicament. We all had our individual talents in this setting.

When the first weekend of August rolled around each year the balloon pilot would try his darnedest not to book a flight during Mountain Man Rendezvous weekend but, being as it was one of the busiest weekends of the summer due to an Arts Festival in Crested Butte at the same time, sometimes it was just unavoidable. So, Trapper had to come out of Rendezvous camp to help.

But that also meant he had on his Mountain Man Rendezvous garb because we had to get started so early in the morning it was just too much to allow time for Trapper to change clothes. Besides, we decided it would give that day's balloon flight passengers an extra special memory.

Our balloon pilot friend is a man who appreciates a good joke. So we had the pleasure of pulling a few on him. One such time was after we received a shipment of battery operated hoot owls to use in deterring woodpeckers from doing their significant damage to some of our customers' homes. We took one of those hoot owls and placed it on the chest of drawers in our guest room and turned on both of its motion-sensor functions – not only head movement but also its loud hooting sound which was the best feature of these owls for our joke on him. After he said goodnight and went to his room we sat upstairs and waited...and waited...and waited. For a long time we heard nothing. I even began to wonder if I had set it up properly. But then we figured he just hadn't gone near it yet. Finally we heard, "Hoo-oo-oo. Hoo-oo-oo." Next we heard him, "Get the gun!" But thankfully there was no loud boom forthcoming even though various guns were available not far from his room.

Although my Mountain Man loves to be a prankster, he is not known for expounding an extraordinary amount of hot air as he is a quiet sort who doesn't care at all for pretentious behavior. However, he thoroughly enjoys the process of fabricating a tall tale or two which he does from time to time as part of his pranks. But with all of our real life and TRUE tales, who needs to fabricate them? He has plenty of material without making up a darned thing. And so do I which is how this book came about.

In addition to hot air balloon crewing, we've crewed for other aircraft, such as when we were part of *The Renegade Crew Of Delta Air Lines.*

The Renegade Crew Of Delta Air Lines

In telling the *Skunk Cookies* story I mentioned that I would tell you about why we were considered an "irregular" crew the winter we both worked at the Gunnison, Colorado airport.

Well, the fact is that in the Delta Air Lines Atlanta headquarters we were truly known as "The Renegade Crew of Delta Air Lines". Most winters when Delta flew into Gunnison they would send in their own professionally trained staff to man the station there.

But that one winter of 1995-1996 a series of things happened just about a month before the ski season was starting and they needed to hire locals of the Gunnison area. That happened during the two years we lived in Gunnison and, since I had some travel industry experience in my background, Trapper and I went together – as a team – to interview for jobs on that crew. We were hired with the understanding that we would receive professional help from Delta Air Lines Red Coats who would come in on every flight.

Trapper and I were about 15 years older than everyone else on the crew and, as shared before, I became Station Manager. Having grown up 70 miles from Atlanta in Athens, Georgia plus having been in the travel industry for several years before my married life to Trapper, I knew the clean cut reputation of Delta Air Lines. So, it was an exception at the time for Delta to hire Trapper with his Mountain Man beard. One of the interesting things we noticed at the end of the winter was that although when we started Trapper was the only one of the crew sporting a beard, by the end of the winter all those who could grow them had them! That was one reason Atlanta considered us "The Renegade Crew of Delta Air Lines" – or so we were told by one of the Red Coats about half way through the winter season. Another is that we did rather unorthodox things in our tenure that winter. Since we did not have Delta's usual training, we didn't really know what orthodox was so, we just did what we had to do to get the job done the best we knew how. The Red Coat assured us that our reputational moniker was a compliment for the way we did whatever it took but with strict attention to the rules as we knew them and according to our training to get that plane unloaded, cleaned, reloaded and back in the sky in a mere one hour about four times a week.

As Station Manager, part of my job was to check folks in at the gate. When the plane would arrive from Atlanta it was time to greet it. This was during the last year before the Gunnison airport purchased jetways from Denver Stapleton airport. So the passengers had to come down the stair truck stairs and onto the tarmac where I stood and directed them to the Arrivals door inside of which they would be able to collect their baggage. Part of my job was also to intercept any smokers who would start to light up after their three hour non-smoking flight and inform them that there was a fuel truck right behind them re-filling the plane's tanks. We didn't really want for all of us to be blown to kingdom come just yet.

Another thing I added to the job was that when I spotted any women who came off of the plane with fur on, and a great number of them did, I would greet them with "Welcome to Gunnison" and then say, "You see that man over there with the beard unloading bags? He's my husband and he's really a trapper. We both thank you for wearing fur." Of course by then I had to be able to know the difference between faux fur and the real thing but my Mountain Man husband had taught me well how to do that visually without even needing to touch it. Besides, I think it would have been a bit forward of me to start petting these women's coats and I don't think Delta or the airport administration would have cared for that. The women seemed to love their extra special "Welcome to Gunnison". I knew from growing up in Georgia that opportunities to wear those fur coats there were few and far between because of the warmer climate compared to Colorado and I completely understood why they would jump at the chance to wear it as they were immediately faced with the outside temperature of Gunnison upon disembarking from the plane that had originated in balmier Atlanta three hours before – and especially since Gunnison is often noted in the weather forecasts as the coldest place in the nation from time to time. I'm sure some of you know that it can easily be a more bone chilling cold in Georgia because of the humidity there even if the actual temperature is higher. Either way, fur coats were extremely functional as well as beautiful on both sides of those Atlanta to Gunnison plane rides.

As for me, instead of a fur coat it was honestly more practical for me to wear my father's Navy pea coat from World War II which he had acquired while in basic training at Great Lakes, Illinois. It worked for him there and it kept me toasty some 50 plus years later.

During that winter with Delta there came the day when, as the plane was backing out of the gate, the head of security there very seriously came to me at the inside gate check-in counter and said, "You have a dirty aircraft." I looked back at him and wondered, "How does he know how well our guys cleaned the plane?" But, thank goodness, before I could naively say that to him he explained, "I saw a Delta Red Coat take a passenger out the back door of the ticket counter and board her without bringing her through security screening." This was in 1996 so a few years before September 11 of 2001 when everything ramped up regarding airport security so, although security was a definite issue, it was not quite as serious as it would be later. Regardless, it was a major infraction and he was right that we had to deal with it.

I went running out onto the tarmac – completely forgetting my training which had instructed me to cross my arms in front of my face at the wrists to stop that aircraft. But the cockpit crew saw me motioning to them with less professional hand motions and somehow they interpreted that I wanted them to halt that plane right then and there. I have to say it was somewhat of a rush of power to realize that I had actually stopped such a big 757 airplane and those fellas sitting WAAAAYYYYY up there in that cockpit. My fellow Renegade Crew members drove the stair truck up to the front door of the plane so I could run up there, get the flight attendants to open the door and retrieve that passenger to bring her and her carry-on bag back down for screening. When the door of the plane opened and I saw the Red Coat, the one who was supposed to be the professional there and was supposed to know and abide by the rules, I just looked at him and said, "What were you thinking?" before then going to the cockpit to tell the pilot what this was about. A full FAA investigation took place over the next couple of weeks and most of the Renegade Crew was required to be questioned by the FAA about what had happened. The bottom line was that we were depending on the Red Coat to know the rules and so he was able to make that move because we figured he knew what he was doing. My how we would do things differently if in that situation today! I think anyone working that ticket counter would have barred the door to the tarmac – Red Coat standing in front of them or not!

Another time that same airport security head came to me at the gate with a little blond boy who had a bowl haircut and gigantic blue eyes. He said to me, "Give him THE TALK." I knew that meant that I was to inform the boy with how serious it was to say certain words like bomb, blow up, etc. on or near a passenger airplane. I have no idea what had happened in the security screening line to precipitate THE TALK but the boy's father was standing right behind his son nodding his head in agreement and cheering me on while I tried my darnedest to keep a serious face because those little boy gigantic blue eyes were filled with crocodile tears and it was breaking my heart to see him so scared. But, we got through it and sometimes I've wondered if that incident was at all life-changing for that little boy. I'll bet if it had been possible to introduce him to a real live Mountain Man at that point it would have been a much happier event for him. But, Trapper was busy out there loading the little boy's bags into the belly of the plane.

Also during that winter my Georgia heritage cropped up when former President Jimmy Carter, also of Georgia, brought a bunch of celebrities into Gunnison for a Habitat for Humanity fund raiser event that he used to put on every year in Crested Butte. When the flight came in they were diverted west of us to Grand Junction because of heavy snowfall so I didn't meet them on the inbound flight. But a few days later we came home to find a call on our answering machine from the Secret Service. When I called the agent back he informed me that I needed to meet with him early the next day before their outbound flight in order to fill out all the gun permit paperwork for his agents and make sure they were in certain seats where they needed to be.

During that process the next day I informed the Secret Service guy that I too was from Georgia. I knew that they were keeping Jimmy and Rosalyn Carter and their grandson warm in the Administrative Building. So I told the Secret Service agent that we needed to establish a signal after the Delta 757 had come in, unloaded its passengers, had been cleaned and was ready for the Carters to pre-board. He said, "Well, since you're from Georgia, why don't you come get them?" Okay. I did that. While the three Carters were putting on their coats I told them that I knew his cousin, Connie Carter. Connie was President of the University of Georgia chapter of Kappa Alpha Theta when I pledged there in 1973 and so she and I had lived at that sorority house together there and were friends. In fact, I was invited to their wedding in Plains, Georgia the summer of 1976 but wound up in Europe that summer – the same summer Jimmy Carter was running for President.

Anyway, after I brought up the Carter cousin then Rosalyn and I talked about Connie and her husband all the way across the tarmac until they boarded the plane. Trapper was out there doing his job and so was watching while I chit-chatted with the Carters. He thought that rather interesting considering what a good conservative he was making of me in the early years of our marriage. Neither one of us knew when that day started that I would be escorting a former President and his family to the plane personally.

As I've said earlier, you never know what's going to happen in life when you marry so outside of your upbringing. But occasionally things happen that take you back to your upbringing in that other pre-marriage life and the Georgia Carters gave me a recollection of my pre-Mountain Man days – including the reminder that my *Life as a Mountain Man's Wife* is a pretty far cry from sorority life at UGA but then I wasn't completely sold out to that while in it in the first place. I appreciated the opportunity to do that and the friends from that time but I wonder if any of them there with me in the first half of the 1970s would recognize me now? I know my life-long friends from Athens with whom I am still in touch from time to time muse, "You sure have changed."

On another day during that airport job winter I saw someone at the gate waiting to leave Gunnison that I recognized...Hank Aaron. He was one of the celebrities who came out to help with the Carter event and seeing him also took me back to my college days. In the summer of 1974 I was a Congressional Intern in Washington, DC for the Georgia congressman from our district. That also happened to be only a few months after Hank Aaron had hit his 715th home run in April of that year which had broken Babe Ruth's record of 714. All of the Georgia House and Senate office employees received a special invitation to be in the gallery of a joint session of congress where Hank Aaron was to appear. As he walked in, the entire place – Senators, Congressional Representatives and gallery alike – erupted into a standing ovation...an incredibly moving thing to be a part of for a college sophomore gal from Georgia. So 22 years later in 1996 I had the profound joy of getting to tap Mr. Hank Aaron on the shoulder from behind and say to him as he turned around, "I'm from Georgia and one of the most moving experiences I have ever had was being in the gallery in the Chamber of the House of Representatives in the summer of 1974 when you were there and received that standing ovation." He shook my hand and with a big smile said, "Thank you for telling me that."

Another thing I didn't know when I applauded as Hank Aaron walked down that House Chamber aisle and spoke to us there in 1974 was what a baseball fan my future Mountain Man husband would turn out to be. Trapper had helped Hank Aaron and his parents with their bags out there in front of the Gunnison airport that day but didn't realize who it was until everyone on our Renegade Crew was buzzing about Hank Aaron being on the flight that had just taken off. It's funny that my avid baseball fan husband did not recognize Hank Aaron but his wife did. But, I'm from Georgia so of course I recognized him! I may not have known a thing about trapping when I met Trapper the baseball fan but I did know who Hank Aaron and the Atlanta Braves were while growing up in Georgia. As it turns out, that was another preparation for marriage that the Lord gave me.

Our Renegade Crew was required to stay at the airport until each flight took off. So, we would stay on duty by sitting up in the restaurant at the airport to watch until we saw wheels off the ground on the runway. One day we saw our Delta 757 at one end of the runway poised to rev up the engines to start down it for takeoff when we saw two coyotes racing toward the plane from the other end of the runway. In his trapping profession Trapper had heard a number of stories of how birds and other animals can get sucked into jet engines and bring down an airplane. We had also been warned in our Delta Air Lines training to work there not to walk in front of a spinning jet engine because it would be awfully easy to get sucked in and...well, I don't want to spell that one out.

We apprehensively watched the coyotes running and the Delta 757 poised for running. There was nothing we could do but wait to see what would happen. Surely the pilots saw the coyotes and would know the potential severity of the situation. Here came the coyotes headed straight for the plane but the plane was already in motion heading straight for them. The pilot skillfully lifted that plane off the ground just as they all reached the same place on the runway and it went right over the heads of the coyotes which then proceeded to run around and around in circles chasing each other! The people in the plane were safe from a coyote caused crash, the coyotes were a might confused and we were free to go home laughing about it instead of another scenario that could have happened.

In the very last days of the season in March we received the news that a close family friend, Kenneth Waters, had passed away in Athens, Georgia. Kenneth and his wife, Grace, had lived a block up the street from our Athens family home, were our family's adopted aunt and uncle, was my Dad's pool-playing buddy (both houses had pool tables in them), was my life-long friend's real uncle (Jody Wilson Boling) as well as the son-in-law of her grandparents who were my adopted grandparents – Dr. and Mrs. Robert C. Wilson – aka Barber and Nana of Skunkie fame here.

It was the day before the funeral and the next to last day of the season. Our jobs with Delta Air Lines would also end the next day. I wanted to go to Athens so badly and here was this big 757 there which could have taken me to within 70 miles of where I wanted to go in only three hours. If I didn't purchase a ticket and get on there today it wasn't going to happen. But I knew I needed to be around to close down the station the next day. They had given me a list of things to do to accomplish that and I felt I was obligated to do them. So, I did my job that day which included going up the stairs on the stair truck, into the plane's cockpit and getting the pilot to sign a form like I was required to do for each flight. I then went back out and waited on the stair truck landing while the flight attendants closed down the door of the plane. The procedure required that I knock on the door to indicate that it appeared closed from my side outside. But this time I patted that door and leaned on the side of the plane feeling remorse that I was outside instead of inside it...thinking that here went my last opportunity of getting to Athens in time for Kenneth's funeral. But of course it was too late and the fare at this late date would have been prohibitive anyway. I knew that. But I couldn't help but be sentimental about it as I patted the plane's side.

It was quite an interesting five months from November 1995 to March 1996 as part of *The Renegade Crew of Delta Air Lines*. But, as you can see , we were only renegade in spirit because the whole crew was extremely serious about doing this work right, in a safe manner and by the rules when it came right down to it.

Although we were grateful for this work that winter, it was a bit out of the usual realm of my Mountain Man's preferred profession which has afforded us with quite a variety of other winter adventures beyond what a lot of people experience. Along those lines, many are the times we have dealt with a *Wintertime Porcupine.*

Wintertime Porcupine

Not everyone knows that porcupines are still active in the winter...even in BIG SNOW winters. We have proof.

We live in a ski resort area and many are the stories of skiers who have seen porcupines on the slopes.

On one occasion Trapper saw a hotel maintenance guy with cuts and scratches and bruises all over him. Thing was – he had seen the same fella the day before and he had been fine.

"What happened to you?" inquired Trapper.

"Yesterday I was skiing, swerved to miss a porcupine on the slope and...hit a tree!" came the pained answer. OUCH!

There is one subdivision up at the base of the ski area in Mount Crested Butte where we were trapping porcupines during the massive snow winter of 2007-2008. Believe it or not, almost every time it snowed that winter it would come down in FEET, not just inches. THREE FEET per storm seemed to be the operative measurement that winter and our county snow plow driver told us at the end of the winter that we'd had 450 inches at our rental house. No wonder we were shoveling UP from our second story deck before it was over!

This one porcupine was giving the subdivision homeowners fits because once porcupines chew the bark on pine trees all the way around the tree (called girdling), that tree is gonna die from that point up at some time in the future. This eventuality does not sit well with those who have paid for landscaping or those who have planned the architecture of the homes around the placement of the trees already there.

Anyway, Trapper put a trap near a culvert in the subdivision where he had seen and smelled sign of a porcupine in residence. But then two things happened overnight and the next morning. It snowed par for that winter's course – THREE FEET. And then, in the wee small hours of the next morning, the snow plow came along and pushed ANOTHER THREE FEET of plowed snow on top of the THREE FEET of fresh snowfall. OH NO!

My Mountain Man is a dutiful trapper and so he dutifully set out to check his trap. Thing was, he hadn't thought ahead to put a snow pole marker where his trap was. He just knew the general area of the little valley there where his trap was the last he had seen it...yesterday. Snow shovel over shoulder, he set out to find his trap – and whatever might or might not be in it.

He dug around and dug around. I went up into the driveway of one of the homes where those people and I tried to get a perspective using our memories from the day before and figure out where that trap might be. With all of our efforts, he finally located that trap. Trapper is 5'9" so he dug down under that SIX FEET of snow there and when he stepped down into it he...disappeared. And then we heard Trapper's muffled voice from way down there below the snow line, "There's a live porcupine in here!" He finished digging it out, dragged that trap across the snow and off we went with it.

The homeowners took photos of this event along with me and we left them the hole for subdivision conversation – which presumably lasted only a few days since pretty soon

ANOTHER THREE FEET and then ANOTHER THREE FEET of fresh powder snowfall obliterated all of the evidence where that had happened.

Before learning of our wildlife services, several trees had been killed by porcupines and we had been on the warpath on behalf of the homeowner and the property manager ever since they first contacted us about the problem there. Therefore, any live porcupine sighting on the premises resulted in a quick call to us.

One of those was on January 4, 2011 when the property manager was there cleaning since the owners had just left to go home right after New Years. She called to say she saw a porcupine near the side of the house and asked how quickly we could get there with traps. It happened to be a day when we could respond in a hurry and off we went up to Mount Crested Butte.

Upon arrival Trapper began unloading traps while I went to say hello to the property manager since I already knew she was in the house. As I approached the front porch I could see her inside. I walked up the stone front steps and reached out for the front door knob planning to stick my head in the door and say hello to her. Oddly enough, she was not coming toward the door and making some sort of gesture to me but I couldn't understand what it was. All I knew was that it was NOT a friendly wave. She had a strained look on her face and was pointing with her right arm stretching over in front of her body, pointing to her left and desperately trying to get a message to me before I got to the door. I realized she wanted me to look to my right. When I did I discovered the reason for her dismay and warning gesture. There was a Christmas Tree leaning against the railing at the corner of the deck to my right, put there during her cleaning with plans of disposal. And there, in that Christmas Tree eye level with me was…that porcupine!

I can only imagine the look that she had the fun and relief of watching emerge upon my face as the situation dawned on me…"Trapper! Come 'ere with a trap! The porcupine's behind the Christmas Tree over here!" And so it was – just sitting there blinking at us.

What to do? We devised a plan. Trapper got ready with a trap and a snow shovel. We dumped over the Christmas Tree onto the front porch and off the ledge the prickly porky dropped and waddled.

But of course it didn't waddle in the direction of the trap. It jumped down to a stone level just below the front porch and was clearly intending to go hide out under the porch through a gap under there. Trapper handed me the snow shovel, grabbed the trap and ran down there.

From above I was able to block off the porcupine's access to the gap under the porch with the snow shovel. This mission involved some teamwork on our part and lots of moving around of the shovel all over the place along that gap. It was quite a strategic effort because this porcupine did everything in its power to avoid the cage trap and we knew that if it got under the porch it would be next to impossible to get him out of there that day. Besides, after it had been so close to capture in the Christmas Tree we became determined not to let it get away from us.

Mission accomplished. The shovel finally guided porcupine into the trap and we hauled it away. The property manager was even more relieved. However she had truly enjoyed the action-packed show.

Since the prospect of getting more porcupines out of awkward places seemed imminent, eventually we ordered a very long, telescoping pole with a heavy duty net on the end of it in order to more expediently extract them and other rascals from places where humans didn't want them making themselves at home.

The occasion of wrangling the Tannenbaum Porcupine was not our first encounter with this particular Mount Crested Butte home. Our very first visit to this house had been a few years before – a service call which resulted in *The Al & The Owl In The Fireplace.*

The Al & The Owl
In The Fireplace

Our first call to the house that later had the porcupine in the Christmas Tree was on December 17, 2004 when the property manager called saying that her maintenance guys let in the window washer and discovered that there was a Great Horned Owl in the glass enclosed fireplace in the living room.

Trapper had been involved in rescue and rehabilitation of birds of prey as a boy in Kansas and so he knew exactly what to do.

When we arrived we found that it was a rather sizeable glass enclosed fireplace. There was that bird flapping around in there scared half to death and wanting OUT.

Trapper opened the glass door, crawled inside and told the maintenance guy, "Close the door."

I had positioned myself at the end of the fireplace where the bird was mostly hanging out so I could take photos of the event and how Trapper was going to resolve the situation. But he had cautioned me before we arrived to absolutely not use a flash as that would traumatize the owl.

We all watched as Trapper quietly approached the owl with his jacket turned inside out.

He talked to it and it began to calm down. He threw the jacket over it but did not grab it. Instead he talked to it some more and waited while the bird came more to its senses and was willing to let Trapper pick him up in that jacket and take him outta that fireplace.

Those of us outside the fireplace ran out onto the deck ahead of Trapper Al and the Great Horned Owl and positioned ourselves to watch the release. This was in the days before we had a digital camera and so I was out there with my Pentax 35mm waiting for them.

I had absolutely no time to make any adjustments for the change from inside light to outside light. So, as they came out the door I hoped for the best and snapped the shot.

When the prints came back from processing we were astounded at this...

The Al & The Owl
emerging from the fireplace together

What a shock! It came out gorgeous and is one of our best moments in our chosen livelihood of Wildlife Management Services.

Since I was not well versed in the habits of birds of prey until this lesson, after snapping that shot I pointed my camera upwards expecting the owl to go UP when Trapper released it.

What I did not know was that the bird needed to go DOWN to catch an updraft when it flew away. By the time I realized it was going down I only had time to catch the tip of its wing on film.

By the time it came back up it was so far away from us that it was too hard to tell where it was for a good photo.

But it was still such a glorious moment for all of us.

As we were leaving the house all of the maintenance guys were on their respective cell phones making calls to various folks and all of them saying things like, "I just saw the most amazing thing..." and then proceeded to share their version of the story.

An extra benefit for us was that we knew the window washer and, since he is also a videographer, he had gone out to his vehicle, grabbed his video camera and recorded the whole thing. He gave us a copy of the DVD.

Unfortunately, just as Trapper was releasing the owl someone stepped in front of the camera. Every time I see it I know that moment is coming and I want to say, "No! Don't go there!" But they do it every time and we just have to use our memory of what it was like out on that deck when the Great Horned Owl took flight and flew away.

A few years after that the newer property manager called us to that house for the porcupine you heard about in *Wintertime Porcupine* but then last summer a hawk fell down into that same glass enclosed fireplace in the living room and she met us up there to watch.

We went inside but didn't see the hawk. Trapper banged around in the fireplace but we still didn't see him. So we all three figured he must have found his way out. Although that would have been a good thing, we were disappointed for her because she had only heard about the owl from 2005 since it was before her time of managing this property.

Just as we were turning to leave I caught a little flutter of something out of the corner of my eye. That hawk was still in that fireplace but was hiding in the logs like a chameleon that blends in with its surroundings!

Trapper crawled back in there and recreated the technique he had used on the Great Horned Owl years before. Again we went out on the deck to release the bird.

The property manager was delighted because she was able to watch this process herself after all.

We sure have dealt with a lot of unusual animal situations at that one house! Here's that hawk in the fireplace where the Great Horned Owl had hung out a few years before.

We have many moments of unusual things happening when it comes to dealing with animals in general that so most of our contracts quote an amount for "CONTINGENCY – due to the tendency for surprises in work involving animals". This book is a testimony that no truer words have been spoken.

Placing himself in tight quarters to deal with animal situations is something my Mountain Man does on a fairly regular basis. But some times are more ripe with aroma and have more potential for heightened activity than others – like the time he crawled into *The Catacomb Tomb Of Mephitidae Mephitis*.

The Catacomb Tomb Of Mephitidae Mephitis

On October 29, 2013 we received a call from a new customer telling us that the property he was managing had been suffering from skunk, marmot and other critter habitation under the deck that goes around two sides of the house.

The property owner had asked him to seal it up so he had done so by pouring a concrete foundation under the deck. But then the aroma of a skunk was so amplified and severe up in the house that the distraught young caretaker needed help fast before the property owner was coming in three day hence!

We felt for the caller so we rearranged our plans for the next day in order to go there – 75 miles away. As Trapper and I mused over the possibilities that the coming afternoon held in store for us, we had imagined a striped skunk (scientific name family of *Mephitidae* and genus of *Mephitis*) sitting there horrified as the concrete poured in, was then unable to leave and possibly dead or, even more sobering, possibly still alive down there. As we pondered the situation, Trapper brought up the Edgar Allan Poe tale of *The Cask of Amontillado*.

When we arrived at the property in question the next afternoon, the *Mephitidae Mephitis* aroma as we walked in the front door was...PHEW!... stout! The primary source location was quickly identified – easy deal – and so a crawl under the house was most assuredly in order for Trapper. But oh my goodness, this crawl was going to be tough. How much room he would find in which to maneuver under there was the big question for he suspected that it truly was a catacomb which is, quite appropriately for this predicament, defined as a human-made subterranean passageway used for a burial chamber.

While he was inspecting the basement area below, I was visiting with the folks upstairs. It just so happened that I shared with them our preponderances of *The Cask of Amontillado* the night before. None of us had read it in a long while so we all tried to remember the story. I offered my version from a long-ago recollection that it was "about a man who was angry at another man, enticed him down into a wine cellar, got him drunk and then built a brick wall to bury him alive in there".

Those who had any recollection of the story nodded in agreement and then it was time for me to go down into the basement to see if I could be of any help.

139

When I hit the bottom of the stairs and walked further into the basement I couldn't believe my eyes, especially considering our discussion of *The Cask of Amontillado* just entertained topside. The first thing I saw was this-------------------------------> and then this...

My husband was nowhere to be seen but I could hear him huffing and puffing – and grumbling – somewhere – nearby or so it seemed. The other guys down there informed me that Trapper had just disappeared through a door that looked to me like it was filled from top to bottom with dirt. How could he possibly be moving around in there?

Apparently he was climbing over dirt and a combination of softball and cantaloupe sized rocks to get to...uh oh...there it was...what appeared to be a dead skunk in the middle of the...no, not the road, but back in the shadows eight or ten feet beyond where he could crawl to. There was a significant amount of trash there too so great habitat for a skunk BEFORE it was filled in with cement.

He couldn't reach it so my bright idea that I called into him for approval was to get a coal shuttle (shovel) from the fireplace. The caretaker brought it plus the poker down and I shuttled them to Trapper through a small rectangular hole in the wall. Neither of those implements was long enough so they scared up a piece of lumber skinny enough to slide through that rectangular hole and was maybe ten feet long. Trapper used that to tentatively move whatever that was back in there and then realized...it was not a furry thing after all but was instead a dark blue broken bottle with a piece of trash paper over it which, back there in the shadows. had given the little pile a dark fur look from his vantage point.

All of us outside the crawl space – both upstairs and downstairs – noticed an instantaneous alteration in Trapper's attitude from that point on. His grumbling turned into fascination and even humming his way around in there for all to hear.

Later I told him we had all noticed his personality change under there and he had an explanation for that:

At first he was worried – extremely apprehensive is more like it – of what he was going to come face to face with under there. I thought about that and realized, well of course! Who wouldn't be concerned about that potential? The possibility was literally ripe, stinky ripe, for finding a dead skunk. But, given the magnitude of the aroma when we arrived, he had seriously wondered if he was going to be confronting a LIVE skunk eyeball to eyeball. There was also the added factor of feeling mightily claustrophobic under there.

He said that as he was crawling around he then started pondering the situation out. My Mountain Man is a man of very straightforward logic, after all. It had occurred to him that, once the concrete had solidified, a live skunk would have had no way out on the outside so by the time we were there it would have come out into the basement and, possibly, upstairs into the house – a reality of which the folks up top would have clearly been aware. No such incident had been relayed to us. So that notion abated his fears of a live one under there. When he had discovered that what he had thought was a dead skunk was not a dead skunk, he had then become fascinated with the old trash that he was finding under there. So, fears relieved, he was a lot more agreeable about being there and had then experienced his attitude adjustment that I and the others could all hear.

But it was painfully clear that a skunk had literally left his mark on his subterranean world under there before he left so our job description then shifted into what to do about that. We had anticipated that need so had brought along a couple of gallons of our own concoction – something we have named *Skunk Smell Solution* which I dispensed into a quart-sized spray bottle a little at a time and then slid the bottle through that little rectangular opening in the wall closer to where he was crawling around in there. That stuff went a long way toward addressing that rather unhappily distinct odor.

Eventually Trapper emerged from the crawl space for the very last time.

He was surely glad that was over.

But he kept that broken blue bottle as a memento of the experience that turned out a whole lot better than he had feared.

Back up in the living area of the house we asked them to open all the doors and turn on the ceiling fans to both air out the skunk smell and move around the more agreeable citrus smell we had put down which was by then beginning to do its stuff to conquer the skunk smell.

Because we had another customer just down the road from this property, we had entertained the idea of stopping by to check in on him before going home but decided we could not subject him to the aroma that was undoubtedly attached to us now – especially Trapper who had crawled around in it in the catacomb turned trash bin under that house.

On the way home we contemplated stopping in Gunnison to grab a bite to eat but decided we could not subject any restaurant or its patrons to ourselves either. So we pulled into a drive-in booth at the Sonic there, ordered burgers to take home and didn't ask the car hop gal if we smelled like skunk to her. It was rather frosty outside so we hope that masked it for her sake.

After we returned to our home in Crested Butte I pulled out my laptop, looked up *The Cask of Amontillado* in Wikipedia and discovered this:
"Amontillado is a variety of Sherry wine characterized by being darker than Fino…A Fino Amontillado is a wine that has begun the transformation from a fino to an Amontillado, but has not been aged long enough to complete the process."

Thank goodness there was not a *Mephitidae Mephitis* under that house that had been "aged long enough to complete the process"…of decomposition.

As for smelling like *Mephitidae Mephitis* in public places, we know all too well how careful we have to be about that.

There was the day we picked up a skunk from a customer's property in Gunnison but had it in a box with a clamp-tight lid strapped down on top of our Subaru Outback car since we didn't have our new truck yet.

There were other cars around us when we parked there in the WalMart parking lot but when we came out of the store we quickly noticed that our vehicle was…all alone out there. Ya know how folks with new cars sometimes park them angled across two places so that no one will park around them and bang their doors into them? Well now we know how to get more room around whatever vehicle we're driving in any parking lot!

There was another day the summer of 2013 that I was in our bank at the teller window. One of our town UPS drivers who knows well our occupation came in with a delivery. When he saw me there he made a comment about our truck which was currently out in the bank parking lot with Trapper inside waiting for me. He said it smelled like skunk – a remark everyone in the bank overheard.

He was correct.

Trapper had just picked up a skunk in Gunnison again but it had not sprayed so he didn't realize that he had contracted the odor which must've been on the trap.

Neither did I because I never got out of the truck while he was dealing with the skunk. Had we realized it we would have saved our bank business for another day, not subjected the bank folks to our aromatic condition and just gone home. I looked at the teller and asked her if she had noticed that I smelled like skunk.

She said, "Yeah – but I just figured you'd been smoking pot!"

Yikes – not me!...or Trapper! Hate the smell of the stuff. Can you believe it?...we actually prefer the smell of skunk over that of marijuana. But we had never considered the possibility that their relative aromas have any resemblance to each other.

I later thanked Craig for creating the situation for me to publicly dispel that potential rumor.

Skunks are prolifically present in our business. For all of Trapper's crawling around under that house, I'll bet he would have been thrilled to have found a *Mephitidae Mephitis* in this condition...

...instead of in the condition he was imagining under there.

143

Sometimes we change their condition...like this hat that we had made from three *Mephitidae Mephitis* captured at the property of one of our customers. After sending the skinned pelts to a tanner we then sent the tanned pelts to our hat maker and it came out gorgeous!

When I was handling Skunkie as a little girl I never imagined I would be handling tanned skunk pelts and ordering the creation of skunk hats.

Life as a Mountain Man's Wife continues to produce creative challenges – like the experience of chronicling these stories and then the ultimate joy of doing the layouts for it in our computer since the old light table method is not acceptable anymore.

As you've been reading you've probably noticed that there are a lot of critters that are prolifically present in not only our business but also our lives in general. We've loved a menagerie of them our whole marriage. The photo on the left below is a bit fuzzy because it was taken through a window screen since I knew opening the back door would make them move.

The cream colored Labrador is loyal Chester who came to be known to us as "Fae's Fae-thful Friend". He died unexpectedly during the night in March of 2006.

Then, four months after Festus left us we met *Oh My Darlin' Clementine*.

144

Oh My Darlin'
Clementine

It's time to introduce you to our second Basset Hound named Clementine and how she came to live with us.

Bridger is such a classic dog (or DAWG as they say in my hometown of Athens, Georgia) that we wanted a pup from him.

After a few years of unsuccessfully searching for a female Basset Hound to create that pup, we eventually resorted to the canine equivalent of a personals ad in two area newspapers. In the ad we bragged on Bridger and his attributes and really had some fun with it.

Bridger was only mildly impressed with how impressive the ad made him sound. The result was a phone call from a woman 100 miles away who had found a lost female Basset Hound, searched for three months for the owner but then had been unsuccessful at that effort.

We loaded up Bridger in the Subaru Outback and headed out to go meet her. Even though we already knew she had been fixed and so would not be able to accomplish our pup purpose, somehow it seemed that she would be worth checking out. This is the very moment they met.

We loved her right off and loaded them both into the Outback. Within only a few miles I looked in the rear view mirror and saw this precious sight...

I turned the camera around for a close-up

...and started singing, "Oh my darlin', oh my darlin', *Oh My Darlin' Clementine...*" Thus she acquired her new name before we made it home.

It was March 20, 2010 and so a bunch of snow was still on the ground. Clementine wasn't so sure about her new home at first but she came around when she discovered that springtime in the Rockies meant that the snow had melted up at the top of those steps when we brought her in.

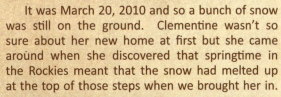

Within only a few months Clementine had Trapper and Bridger thoroughly trained to her satisfaction.

A few months before we met Clementine we also met a fine man by the name of Bob McConnell who was running for United States Congress from our 3rd District of Colorado. Partly because Bob had been an Army Ranger, he and Trapper connected right away due to their mutual military involvement and interest in survival skills. We all became fast friends and we knew this was a man we wanted to see elected as our Congressman.

Neither one of us had been heavily involved in anyone's political campaign before. When Bob started asking us to speak in our area on his behalf, we decided it was time to step up and get active. We also decided our bassets could help out in the effort too.

So, I made sandwich boards for them (very SHORT sandwich boards) that said "Bassets for Bob" and "Of the People Not the Party". The signs also sported the "Don't Tread on Me" Gadsden Flag and a photo of Bob on horseback carrying a waving American Flag.

First we entered them in the Crested Butte Fourth of July Parade.

The reaction to their campaigning was so enthusiastic that we did it again a couple of weeks later in the Gunnison *Cattlemen's Days* parade. For a long time people who knew us would see our bassets and talk about the Basset Hounds in the parades.

They had never even seen us with them. Yippee – that was the idea!

Darn – Bob McConnell didn't win the August primary. But in October about a month before the election we dropped by a Meet and Greet in Gunnison for another fella we had become acquainted with during the campaign, Ken Buck, who was running for a U.S. Senate seat. We commiserated about McConnell's campaign loss but then Ken mentioned that McConnell had won Gunnison County. "That's because of our Basset Hounds!" we boasted.

Ken Buck thought about that and then spoke his revelation with a big grin:
"Hmmm. Bassets for Buck.
Works for me."

So, we made new very short sandwich boards and took them on the road to be greeters at an event in Grand Junction.

This good man did not deserve the mud slinging he received from the opposition. The ads since the primary had become vicious and everyone was sick of them. So, for these signs we decided to do our part to counter that and be above it. So the sign added to the top under **Bassets for Buck** read:

We'd rather make ya laugh than sling mud

In November we sponsored one last Meet and Greet for Buck in Gunnison two days before Election Day. Folks were waiting for him in the restaurant and it was brutally cold outside.

We figured Ken would be anxious to get inside to the voters as soon as he arrived. Instead he seemed completely content to take some time outside to scratch both bassets behind the ears. In fact, maybe that time gave him a welcome break from the final push of the campaign.

Another darn – Ken Buck was defeated in that campaign for the Senate in 2010. But we are happy to say that he did win his 2014 campaign and is now a U.S. Congressman for a section of the eastern part of Colorado. Since that was a district race on the Front Range of Colorado and we're on the Western Slope, we were not actively involved in that campaign. But we sure are glad he finally made it to Washington, D.C. Our Basset Hounds are ready and hopefully they will be able to be **Bassets for Buck** if he runs a statewide race again in the future.

Clementine quickly became a part of our lives and activities by enthusiastically jumping right into the political campaigns only three and a half months after she came to live with us. What she loved the most was all of the petting she got from parade on-lookers, candidates and such. Our first Basset Hound, Bridger, has been with us since six weeks old when we picked him up from his birth home in La Junta, Colorado in 2003. He's one of the best decisions of our marriage and gives us volumes of material and laughs. One of the best times is here – a story we call *Bridger Goes To Rendezvous*.

148

Bridger Goes To Rendezvous

You folks interested in Mountain Man history will recognize the name Bridger – as in Jim Bridger of the 1820-1840 Rocky Mountain Fur Trade Era. So, when we acquired our first Basset Hound pup in 2003, Trapper came up with the idea to name him "Bridger" after this most famous of the Mountain Men.

Notice the big brown hat on Jim Bridger here. Look familiar? If not, it will soon. Hang onto yer...well...HIS hat.

There was a day when the original Jim Bridger truly did go to Mountain Man Rendezvous and nowadays there is a reenactment of that annual event which is actually held at Fort Bridger, Wyoming.

Sculpture of Jim Bridger by David Alan Clark in Fort Bridger, Wyoming

We have never attended it but we have attended Mountain Man Rendezvous reenactments from time to time over the years as there are one or more of them in the Rocky Mountain area every summer weekend as well as in other areas of the country. When Trapper and I attended these reenactments together I used to sell my cooking at them – which earned me the moniker of "Fry Bread Fae". In 1996 we even attended a couple in north Georgia not far from my hometown of Athens.

One such Mountain Man Rendezvous has been put on every first weekend of August by our local contingent of re-enactors – called the East River Free Trappers. I no longer have the desire to attend the Rendezvous for the entire weekend but Trapper, being the only full-time trapper in our area, does have the desire to celebrate the heritage of his chosen profession and so he still attends our local Rendezvous.

For eight years the Gunnison National Forest was literally in our backyard and each year the Rendezvous site was conveniently located just two miles up Washington Gulch Road from our house which meant that we could take one vehicle load of gear up to the site and then I would go home.

Trapper would set up camp early and then come back home for the night. The next day I would happily wave goodbye to him as he drove back up there on our red ATV which he then properly parked in the designated parking area out of view of the camp since it's not period transportation.

Once installed at the site of any Mountain Man Rendezvous it is imperative to dress the part – as an 1820-1840 Fur Trapper. Deer hide britches with white fabric suspenders, beaver fur hat, leather moccasins and a calico print shirt are Trapper's preferred and historically accurate attire for any Rendezvous he attends.

Sometimes he switches to his much loved brown beaver felt Mountain Man hat.

Most years I would drive up to the camp for a day visit at some point during the weekend. Just as I was about to walk out the door to go there on Saturday during the 2009 Rendezvous it occurred to me to take Bridger to camp too.

And then my eyes fell on Trapper's previous beaver hat which now had worn out places on it. So he had his new one up at camp but the old one had become a part of a Mountain Man display in our home.

At that point a most a marvelous Mountain Man notion came to mind – to put that hat on Bridger. I knew that the guy who had made both hats was also up at the Rendezvous and so I was hoping this would give him some chuckles too.

There was a need to find a way to keep the beaver hat on Bridger's head. The best I could think of in a hurry was a piece of fabric in a scrap bag leftover from some trader's shirts we had made and sold at the Rendezvous in years past so I figured that this fabric would be historically acceptable. I attached it with safety pins that could be hidden, loaded Bridger into the Subaru Outback and off we went to Rendezvous.

It took an eternity to drive those two miles because every time I looked at Bridger I started laughing and stopped the car to take a picture.

Bridger's Photo Shoot
Enroute To Rendezvous

We finally arrived and I parked where it was okay – away from the camp so as not to drive an out-of-place and historically incorrect modern vehicle in there.

We then began walking down the road toward the tents – beaver hat on top of this short-legged furry friend.

151

As we approached folks started laughing and when we arrived at Trapper's tent he appeared wearing his new matching beaver hat. Then Terry the hat maker showed up and exhibited a big grin at what had become of both of his hats.

I admit that our Bridger dog looked like he had a toothache with the makeshift hat holder I came up with but it did the job. Those big brown Basset Hound naturally sad eyes added to the look but he was tail-wagging happy all day.

"Hilarious" was the word Terry used for it. Part of what made it so funny was that Bridger took to wearing a beaver hat so naturally – as if of course he should be wearing it! He didn't ever try to take it off or mess with it. He was named for Jim BRIDGER, after all.

And so our Bridger posed and I laughed all the way to Rendezvous and back and the Rendezvousers, especially Trapper, found it quite comical – which was the point anyway. It was just one more way I got the message to Trapper that I honored who he was – in a somewhat ridiculous way – but honored he was anyway.

Bridger the Basset Hound has a way of accentuating many of our animal capture moments, like the time he was party to the serenade of *Chirp Bark*.

Chirp Bark

From June through October of 2004 I took a temporary job that required that I drive to Gunnison 28 miles south of Crested Butte every day. Since I knew it was only going to be for five months and that those months would mostly – if not all – be without winter snow driving conditions, I agreed to do it.

During that summer we received a call from a new customer having marmot problems under his deck at his Gunnison home. For those who are not familiar with marmots, they are quite common in our area and are similar to ground hogs known in other parts of the country. We catch of lot of 'em where they're not wanted and then take them out to where they will have plenty of land and water and rocks to run around in.

Although at times they're easy to capture, sometimes they have some fun with us as you can see in this photo. Marmots have a very shrill chirp and the ranchers around here call them "Whistle Pigs". That high-pitched chirp is rather ear piercing in an enclosed area – such as in the back of our Subaru Outback.

One day while I was at my Gunnison job we received the call from our customer who said that we had captured a marmot in our trap. Logistically and practically speaking, it didn't make sense for me to drive the 28 miles up to Crested Butte to pick up Trapper, drive back to Gunnison and then drive back to Crested Butte just so he could pick up a trap that I was perfectly capable of picking up – with thick gloves on, of course...these critters have some teeth on 'em!

Well, it just so happened that I had Bridger with me at the office that day because our vet in Gunnison was willing to come there to give him his rabies shot that was due. Naturally THAT was the day the marmot got into one of those traps there so I now had the need to get both of those animals successfully from Gunnison to Crested Butte without a critter fight in the car. I must say I wondered if I would make it without a clash of the critters.

153

When I arrived at the customer's house I enlisted his help. I had been thinking this whole thing through on the way there. After I carried the live trap cage with the marmot inside and placed it on the ground at the back of our Subaru Outback, I asked his assistance with these instructions: "I'm going to open the hatch on the back of the car and then I'll get into the driver's seat and hold onto Bridger's leash that I've shortened so that he'll stay in the front passenger seat." I asked him to then just lift the marmot trap into the way-back of the car and close the hatch.

He was glad to help, It all worked perfectly and we drove away. Considering that I was holding the leash and shifting gears on our manual transmission Outback at the same time, it went exceptionally well...except for one thing. As you can imagine, Bridger has a deep Basset Hound bark and the marmot, well, they don't call them "Whistle Pigs" for nothin'. A short distance from the house I pulled over to the side of the road and dialed Trapper on my cell phone. When he answered I told him, "Ya gotta hear this" and, just as the two critters had been doing as we drove away from that house, they continued alternating their native animal sounds. The marmot would let out an ear-piercing "CHIRP" to which Bridger would answer with a low pitched "BARK".

So, "CHIRP BARK", "CHIRP BARK" we started off onto Highway 135 and headed for Crested Butte. As entertaining as that was, I had notions of having busted ear drums by the time I got home. So then I had an idea. We just happened to have a few CDs in the car of piano music by an extremely talented gentleman we had recently met named Huntley Brown.

I figured it was a long shot but worth a try. I plopped one of those CDs into the car CD player and, as Huntley's fingers majestically tickled the ivories all over the keyboard, my critter cacophony came to an end. To my total surprise since this approach truly was that long shot, both the marmot and Bridger immediately settled down, stopped their "CHIRP BARKING" and the rest of the drive to Crested Butte was amazingly and contentedly peaceful.

Some time after that we ran into that particular customer. Before I had a chance to tell him my side of the story from the inside of that car, he told his friend standing there with him his own perspective of that event which we had not heard before: "As they drove away I could hear 'CHIRP BARK', 'CHIRP BARK' until they were out of sight". I might add that he did a rather good imitation of the two animal sounds in the process of the telling. So then I told him the effects of the piano music on the "CHIRP BARKERS" and we all had a good laugh. Now it's been 11 years since that happened and when we saw him again I told him about this book and that "CHIRP BARK" was definitely included.

Many have been the marmots that we have dealt with and relocated. We have taken several of them to the same location so they can find each other if some of them will only send out a chirping message to suggest to all marmots within earshot: *Shall We Gather At The River.*

154

Shall We Gather
At The River

Marmots are generally harmless and so we usually release them – but far enough away from where they are captured so that they will not return to that place.

However, marmots can cause some considerable damage. They chew on houses plus burrow and live under decks where it begins to stink from excrement after awhile. They sometimes also chew on wiring – of houses when they can get to it but more commonly under the hoods of vehicles.

One customer has had the experience of both wiring issues. Before she knew about us some marmots got under her log cabin and snacked on her electrical wiring such that, because of the age of the cabin, she wound up having to have the whole place rewired to bring it up to more recent code. She was so happy to find us that we became friends quickly and so every time she saw a marmot near her place she called us immediately.

Such was the relationship on the day she called us that now a marmot had lodged itself under the hood of her vehicle, chewed the wiring and at that very moment she was having it towed to a mechanic. The thing was, the marmot was still there under the hood and the mechanic wanted it outta there before he would fix it. I can't say as I blame the mechanic for not wanting to put his hands down in the engine area with that furry face adorned with those very big teeth staring back at him.

We were at another job where Trapper was doing some bat exclusion work when we received our customer friend's URGENT call for help ASAP and we suggested that they not open the hood until we could get there.

We got to her vehicle as quickly as we could – but not quick enough. Our message to wait for us to get there did not get to her or the tow truck driver in time which had unhappy consequences.

Both of these marmots were captured by Trapper behind this same customer's shed on the same day.

155

When the tow truck delivered her vehicle to the mechanic, someone opened the hood right away without knowledge of what was trespassing in there and...out jumped the marmot and into the engine of the car next to it where the hood was also open.

We arrived momentarily after that and now we had the quandary of getting the marmot out of that OTHER vehicle which the mechanic put up on the rack. We could see it's furry self up in there and did all sorts of creative things to get him outta there – not an easy trick when they burrow in and do not want to come out. It took awhile and a number of creative attempts at solutions but finally he came out of his own accord and wandered away without doing any damage to that or any other vehicle – as far as we know.

We have received a number of these marmot-in-the-engine calls. Trapper can sometimes get to them and sometimes they are so ingeniously snuggled in there that it is a most difficult endeavor to get them out. Some of the customers already know of the damage that can happen to their vehicles if a marmot is left to snack in there. Some start out worried about the fate of the critter and then find out the fate of their vehicle if the marmot does not leave or is not extracted.

Such a fate almost befell the engine of the sixteen passenger van at our church. A marmot was living under the deck at the entrance to the church, was darting under the van parked nearby to hang out and, potentially, into the engine of the van. The church hired Trapper to relocate said marmot "to a better place" as they say in church circles. We were not talking about a heavenly place, just a better place on Earth – anywhere but anywhere near that van.

Trapper promptly caught the marmot and we headed out to that better place – far from the church but near a river where we had already released a significant number of marmots that summer. Just as Trapper sat the marmot occupied cage trap down and faced it toward the river, he said, "Since we caught this marmot at the church, we should sing a hymn" and launched into "Shall We Gather At The River". The marmot took off for the river and we assume the other marmots did gather there with him that evening.

The Neighborhood Services officers of the Gunnison Police Department have often referred us and called us themselves for animal assistance. One day they knew Trapper was in Gunnison on another job and brought over a car driven by a Texan who had discovered a hitch hiking marmot under his hood. Trapper was happy to help them out and relocated it into a cage that the officer had on hand. That marmot therefore acquired a new home in the mountains near Gunnison at the hands of the Gunnison police after being coaxed out by Trapper.

Trapper does a significant amount of beaver trapping. It's one of his favorite critters to capture and, as I learned during my *Mountain Man's Wife* studies early on with that education continuing all the time, beaver are some of the most fascinating animals on the planet. He highly respects them, their behavior and their habitat but he also realistically handles the problems they prolifically create around here as water is a big issue and at a premium in Colorado.

One day in October of 2007 we received a "come quick!" call from folks who owned a landscaping company and nursery right down by the riverside – unfortunately for them on one occasion. The day before their call they had received a semi load shipment of brand new aspen trees ready to sell and plant at the primary and secondary homes of their various customers around the area.

We absolutely did "come quick!" and with them inspected the magnitude of the situation. Overnight the beaver had come up out of the river and chewed down about 40 of those tasty brand new trees.

Traps were set and attempts at comforting the business owners were made.

At some point during the job, in the privacy of our home and out of earshot of the customers, Trapper made the observation that, "Ya know, I'll bet those beaver were on the other side of the river, saw that semi back in there and unload all of those trees, watched as the trees were lined up in straight rows, folded their paws up under their chins and prayed:

'Father, thank you for this meal of which we are about to partake.' "

We eventually shared that with our customers when we felt like the time had come when they could laugh about it.

We understand — kinda like how writing these tales now is helping me laugh about a lot of things that weren't necessarily funny when they first happened.

But my Mountain Man's ability to come up with such statements and antics is partly what has helped me deal with various moments in our own lives.

He truly is quite creative in the ways he handles difficult moments, like when he became *The Ghost Of Carbon Peak.*

The Ghost Of
Carbon Peak

Somewhere along the way a Hereford cattle ranching couple of Gunnison, Bill and Ina Sanderson, adopted us. They lived about five miles from us...as the eagle flies. But since we're not eagles, it was necessary for us to drive either 40 miles or 25 miles around the mountains to their place at the base of Carbon Peak, depending on whether there was snow on the mountain pass between us during the winter months of the year.

This is the same area where eventually we said our tearful *Farewell Most Excellent Festus.*

His grave is just in front of the two stumps in the clearing between the trees and the Festus Tree is just to the right of that.

It's a place not far off of Ohio Creek Road in the West Elk Wilderness where we have spent much time in the 21 years of our marriage – including not far from where we took that 1993 horseback ride when Trapper decided to ask me to marry him.

Carbon Peak with Festus' grave in the clearing in the middle of the photo

Trapper and Bill had a deal. Trapper would control the beaver population that flooded the roads and pastures up there in trade for accommodations in the calving trailer on their place where he could also skin animals as needed.

159

While they were still living there we would both go visit them for a week or so in November of each year, stay in the trailer and spend the evenings having dinner with them and listening to Bill's precious stories of cattle ranching in Gunnison. Bill also had an amazing pen and ink drawing talent. For years he did a drawing for their Christmas cards and one time he made some letterhead just for us and they had 500 copies printed up as a very unique gift.

Eventually Bill and Ina moved to town where, in 2008, Bill joyfully went to eternal storytelling and cattle ranching – we figure that's a reasonable description of what heaven is like for him. Whatever he's doing now, he's definitely reached his heavenly reward.

Shortly before he died Bill asked Trapper to continue to honor the trapping trade for the landowners up there as a favor to him and so Trapper and Bridger continued to do that for quite a while after that.

So, for as long as the landowners allowed the Sanderson Herefords Calving Trailer to stay on the place, Trapper continued honoring his deal with Bill Sanderson.

At some point I decided to stay home and Trapper then would go up for a week or so by himself. I always treasured those times of Trapper having a chance to have some time alone up there and then I would enjoy some dedicated time alone at home to do various projects that there was no time to concentrate on when Trapper was around keeping me occupied.

I'm thinking many of you wives out there reading this have a similar approach to time when your husbands are away. As much as we may love them, we need time just for us just as much as our men need time just for them, right?

This was the view of *The Castles* from the Sanderson Ranch so he was in his element up there.

So it was that Trapper was up there in 2010 at the base of Carbon Peak for one of those weeks and reached the end of the day at his Calving Trailer Mountain Man trapping camp.

He turned out his light to go to sleep but was yet still awake when he heard some scuffling of feet out in the darkness in front of the camper. And then...

"C'mon. You've done this before," urged a young man's voice.

His female companion was apprehensive. "I don't know. I think somebody's in there." She was apparently an observant young lady and had most likely noticed a red ATV out front this time plus various other tools and supplies Trapper had out there.

Trapper quietly listened as they tried to work this out but he didn't make a sound.

He did get out of bed, flashlight in hand, and quietly snuck his way to the screen door of the shed attached to the camper.

He waited crouched at the lower aluminum-fronted portion of the screen door for something that made it the exact right moment to confront the young trespassers.

And then the fella there unwittingly handed Trapper the perfect moment with, "What's the matter – are you afraid of ghosts?"

With that Trapper put his face in the upper screen of the door and the flashlight under his chin, suddenly turned it on so that the light shined eerily up on his face and said, "I don't know about her but I am!"

Trapper says he's not sure their feet hit the ground as they headed the 75 yards that you can see in the photo below toward their vehicle. He did hear them hit the big wooden gate and then fly over the top of it. They must have been so frightened that they were afraid they'd get caught if they stopped to get in their vehicle. He doesn't know where they went but it was maybe a half hour before he heard their vehicle start up out there on the road on the other side of the gate and then they hit the gas to get outta there!

As disconcerting as it was to hear that they had "done this before" in their trespassing, we're imagining that Trapper (aka *The Ghost of Carbon Peak*) cured them of ever doing it again – hopefully there as well as anywhere else.

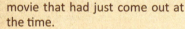

When we moved the Calving Trailer off the ranch in November 2012, it was a day of reminiscing about all of the good times there – including this one a few years earlier when a friend was about to take this photo but just before she snapped it I unexpectedly SUNK into the snow there and she managed to capture the moment. It reminded us all of the wedding cake in the first *Shrek* movie that had just come out at the time.

Many are our memories of this ranch. We always enjoyed seeing *The Castles* from there but sometimes that view was shrouded in a gorgeous sunset display of *Fire On The Mountain*.

162

Fire
On The Mountain

Fire is an absolute staple to a Mountain Man – for heat as well as for cooking. But wildfire on the mountain is a terrible thing and has been happening in gigantic proportions in Colorado over the last few years.

I am happy to say I do not have a story about living through a wildfire in our area but we have had evacuation supplies ready since it could happen so easily.

The Rocky Mountains around us are prolific in providing fantastic sunrises and sunsets such that it looks like fire in the sky over the mountains.

And then there was this jet stream extravaganza one afternoon at the end of the day – right out the front window at home.

Alpenglow Fire On The Mountain

Mount Crested Butte – afternoon view from the deck of our home at the time

One morning I was reading about God's Shekinah (shining) and glorious presence. I figured that would be an incredible thing to see so I boldly yet quite respectfully asked Him for a display of it sometime not knowing that He had it ready to go and immediately forthcoming.

I can honestly marvel at oh how He must love such requests because moments later as I walked to the kitchen to simply get a cup of coffee, this is what He presented to me off the deck of our home at the time in the Rocky Mountains.

So now I have a sense of how Moses felt when God showed His glory to him because I too was temporarily yet joyfully blinded by it.

Almighty God Himself gave me the idea and told me through Scripture that it was okay to ask for Him to show me His glory. You'll see more about that in the part of Exodus 33 coming up in *Modern Day Mountain Man Moses*.

Do you remember the *Mountain Man Tinder Box* and fire starting techniques shared in the very first story of this book? Well, here it is all packed up and ready to go to my Mountain Man's next camp.

Yes, fire starting is most prevalent in our lives. I am grateful to be married to a man who knows so much about it.

A true Mountain Man always has a way to create fire. If the sun's not out, another way is with something called a flint and steel. We even used to sell these items in our Mountain Man Possibles supplies years ago. In 1996 we decided to drive those supplies to my home state of Georgia, see family and friends and then attend a couple of Mountain Man Rendezvous there.

One of the companies with which we had opened a wholesale account for those supplies was Lodge Manufacturing – makers of cast iron skillets, dutch ovens and much more that is traditional open fire cookware. When we realized that a day in our journey South in 1996 would take us through Chattanooga and so very close to South Pittsburg, Tennessee where Lodge Manufacturing is located, we decided to go there, meet them and hopefully see how they make their products.

The folks at Lodge could not have been more hospitable to us! The President, Bob Kellermann (the great-grandson of Joseph Lodge who founded Lodge Manufacturing), greeted us and then came out with a most unusual request for Trapper: "Do you know how to do flint and steel?" to which Trapper replied, "Yes. We have some with us." Kellermann was delighted: "My boy has to do a flint and steel demonstration at his Boy Scout troop meeting tonight. Can you show him how to do it?" Of course Trapper knew how so Bob went to the school to get his son. By the time they returned Trapper had donned his Mountain Man clothing to give as much authenticity as possible to this activity. The result was Bob, his son and Trapper out on the sidewalk in front of Lodge Manufacturing teaching and learning flint and steel how-to's.

Darn. I didn't think to take a photo of the flint and steel lesson. But Trapper took one of me with ol' Festus who took this trip with us.

Now, 19 years later, we wonder if that Kellermann boy still remembers and uses his flint and steel lesson.

Speaking of the importance of fire to a Mountain Man, there's a scene in the Robert Redford movie, *Jeremiah Johnson*, where he is in the process of his education on becoming a bona fide Mountain Man. He quickly learned not to build a fire under a pine tree with snow on it because the heat of the fire warmed up the snow above it which unhappily fell off the branch and...snuffed out his much needed fire which he had struggled valiantly to get started with, as I recall, a flint and steel. The first time (of many) that we watched that movie together Trapper informed me that he had experienced that very same thing at some point and so he had learned the same lesson the same unfortunate way that Jeremiah Johnson did.

Fire pits are always present at Trapper's campsites — unless his camping happens to be during one of Colorado's many summer droughts and so there is a fire ban on at the time. Regardless of the laws, he does not want to be the person responsible for starting a Colorado wildfire — or a wildfire anywhere!

In days past we have taken whatever canine critters are currently living with us camping and have also put them to work collecting firewood whenever they felt inclined to help out.

Here's red heeler Festus and lab Chester during and after a productive session of firewood collecting for the camp.

They were not above creating a tug-of-war to see which one could bring the most firewood to the fire pit.

To celebrate the occasion of our 15th Wedding Anniversary and Trapper's Birthday on June 18th, 2009 we discovered that the Wyman Hotel in Silverton, Colorado about three hours southwest of us in the San Juan Mountain Range offered most intriguing and private accommodations — *The Candlelight Caboose* featuring a private courtyard which had...a fire pit.

I called over there to ask questions of the owner and to especially find out if we could cook on the fire pit. That seemed a natural thing to do on our private fire pit from our perspective. He responded that, "Well, yes you could," he supposed. We left it at that and booked *he Candlelight Caboose* for a couple of nights. So we then planned and packed all the necessaries for a seafood feast to grill on our private fire pit in our private courtyard in front our private caboose. We never even considered that the fire pit in question was the kind we see everywhere nowadays — a metal container for fire for warmth and ambiance but NOT outfitted with a grill for the purpose of cooking.

When we checked in and discovered our error we were quickly informed by the owner that he had anticipated the dilemma and, being the amazingly accommodating inn proprietor that he turned out to be, had purchased a very nice propane double burner gas grill just before our arrival and had placed it out there for us so that we could truly grill our seafood feast.

Thank goodness he did that because otherwise we would have been stuck with a bounty of seafood and other fixins we had picked up in Montrose on the way there.

So, we enthusiastically enjoyed both the ambiance of the fire pit and the ability to still be able to cook on an open flame – just not the type of flame we had anticipated but an open flame nonetheless. We were honored by the owner's attention to this detail on our behalf but when we told him we did not mean to cause him such an effort he responded with, "I've been needing to get a grill for out there anyway. This just got me to do it."

The Wyman Hotel folks were beary helpful in creating some other ambiance too. By prior arrangement, upon our arrival and when Trapper was not looking, I snuck the owner some bear salt and pepper shakers as one of my Anniversary/Birthday gifts to Trapper. The pre-arranged plan was for them to be placed on our breakfast tray being delivered to the caboose the next morning. That gave the hotel folks the idea to seriously follow a bear theme for us. When the owner took us into the caboose, there on the bed lay a bear skin which he had borrowed from his son – just for us. Roses and champagne were also awaiting us on the top of a chest of drawers in there. I understood why they had come up with the bear theme but knew that Trapper wouldn't fully understand it until the bear shakers showed up the next morning. But Trapper still quickly joined in the fun by throwing his brown beaver felt hat onto the head of the bear on the bed.

But there was more beary stuff to come on the part of the hotel personnel. The gal who fixed our breakfast got creative with the strawberries (strawbearies?) and these bear faced berries showed up on the breakfast tray outside our caboose door:

In all this we discovered that even when our *Mountain Man and Wife* approach to life is different from what others anticipate, the results can be most entertaining. We thank the Wyman Hotel and Inn for truly fond memories beyond our own anticipation.

Although bear sightings are frequent in our Mountain Man Life, Trapper deals with beaver more than bears so he often encounters a *Beaver Slide.*

Beaver Slide

The folks who decorated our car before we left our wedding reception had great insight. They very prophetically painted the windows of both sides with picture frames so that our faces would show through:

We posed in our respective frames before washing the car during our honeymoon.

Their meaning was clear at the time. Trapper's face showed through the "Trapper" frame and my face showed through the "Trapped" frame.

However, over the years there have been some significant role reversals from time to time.

For example, only a short time into our marriage Trapper was doing some beaver work on Danni Ranch just south of Crested Butte again. I was visiting with the family up in the ranch house while he was doing that. As we sat there around the kitchen table drinking coffee, suddenly a fella showed up at the back door with the news that, "There's a guy down there with a trap on his foot."

At that point I calmly, knowingly looked up and commented quite matter-of-factly, "That would be my husband."

I was surprised when everyone laughed because as far as I was concerned it was just a logical observation on my part.

I drove our car down the hill following the messenger who took me to Trapper. Sure enough, there he was standing on the side of the ranch road with a beaver trap on his foot and this story:

After setting his traps in the "crick" – as Trapper calls it – he was climbing up the steep bank to get back on the road and was planning to walk over to the pond where he was supposed to meet Al Van Dyke for some reason. The bank was slick and he was climbing it in irrigation boots which caused it to be difficult to make a good foot purchase. He said that when he started sliding back down the bank he heard in his mind the click of the trap firing even before he slid into it in the "crick".

He tried but he couldn't get the trap off down there so then he began climbing that bank in his irrigation boots with a square trap attached – a bit cumbersome to say the least. He finally made it to the top and tried again but he could not get the right leverage to open up the trap on his own. So it was a great relief when someone showed up driving down the road. That fella had offered his help and had tried too but he couldn't get it open either, which led to his decision to be our ranch house messenger.

I made sure Trapper was okay and then drove over to the pond to get Al. I got out of our car and walked up to Al's truck passenger side window. As I began telling Al what was going on with Trapper the absurdity of the whole thing struck me so my words came out in disjointed laughter, "Trapper's okay, (laughter) but (laughter) he's over by the creek (laughter) with a trap (laughter) stuck on his foot! (out of control laughter). Can you go over there (laughter) and help get it off?" Now Al Van Dyke was laughing too – possibly at me if not at the situation – maybe at both.

Al did that and since then we've talked about how Trapper has been trapped himself, not just his wife on the day of our wedding. After all, Al was our Best Man and was one of the ones who helped decorate our car at our wedding reception – not only with shoe polish or shaving cream but also with some natural ranch decorations – a fact that he denied but we have the goods in

170

a living color photograph that someone just happened to take as they were transporting that stuff to our car. That's another photo I couldn't get my hands on in time for insertion here but we do have it.

I may have been red-faced when I met Al Van Dyke on my first night in town back in 1992 but then he was caught red-handed at our wedding reception in 1994 along with Trapper's brother-in-law and our Matron of Honor's husband – all bearing PLATES of what horses leave on the ground at ranches such as that one.

At least they mostly left the stuff on the plates on which they brought it to the car...before the plates were inserted onto the front seats and elsewhere. Our wedding video shows cousin Lee pulling one of those plates off of the driver's side seat and carrying it over his shoulder as if he is serving it. Let's just say that, if you were to step in what was on those plates, you would definitely SLIDE.

Over these years as a Mountain Man's wife I have learned that one of the signs that Trapper looks for in deciding where to set up beaver traps is a Beaver Slide – a place where they have beaten down a trail while traversing back and forth – usually dragging trees.

I've even learned how to spot them myself and tell Trapper where I see them. But Trapper's antics of a Beaver Slide into his own trap was not part of the planned education for his bride.

From time to time in the operation of our business we will tell our customers: "Do not touch the equipment". We ask them to leave that to Trapper. Sometimes it is necessary to make the point more definitely so that they will properly respect our request. We have been known to evoke this story as a means of telling them that mishaps even happen to Trapper who knows what he's doing! And, if Trapper had not had on those irrigation boots (which were what made it so difficult to climb that bank in the first place), that trap slamming down on his ankle would have surely broken it all to pieces.

Although we try to be serious in making our point, it has always been hard to tell that story without laughing. And Trapper tries not to be offended at making light of his pain. After all, I told him I made sure he was okay before I started laughing about it – similar to the ATV on the freezer incident. But sometimes this stuff is too comical after the fact to stay serious about it even though it is a serious moment at the time it actually happens.

Necessity even caused me to create a Beaver Slide myself one day in January of 2013. Trapper was away from home but called to tell me that he needed two beaver that were in HIS freezer waiting to be skinned.

I said I would deliver them the next day.

Shortly after Trapper's call someone thankfully showed up at our door to drop something off for Trapper so I enlisted his help in getting those two beaver out of the freezer and into the utility room where hopefully they could begin to thaw out overnight.

The next morning the time came for me to load my furry delivery into the Subaru Outback. You may recall from another story that I am not a particularly strong gal so when I tried to pick up the bigger beaver, which weighed about 200 pounds (okay — more like 65 but it felt like 200 to me), I could not carry it very far, especially because it was still so solidly frozen that it was not at all pliable. No one was around to ask for help this time so I had to get creative. I mustered up all the adrenaline I could but only managed to get it to the snow just outside our garage door where the car was waiting with the hatch on the rear open. It would have been intelligent of me to turn the car around. But that notion did not occur to me at the time so this silly event has been added to our tales.

Now that the beaver was sitting in the snow by the headlight at the front end of the passenger side of the car, it occurred to me that there was a downhill slope there and the snow was fairly deep being that it was January. I lined up that beaver and did...A BEAVER SLIDE – gave that guy a healthy push and down he zoomed, sliding on his back with his head pointing downhill and his paws in the air parallel to the side of the Outback until he came to rest at the rear of the passenger side. "Good work!" thought I as I rallied my strength for the next phase of this endeavor. Thankfully my Mountain Man had left that rack on the back of the Outback (see *Alive In The Outback*) and I was able to maneuver that beaver up onto it a little at a time and then onto the mat in the back of the car. After all of that effort, carrying the smaller beaver to the back of the Outback was no big deal.

No more than five minutes after I finished doing all of that, our employee showed up to pick up supplies for the jobs he was doing for us that day. Oh for heaven's sake! I could have waited for him and his strong arms to arrive to help me with this situation. But then the comedy of my own creative Beaver Slide would not have happened.

Trapper would have unquestionably been able to handle this whole thing quite differently but I seriously needed to handle it without him. I would say I man-handled that beaver but, since I'm a girl in the West I'll say that I "gal-handled' it. Sometimes we all have to get serious about solving a predicament – especially one that is out of our usual realm. It's only later that the humor in it is so obvious.

Another thing people take very seriously is running business meetings. Those generally do not provide much in comedy. However, my Mountain Man's way of handling such a thing so out of his usual realm made even that amusing with *Trapper's Rules Of Order.*

Trapper's
Rules Of Order

Parliamentary Procedure was not something at which my Mountain Man was proficient when we married. Nor had he ever considered the possibility of being proficient at it in his lifetime.

As most of you have experienced whenever you've attended a meeting of almost any organization, there is a certain way in which discussions are held and actions are taken. Usually that is done by means of Parliamentary Procedure as dictated by a book called *Roberts Rules of Order.*

Most of us have been to enough meetings in our lives that we are reasonably familiar with how that procedure goes. But Trapper was not a prolific meeting attendee in his earlier years and so he was not that familiar with it.

Over Labor Day Weekend of 1996, just a little over two years into our marriage, we attended the Colorado Trappers Association Rendezvous. He had attended it from time to time before we met and we had attended it together the two summers since our wedding but Trapper was not at all involved in the running of the organization.

This is an annual family camp out of those who do contemporary Wildlife Management, including trapping, in the state of Colorado – either for income or for other reasons.

Although they are all familiar with the Old West heritage of their profession, this is a modern-day camp of about 150-200 people or so and not a reenactment of the 1820s - 1840s Fur Trade Era as described elsewhere in this book.

At some point in the weekend Trapper expressed to someone, "I'd like to be more involved in the CTA." Those fateful words led to a most unexpected development...his nomination as President of the organization.

That night after receiving word of his nomination, we sat in our tent and discussed whether or not he wanted the job if elected.

We agreed that he "might as well accept right now that, no matter what you do you can't make everybody happy" because that is simply the nature of relationships in most organizations. So he accepted the nomination the next day with that in mind.

By golly, Trapper (known as Al there since most everybody in attendance is also a trapper) was elected as the new President. As we left the event to go home that September 1996 Labor Day, we both recall just shaking our heads wondering how on Earth that had happened. If before that weekend we had been told that we would leave there with Trapper as CTA President we would have laughed off the notion as impossible. We have more proof positive now that absolutely nothing is impossible. He had never even been a board member. I'm not completely certain if he had ever bothered to attend a membership meeting in those years he had shown up at the CTA Rendezvous before. Meetings of any kind were just not his thing.

The CTA procedure for turning over the Presidency was for the previous President to run the Membership Meeting and then, as the last order of business, turn the meeting over to the new President with one required action – to maneuver the meeting to adjournment as prescribed by *Roberts Rules of Order*. Since the current President had recently moved out of state, the Vice President – Marvin Miller – was running the meeting. The time came to turn it over to the new President, Al Davidson.

Well, when that moment arrived the new President was missing in action – in absentia – in the porta potty. The group looked at me and someone said, "Fae, you adjourn the meeting." Being as this was during the last few months of the first term of America's current President, Bill Clinton, I replied, "My name's not Hillary. Marvin can do that but I can't do that." I knew my Parliamentary Procedure from an unfortunate number of meetings that I, unlike my down-to-Earth Mountain Man husband, had attended in life.

At that moment our new leader returned to his chair – with me on his right and one of the original founders of the CTA, Major Boddiker, on his left. We both simultaneously informed Al that the meeting had been turned over to him and that he was to adjourn the meeting. He took his cue:
"The meeting is adjourned," pronounced the new President.
"You can't do that," Major and I informed him from both sides. "Someone has to make a motion."
Being the man of action to just get things done that he is, Al said, "I make a motion to adjourn the meeting."
"You can't do that," Major and I informed him from both sides. "You have to ask for someone else to make a motion."
He was catching on. So he said, "I need a motion to adjourn the meeting" and someone did that.
"The meeting is adjourned," said Al with authority.
"You can't do that," Major and I informed him from both sides. "You need to ask for a second."
"Does someone second the motion?" a frustrated new President inquired.
Gratefully someone else complied with the request.
"Are we done now?" said Al looking quizzically at Major on his left and me on his right. We both nodded.

With great enthusiasm and relief Al (Trapper) proclaimed, "The meeting is adjourned!"

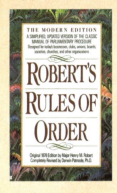

All were laughing and in this moment when his Presidency officially began, the CTA Secretary walked up to him with a box of stuff which included what we soon discovered is, to us, one of the boringest books ever published: _Roberts Rules of Order_. However, thank goodness there are those who have read it and understand how to properly apply its contents in more complicated meeting moments.

Although I had always heard of _Roberts Rules of Order_, I had never expected to actually peruse a copy.

As obviously as Trapper needed to know it's contents, I admit that neither one of us could ever get ourselves to read it and from that point forward he chose the trial-by-fire, on-the-job training method of getting a handle on Parliamentary Procedure for the next six years.

As his first two-year term in office moved forward we talked about the fact that the one person who is in the position to keep a meeting running efficiently and without time-killing, anxiety-producing boredom was the person presiding over it – a position in which he now found himself.

So, he actually did some work while preparing his future meeting agendas and then in the presiding to make sure these meetings kept moving and didn't drag as much as he possibly could be in charge of that.

More than anyone there I knew how much he worked at that and I watched this metamorphosis of a Mountain Man Trapper into a Presiding President with great interest, joy and amusement as I followed his progress and typed up his agendas for him.

In 1998 and again in 2000 Al was re-elected for two more two year terms. In the process the members of the organization got to know us so much that CTA hired me to be their fund raiser for an effort to try to overturn an Amendment to the Colorado Constitution which restricted some of the equipment of trapping in 1996.

As Director of this effort under the name of Wildlife Organizations Legal Fund which existed from 1999 to 2003, I was required to make speeches to various wildlife, agricultural, hunting and other related organizations all over Colorado, design printed pieces, write and send out press releases to the media all over the state as well as to publications all over the country, generally handle the public relations otherwise, do the bookkeeping of the funds raised and more.

The time came for the Labor Day CTA Rendezvous of 2002 . As we were driving to the site near Cerro Summit between Gunnison and Montrose, we both knew that Trapper Al was trying to decide whether or not to continue if they wanted to elect him as President again. We all found out his decision when he proficiently and decisively – just as he had learned – opened the Membership Meeting with:

"This meeting is called to order. As the first order of business I am announcing that I will not accept a nomination to be re-elected as President,"

at which time he slammed down the rock in his hand that he was using for a Presidential gavel.

My how far we had come on Parliamentary Procedure in those six years! You may have noticed that he didn't ask for the reading of the minutes of the last meeting, the Treasurer's Report or other such customary meeting starters before making his announcement but he had his reasons for doing it that way – according to *Trapper's Rules of Order*. And, true to my Mountain Man's style, a rock suited his personality much better than a formal wooden gavel. I know he was relieved to have made up his mind.

As we were packing to leave that Rendezvous I was thinking about it all and it dawned on me that we had been married eight years at that point, six of which he had been President of the CTA and for the last half of those years I was their fund raiser regarding the effort to overturn Amendment 14. I stopped packing and shared that with the gal helping me and also shared this revelation, "Wow! We've been doing this for three fourths of our marriage. No wonder it's been tough!" Looking back, so many of our dinnertime conversations focused on this or that having to do with CTA and Wildlife Organizations Legal Fund. Now we could get on with our marriage otherwise – minus so much of this outside influence on a daily basis.

It's a funny thing how fast notoriety comes...and goes. In 1994 we attended the CTA Rendezvous as just another couple – no involvement. In 1995 we attended the CTA Rendezvous as vendors with a business name of *Trapper's Trap Line* carrying a line of trapping supplies and an accompanying catalog but we didn't have a big sign at our booth yet. We had contributed a gift certificate to the Saturday night auction and when it came up for bidding Marvin Miller said, "*Trapper's Trap Line* ? Who's that?" to which we waived at him and said, "We're right here."

The next year, at the 1996 CTA Rendezvous, Al became President of CTA with Marvin Miller as his Vice President. So, in one year we went from "Who's that?" to President of the same organization. That's really rather surprising but at the same time they were glad to find someone to take the helm during such a difficult time in the life of CTA because of the arrival of Amendment 14 into the Colorado Constitution during that time.

Clara Fae with Helen Fae at CTA. Bridger was Clara Fae's buddy all weekend too.

In 2003 we received the news that Major Boddiker's daughter and her husband, who we also knew through CTA, were having a baby. When their little girl was born they called us and said they were naming their daughter – Clara Fae – the second name after me, because they like the way I spell it which is how it was given to me by my parents who named me Helen Fae after my Mother's best friend at SMU in the 1930s.

It's interesting that I, as a gal who knew nothing about trapping before meeting my Mountain Man, have a namesake in the very same world I knew nothing about. So, our notoriety at CTA carries on in a whole unexpected way. And it's kinda fun to now go to the CTA Rendezvous and enjoy the weekend without having so much work to do there or agenda planning to do in advance.

During Trapper's tenure as President and me as Fund Raiser we learned a lot about the people in state government who are involved when it comes to Wildlife Management and the profession of trapping.

In fact, one time his CTA office caused him to have a direct conversation with the Governor of Colorado at the time, Bill Owens, who looked Trapper straight in the eye and respectfully engaged him in conversation with a firm handshake on both ends of that conversation. We were impressed with that when most of the other politicians in the room were looking about during their own conversations with folks to see who was more important to talk to instead of the person in front of them. At another time a state senator called us from the floor of the senate while a vote on the legal interpretation of Amendment 14 was going on. We could even hear the audible vote in progress behind him. Interesting times.

Also during this time we wound up in mail, phone and in-person conversations with Scott McInnis who was our United States Congressman at the time. One of his personal letters to us, written not long after 9/11 in 2001, referred to Eco-Terrorism – "terrorism is terrorism". More interesting times.

This period of our marriage gave us both an education much more than we had ever anticipated needing to know about the politics involved in the Wildlife Management arena and some significant amount of knowledge of how to walk through that mine field.

Since then we have learned that there is a substantial amount of Public Relations that is helpful for a successful Wildlife Management Services business like ours, which has led to some very creative solutions to various *PR Predicaments*.

PR Predicaments

At Trapper's request, I am the primary human resource in the PR (Public Relations) department of our Wildlife Management Services business. Trapper generally prefers for me to deal with customer communications – either by email, telephone or in person. On the job he explains the technical side of things and then it's my turn to deal with explaining our Estimates, Contracts, Billing and other administrative type stuff. All that works out fairly well but there have definitely been some creative moments worth recording here.

In the late 1990s, before the time of most of us having cell phones, there was the summer day that a woman called who was very distraught about a marmot that was – at that very moment – mowing down her flower garden. I told her that my husband was not present but I would send him out as soon as he got back, although I was not sure what time that would be. Thus began the wait for Trapper's return.

In the meantime, however, she continued to call me approximately every five to ten minutes with a play by play of what she was viewing out her window. She would say the name of the particular type of flower on which the marmot was munching at that moment (some names of which I recognized and some names of which I did not) and then would fill me in on its movement to the next type of flower. I felt for her but there was nothing I could do to reach Trapper sooner.

All the while, with each successive phone call I could hear the ice clanking in her glass and the increase of the slur of her words. She never said what she was drinking and I never asked.

At long last Trapper showed up and I gave him and the friend with him directions to this poor woman's home. He said that when they arrived there she showed up at the door and promptly...tripped out of it – alas, completely blasted. He quickly put out a bunch of cage traps and left there. Overnight he successfully captured the culprit so released it that day into one of those much better places far away from her home which gave this woman some peace although she had very little of her garden left by that time. She was grateful anyway and I was grateful to meet her in a more sober condition a few days later when Trapper and I went out together to pick up the equipment.

I never let her know that I noticed her inebriated condition earlier.

Very often my Mountain Man must carry a pistol on his belt because he is going into precarious situations that could likely take him face to face with very large critters like bears and mountain lions.

Yes – it has happened on a number of occasions.

One such time was when he had beaver traps at an irrigation ditch head gate which we had to access down a steep little hill into a very small open area that was flooded by the beaver activity there. For a couple of weeks we went there daily and no one else was around except for the bear of which Trapper had definitely spied sign. So every time we arrived he would get out, immediately put on his sidearm and irrigation boots and head out to do his job.

However, Memorial Day weekend came around during that time and on Friday of that weekend when we arrived at the head gate area we encountered not one...not two...but THREE great big RVs parked there! How they maneuvered all three of them down that hill and parked them in there is still a mystery to us.

Anyway, after we drove down the hill Trapper got out and started doing his usual thing without thinking a thing about it – sliding his pistol holster onto his belt and putting on his irrigation boots. Of course he chose THIS particular time to double check his ammo before putting the pistol back into the holster – again not thinking a thing about it.

He didn't saw what I saw right then...some women and children sitting in chairs between the RVs. In the split second that I saw them and then began to say to Trapper there handling that pistol, "That's not a good idea" they looked over at him and then all jumped up and ran into one of the RVs for safety.

Since I saw them before Trapper could, I knew that a quick response was critical to the situation. So, as they say in the military, it was definitely time for me to "SNAP TO" and engage in some *Mountain Man's Wife* PR.

I grabbed the Colorado Division of Wildlife permit we had with us for this job and went over there to tell these people that there was nothing to fear. It took awhile and there were some very tense moments but finally they believed me. Their men came back from wherever they had been, talked with Trapper and then everything calmed down – to the point that before we left we sat down between the RVs and had a congenial beer with them.

I don't recall that any of my PR courses during my 1970s studies at the University of Georgia's Grady School of Journalism included any preparation for handling a situation like this. Well, maybe they did – in the sense of recognizing quickly that some PR was in order post haste instead of letting the situation escalate unaddressed.

In 2012 we decided it was time to order some magnetic signs to put on the doors of our business truck. We employed our two basset hounds, Clementine and Bridger, as our mascots for the signs. They were happy to comply for a photo shoot on the deck with a blue flannel sheet behind them.

But the trick was to get them both to look at me with the expressions I was after on each of them and at the same time.

That was finally accomplished and then I realized that I had not put enough blue flannel sheet in front of them for words to be put over that on the sign. So, we had to do it all over again.

We paid them with peanut butter flavored dog biscuits. To the IRS and Social Security – sorry but there was not the option to withhold anything from their paychecks because they absolutely gobbled them all up!

That night I downloaded the photos and began working up the signs on the VistaPrint site with plans to order them right away. After some time everything was done but then I had the bright idea to call the dogs something on the signs. Trapper was watching the evening news when that notion came to mind. As I was pondering what title to give the hound dogs – or whether to give them one at all – one of the news stories on the TV mentioned something about a company's "Human Resources Department".

That was it! But they're dogs, not humans. So a little more creativity was in order such that they became our CANINE Resources Department and the upper right-hand corner now reads:

We figure the presence of the Basset Hounds on the signs dispels some of the misunderstandings that various folks have about trapping. The photos alone tell them that we're animal lovers too and it helps bridge a variety of situations. But, more than that, the dogs draw attention to the signs which is the very idea of such marketing anyway. One day we walked out of WalMart in Gunnison and found a guy standing behind our truck reading the sign on the back of it. He laughed as he read the upper right-hand corner of the sign and then we introduced him to the actual Canine Resources Department wagging their tails inside on the folded down back seat of the truck.

We have also found a way to employ my pre-Trapper lack of education in our PR practices. From time to time we encounter someone who is against trapping or is sensitive about what is to become of the critters we capture on their property. At those times I can be there to genuinely empathize with where they're coming from because I've been there myself. We've found this feminine approach quite helpful not only with our female customers but also when I donned *Lace For The Game Wardens*.

Lace For
The Game Wardens

After we married in 1994 Trapper did some wildlife management work on his own but primarily worked elsewhere for steady income for the next three years. We were just getting things going on our own business when we decided to move to Saguache about 100 miles southeast of Crested Butte.

In the Spring of 2004 we decided to move back to Crested Butte. During that summer Trapper took other work and I had a five month job that took me to Gunnison every day while we were reestablishing our Wildlife Management Services business in the area. So we asked for and were provided the opportunity to attend a meeting of the area Game Wardens to re-introduce ourselves and talk about our business with them. I drove to Gunnison and went to my job in a lace-collared beige blouse and pastel patchwork skirt with crochet beige flats on my feet. To the left is a photo of the lace adorned outfit I was wearing that day.

Trapper was planning to catch the shuttle bus to come down later in time for the meeting and then we were planning to drive back up to Crested Butte to go home at the end of the day. However, when a piece of equipment revolted on the guys at his job that morning, he did not have the option to up and leave at the appointed time. He called me and we agreed that we could not pass up this opportunity over at the Colorado Division of Wildlife office a few blocks from my office and so it fell to me to go...by myself.

After I sat down at the table and each of the Game Wardens in their uniforms came into the room, their boss who had invited us and who was sitting to my left leaned over and whispered to me, "Where's Al?" Only a few seconds before he said that I had concocted an opening to our presentation so, instead of directly answering his question I just whispered back, "You'll find out in a minute." I was very nervous about this turn of events that had put me at that table without my Mountain Man husband in attendance with me. We had initially thought that my being there would be a good idea so that we would have a professional appearance as a husband and wife team which is why I intentionally wore the lace.

But me being there by myself – well, that was not in the original plan and seemed ridiculous but it had to be handled.

When I was introduced I matter-of-factly said, "Hi. I'm Al Davidson." When they all started laughing and looking at me in my lacy glory I calmly and quizzically said, "What? Don't I look like a trapper?" By that time they had all taken one of our business brochures that I had sent around the table and I explained what had become of the real trapper and that I was active in the business doing the office work and PR with the customers plus would be, along with my husband, handling whatever communication would be needed between our business and their office.

Since I was speaking of meetings in the last story and we all know how boring they can sometimes be, I hope I added a little levity and unusual stuff to their meeting. I left the room before they continued so I have no idea how lively or boring the rest of that meeting was. But at least it started off with a jolt and a laugh. And to this day we have a good relationship with our local office of what was then called the Colorado Division of Wildlife but in 2011 merged with another state department and became Colorado Parks and Wildlife. They refer our business quite often for professional Wildlife Management Services and we are grateful for that and for our on-going friendships there.

Speaking of being on good terms with the Game Wardens, one day while we were living in Saguache some friends from Crested Butte paid us a surprise visit. They had been there awhile when we saw through our living room picture window a Colorado Division of Wildlife truck pull up in front of the house. When the doorbell rang Trapper opened it to find a young man in a CDOW uniform standing there with his hat in his hand. Very respectfully he said, "Hello. Are you Al Davidson, President of the Colorado Trappers Association?" Our friends knew of the tension at the time between the CDOW and the trappers because of Amendment 14 so they decided it was time for them to depart – RIGHT NOW – and they ran out the door. We then sat down in our living room with the young man and immediately became friends with Brian Bechaver, our Game Warden at the time from the Monte Vista office of the CDOW.

Because of the aforementioned tension, Trapper said to Brian, "You're a brave man. For all you knew I was going to meet you at the door with a shotgun." Brian said he'd considered that possibility but after reading an article in one of the nationwide trapping magazines where he discovered that the new CTA President was in his own CDOW area, he decided to take his chances and come introduce himself. It is a happy thing in our profession to be on good terms with the Game Wardens.

That comes in handy in various situations…including sometimes when we receive calls that require the involvement of Colorado Parks and Wildlife and our customer needs our help in a hurry because of some sort of animal *Emergency!*

Emergency!

In our Wildlife Management Services business we frequently receive "Help!" calls and my Mountain Man has been a hero to many folks besides me during our marriage. There are those who do not understand the need for our services – until they have their own encounter with some pesky pest.

One of those was an amazing dead ringer event at a customer's house in town. During the night a guest there had awakened to a live bat crawling on her shoulder. She had knocked it off her shoulder, across the room and accidentally into a trash can which, as happenstance would have it, had a plastic bag liner in it. She had the presence of mind to get up and tie the bag closed with the bat inside. They called us the next morning and we went down to the house. Trapper drowned the bat and they took it to the county Health Department in Gunnison that day. It thankfully tested negative but had she not had the actual offending bat she would have had no choice but to take rabies shots since a pin prick sized bat bite is almost imperceptible unless you know it has happened. Then, if a person waits until they exhibit rabies symptoms nothing can be done and it truly is fatal. So, her two-pointer saved her the $3000 cost of a just-in-case rabies shot series. We often tell people this story to try to help them understand that dealing with bats is serious business.

And then sometimes we have our own emergencies.

On October 19, 2012 Trapper came in from a full day of wildlife work with one of our employees at around 3:00 pm, said he wasn't feeling well and sat down in his La-Z-Boy chair. I was busy in the kitchen and all of a sudden I heard a thump in the living room and then encountered my Mountain Man crawling on the floor toward the bathroom. When he got there he...well, it wasn't pleasant...and then said he was so dizzy that he couldn't lift his head. After quite a bit of trying to figure out what was going on, a doctor's office suggested that we call the EMTs. They came and gave him some medication to stabilize his dizziness and then transported him in an ambulance to the Gunnison hospital 28 miles away.

This was the second time in our marriage I had followed behind an ambulance with my Mountain Man inside (see "*I Feel Like A Fish*"). Once every 10 years or so is not that bad but it has been worrisome both times. I was glad to see that the ambulance in front of me did not have its lights or siren on but I thought about it and figured that if they turned either of those on perhaps that would be the time to be more concerned. In the meantime, I decided to leave this situation to their professional judgment and rode along praying that all would be okay.

At the hospital they couldn't figure out what was wrong with him right off so the doctor decided to test him for appendicitis. That meant he needed to spend two hours in preparation for a test by drinking some stuff they gave him and, since it was October, getting dark, and the bears were out bulking up for their winter snooze (we had seen a lot of them at our house), I decided to drive back up to Crested Butte while Trapper drank his stuff, get our two Basset Hounds out of the dog pen and take them back to Gunnison with me in the car.

Before I left the hospital Trapper and I briefly discussed the fact that we had a headlight out on the Subaru Outback I was driving that Trapper had tried to fix a few days before. Changing the bulb had not done the trick but he had not had time to investigate further yet. I had seen the Colorado State Patrol in Almont, a little town between Crested Butte and Gunnison, on the way down so we agreed to simply tell the truth if I got stopped on my Basset Hound rescue run.

Sure enough, it happened. The Colorado State Patrol trooper walked up to the car window: "You have a headlight out."

"I know." I was honest about it as Trapper and I had agreed that I should be. But then, honesty is a big deal to us and something we profess to anyway.

"You know?" He seemed genuinely surprised that I didn't act dumb or babble excuses.

"Yes. My husband tried to fix it this week but a new bulb didn't work and he hasn't had time to work on it more. But right now he's at the hospital and they're testing him for appendicitis. I just went to Crested Butte to get our Basset Hounds to protect them from bears."

He shined his flashlight on Bridger and Clementine with their sad eyes and wagging tails in the back of the car. He then inquired, "Are you headed to the hospital right now?"

To my "Yes" he said, "You better go on and just fix the headlight as soon as you can." We did that later.

The whole conversation took only about 45 seconds and then I was back on the road headed for the hospital. It truly DOES pay to be honest – not a surprise. Those guys have to know when folks are squirming but by being real with my predicament I discovered a very understanding trooper.

Back down at the hospital they were able to rule out appendicitis but never did figure what all of that was about. We and our dogs wandered back to Crested Butte and fell into bed just happy to be there instead of still at the Gunnison hospital or moved to one of the bigger hospitals in Montrose or Grand Junction for surgery.

In August of 2013, while Trapper was at the Crested Butte Mountain Man Rendezvous up Washington Gulch Road two miles away, on Saturday morning he broke the rules and called me on his cell phone. "Get here in a hurry. It's like October all over again." I knew what he meant and I jumped into the car. Contrary to usual Mountain Man Rendezvous protocol, the group there allowed me to drive our Subaru Outback right up to Trapper's tent, give him a dizziness stifling pill leftover from the October incident and get him stabilized in about a half hour. We then poured Trapper onto the back seat of the Outback where I had propped up a bunch of king sized pillows to keep him upright.

One of the Mountain Man re-enactors followed us home and helped get Trapper into the downstairs guest bedroom where Trapper slept the rest of the day and eventually shook this whatever-it-was off. In the meantime, the guys at the Rendezvous graciously offered to pack up his camp for him and brought it home to our garage. As they were leaving one of them said, "I'm gonna have to remember this trick of a way to get my camp torn down." We were grateful for all of the help. We still have no idea what is causing this physical phenomenon from time to time.

Occasionally we receive an emergency call when Trapper is not around for some reason or other and it falls to me to try to deal with the situation the best I can.

One weekend my Mountain Man went camping with a couple of guys and I was enjoying a little time alone again. I love it when he goes camping because I know how much he needs some times like that – especially guy time. He tells me he would like for me to go camping with him more but at least he gets to do that with the guys.

They had left earlier that Friday afternoon and then I was awakened from a sound sleep at 1:00 am by the telephone on my bedside table ringing.

"Hello," I groggily said. It did not occur to me to answer with our business name at that ridiculous hour.
"Is this Davidson Services?", said a female voice. That was the name of our business at the time before we changed it to Davidson Wildlife Services LLC in April of 2013.
"Yes," now I was waking up. "Who is this?"
"This is the Colorado State Patrol. Who am I speaking to?"

Now I was wide awake and sat straight up in bed on full alert.

What went through my mind was that my husband and two other guys had been traveling earlier in the day and that something had happened to them on the highway. I was still scratching my head as to why they were asking for our business name instead of making sure this was our residence so I just acknowledged the question of the State Patrol with, "This is Fae Davidson."

I was probably holding my breath at this point. Although I am an optimistic person, I am absolutely certain that I was expecting some kind of terrible news from the Colorado State Patrol.

"We have a gentleman on the line with a bat in his condominium in Mount Crested Butte and he's pretty upset. We found you in the Yellow Pages." Ah the value of advertising...questionable at in my sleepy, panicked condition.

Exhale!

The County Sheriff's Office, area town animal control police officers plus the area office of Colorado Parks and Wildlife all know us well and refer us often to handle such problems...but usually during the daytime. Why in the world was the Colorado State Patrol calling us – and at this hour? This was very odd.

"We've had him on the line off and on for four hours, finally decided to try something else and called you. Do you have any suggestions of what he can do? I told him I was calling someone for help but I have not given him your phone number because I know how long we've been dealing with him and don't want to put you through that." I thanked her wholeheartedly for that courtesy toward me. I gave her some ideas for the guy to try. She gave me the gentleman's phone number to call later in the morning, which I did at a more reasonable hour, and we hung up. Finally I accomplished going back to sleep. But not before laying there in the dark thinking about how it had felt when I first answered the call and had wondered if something dreadful had befallen my Mountain Man.

This thing of helping each other out is not one sided. Trapper has done his share of that on my behalf. I am also thankful that my covering on Earth is a Mountain Man. Several times in the past few years I have had occasion to say, "If this country goes completely haywire one day, I am absolutely married to the right man." I know he knows both survival skills and the Lord so I am all the more grateful for being given my Mountain Man as my covering here.

Many are the times that Trapper has been a hero to other people for handling animal matters causing them fits. But my Mountain Man has certainly been my hero on many other days in many other ways. Those moments really make you stop and think about the importance of our priorities in life, don't they? We had already learned this lesson in a big way in 2003 (see *Praise, Pelts and...PRIORITIES*).

However, sometimes other people's animal emergencies take over our lives like what happened on *A Sunday Of Unrest*.

A Sunday Of Unrest

Some time ago we came to understand much more about God's plan of having a Sabbath day of rest. We all need it and He created it after He did an awful lot of work for six days in creating the universe. So, we see the wisdom of this rest and also understand His additional intent as a restful time WITH HIM.

We used to consider Sundays our day of rest but in October of 2013 we decided to start observing Saturdays as this day. Either day we choose, we seem to run into obstacles in observing it so we now know we need to be more intentional IN ADVANCE about making sure our rest in the Lord actually happens as He commanded for good reason and for the benefit of all – Him, us and those around us.

So we were still considering Sundays our Sabbath when Sunday June 23, 2013 began. We started the morning easily enough and anticipated a "nice, quiet, restful, relaxing Sunday." Not long after we awoke we received an emergency call that a skunk had managed to get caught in a trap we had out for a marmot...at a property west of Gunnison. No matter how we figured it, we decided we had no choice but to go get the skunk about 35 miles away.

We hopped in the truck, went down there, retrieved the trap with the live skunk in it and came home ready to start observing our "nice, quiet, restful, relaxing Sunday" at which time we received another emergency call regarding a live bat inside a house 5 miles away down in the town of Crested Butte.

We hopped in the truck, went down there, captured the live bat and came home ready to start observing our "nice, quiet, restful, relaxing Sunday" at which time we received yet ANOTHER emergency call from a gentleman with a marmot stuck in the engine of his car.

We quoted him our fee but Trapper told me to tell the fella, "we'll charge less if you bring the car to our house." We were tired and we had absolutely not done any of that "nice, quiet, restful, relaxing Sunday" so far.

The customer assured us that the marmot was in a place where starting the engine would not injure it and they both soon arrived in our driveway.

By the time they got there the marmot had thought better of staying under the hood and instead had moved under the car above the skid plate.

Trapper and the owner of the car spent the next two hours trying to coax that marmot out of the car. Most of the time it was high-pitched, ear-piercingly chirping unmercifully at them but kept itself in such a place as to make it impossible to get the rubber covered loop of our catch pole over its head and pull it outta there to freedom. Similar to the situation expressed in *Captured Coon's Life Lessons,*

the critter could not fathom that he would be much happier outside out from under the underside of this man's vehicle. Finally their poking and prodding paid off and Trapper was able to get that loop over the animal's head and pull him out. After that he released him into the freedom of which the marmot had been so fearful.

When this emergency was resolved Trapper scratched his head and said, "I'm not taking any more calls today." Good thing since the day was about over anyway.

Like I said, we've learned to be more intentional about setting aside a day of rest.

But we figure we're in good company because Jesus even helped a lot of people on the Lord's prescribed day of rest – for which He shouldered a lot of criticism. I don't think any of the people He helped on those days complained and we didn't hear any complaints from the people we were given the opportunity to help. We figured we could either be legalistic about it and say no to helping them or go help them out of their emergency situations and feel blessed – albeit tired – from doing that. The animals didn't complain either.

Our business provides many opportunities to go above and beyond to help our customers even if it is a stinky process. We do not always get it exactly right for everyone but we do try.

As you can see, quite often a day starts out one way and winds up a whole different way than expected. Betcha that happens to you too. Such was the general theme when all of the following happened at about the same time... *Bats, Bovines, Birdies & Brownies.*

Bats, Bovines, Birdies & Brownies

As part of our business Trapper builds a lot of fences – primary barbed wire cow fences but sometimes a barbless wire horse fence. After all, keeping cows and horses outta where they shouldn't be gong is animal control work too.

August 22, 2013 was entertaining. It started out as the day that Trapper began building a fence to keep cows out, that is...OFF, of the local golf course! The guys who work at the golf course had reached their limit of patience with the bovines and were perturbed about the significant amount of damage the munching and hooves of the cows and their pies were doing to the greens and other parts of the course.

We had a great time getting Trapper to the place where he was to build that fence. First it had required that we drive a golf cart to inspect the job with the manager. I had never driven a golf cart in my life so I thought this was loads of fun. It helped a lot after we arrived at the location when the manager showed me how to put it in REVERSE. Although I'm rather proficient at not getting myself into dead end predicaments as I said in *Mountain Man Hot Air*, I was happy to learn the backup procedures on this smaller, more maneuverable vehicle.

That first day I sat on the golf cart I was driving, camera at the ready, trying to find some errant bovines out there on the golf course. I knew that after Trapper had finished the fence then there had better not be any of them on the course so this was my one shot to capture the moment. But, alas, none would trespass that day. We were out there early enough that we didn't see any of the day's golfers either so the option of seeing them trying to make birdies around the bovines did not happen either – to my disappointment but not something the golf course staff was interested in seeing again. They had had enough of herding cattle.

At first they asked Trapper to use a gray maintenance type of cart to go out to inspect his prospective fence building site. Delivery of several heavy posts and rolls of barbed wire plus other supplies were needed for this job.

After that he was allowed to take his ATV to the job site and that really was more appropriate for his needs – as long as he stayed on the golf cart path. Somehow a Mountain Man on an ATV on a golf cart path struck me as entertaining.

When he was done with that day's work at the golf course we went to a customer's house to deal with bat issues.

Trapper located the entry point on the inside of the house and sealed it up so that the bats could no longer gain access to the interior of the house. This customer and her husband had become friends during our various dealings with animal situations there but this day she had a new dilemma. Her husband, who was also the president of their homeowner's association, was out of town. The cows (aka bovines) of a rancher who grazed them on a nearby pasture were getting through the cow fence that was in disrepair and getting into the subdivision. The president's wife had been receiving calls to DO SOMETHING about the cows and she had been trying her best but...she had a problem and the calls kept coming. Just like the golf course maintenance guys – she had had enough of herding cattle.

As we left their house that day she said, "When you get to the road please let me know if the cows are out again." When we got there, sure enough, they were where they shouldn't be. We called her on our cell phone and she came down to deal with it at which time we offered to help. I don't think she knew before of Trapper's experience dealing with cattle but I did and I even had a little of my own from dealing with various cattle drives on the highways of our area over the years plus being party to Trapper's work at Coleman Ranches a few years before in Saguache.

As she came down in her vehicle it started raining. We didn't care. We were glad to help so Trapper got out and positioned himself by the gate where they needed to go. She got out of her vehicle and went to find out his plan. I drove the Outback a little further on to see how far down the road the bovines had wandered. When I spotted the last of them, at that point I had the good sense to start using the car to herd the cattle back toward Trapper. Just as I started doing that she arrived and said, "Trapper wants you to use the car to herd them."

I'll be darned...after those early years of feeling like such a greenhorn I had actually already come up with the right move according to Trapper. She just didn't know that I was already on track because I was just getting into the car.

It was a scary moment when a cow and a calf jumped over a fence right in front of both of us and for a moment we wondered if they were going to get tangled up in that barbed wire. Only a day or two before Trapper had received a call from a neighbor about a dead cow in the barbed wire fence around our subdivision. She knew about that so it was not a far-fetched notion. But they both got out and got up and we were relieved.

At that point the cows started going around the Outback. So I got out and, to my surprise, they obeyed my command to come down offa the nearby hill and follow each other toward where Trapper was waiting at the gate. Of course I didn't do that with words but with whistling and hand gestures. I've learned a lot in this *Life as a Mountain Man's Wife* over the years!

Our friend was grateful for the help but, frankly, even in the rain I thought it was a lot of fun. I'm pretty sure Trapper did too 'cause he misses working with cows like he used to.

Anyway, she knew we were headed to a local restaurant for dinner, enthusiastically thanked us for our help and off we went to top off our day of such a variety of animal issues. When it came time to pay our bill at the restaurant, the hostess came over to us and asked us about our day. It was kinda odd that she said that but we didn't catch it and just said it had been a crazy day, to which she replied, "I know about the cows." Huh? How could she know about that? Well, because our customer friend and fellow bovine herder had called the restaurant, given her credit card number for our bill but had asked the hostess not to tell us of the gift until after we had finished our dinner.

A couple of months later we spotted a silly thing on the grocery store shelf.

These were too much fun to pass up so we purchased all they had in order to give them to this special customer as well as several others for whom we have been dealing with bats – a constant issue in the summertime here. Because bats can carry rabies and that is a very serious concern, bats are no laughing matter. But at least these brownies gave a little comic relief to this particular summer of dealing with them.

There is usually comic relief from life's pressures if we can step away and look for it. In our lives that often takes the form of spontaneous moments - like this one when it was *Bridger's 70th Birthday*.

Bridger's
70th Birthday

We're about to take you on a *Journey* – a *Journey To The Land*. But, before we do that we're sharing one of the most memorable comic relief moments we have in our packbaskets. When I took this photo the sun was in my eyes. I couldn't see the camera screen so didn't know what I was getting – similar to what happened in our pre-digital days of using a 35mm to photograph the Great Horned Owl in *The Al & The Owl In The Fireplace*.

What I did know was that it was a precious moment of those short little legs running full speed. It was not until downloading this on the computer later that we realized Bridger was in mid-air in this photo of his birthday celebration jaunt while beaver trapping with Trapper – something's he's loved doing all his life.

Bridger's 70th Birthday
June 5, 2013

Our line of work creates quite a number of situations in which protection is needed – protection for people from animals and protection of the animals from harm. When it comes to protection for us as the people dealing with the animals as well as in life, we know in whom to put our trust, especially when this *Mountain Man and Wife* were able to *Journey To The Land*.

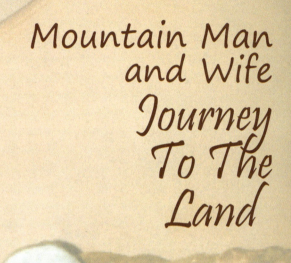

Mountain Man and Wife
Journey To The Land

Middle East

Journey To The Land
Overview

When my Mountain Man and I married in 1994 we never imagined that:
1) we would be filled with a passionate desire to study Israel and Jewish history in 1998;
2) we would both begin dreaming of going to Israel;
3) in 2010 the Lord would eventually gift us with a *Journey To The Land* that we traveled in 2011;
4) we would someday be referring to Jesus as Yeshua – his packed-with-meaning and beautiful Hebrew name – and then be using that precious name in my own writing as I now do here whenever I refer to Him.

Our *Journey To The Land* from October 5 – November 15, 2011 took us to Israel, God's Chosen Land for His Chosen People, plus to two of the countries through which the Israelites traveled (Egypt and present-day Jordan) on the way to their Promised Land something around 32 centuries ago...a mind boggling concept.

Many have asked us if we were afraid to go there, especially during this time so soon after the Egyptian Revolution that had begun eight months before during the last week of January 2011. That event only heightened our experience because our trust in the Lord's promise of His protection before we left was rewarded with an overwhelming abundance of it while we were there – as you'll soon read.

Back in the Fall of 1993 when my life-long friend in Athens, Georgia asked me more about my fiancé, I told her that he was a Mountain Man trapper. The words she said then (see *That Bible Totin' Trapper*) had a powerful impact on me as I tried to imagine the life for which I figured I was headed:
"I envy you. You're going to be living so close to the land."

She and I both thought at the time that she was referring to the land in the Rocky Mountains and especially in Colorado. That has certainly been true just as this book has been describing to you, even though neither of us had any idea then how comical it was going to be.

And we surely had no perception then that her words were prophetically referring to THE LAND – *Eretz Y'israel* (The Land of Israel) – the destination calling my Mountain Man and me for years before we finally made it there in the Fall of 2011 some 18 years later.

Before we left Crested Butte I wondered how this was gonna go – not only thinking about the safety aspect but also...what was it going to be like traveling in the Middle East with a Mountain Man??? I had enjoyed quite a bit of international travel before meeting Trapper but had long since lost interest in that with the one exception of going to Israel. However, since our God is a master at employing all past experiences that He has allowed into our lives in order to bring about His purposes, although we had not traveled internationally together in our 17 1/2 years of marriage at that point, the travel experience I had in my background combined with Trapper's survival instincts as a Mountain Man turned this *Journey To The Land* into the most extraordinary experience of each of our lives up to that point and the genesis of a gigantic further bonding to each other in our marriage.

The first week was filled with flying into Cairo to spend a couple of days in that area, then by bus to the southern tip of the Sinai Peninsula, next up to Jordan and then across the Jordan River into our primary destination – *Eretz Y'israel* – at very, very close to the same place the Israelites originally crossed into The Land some 3200 years before us.

Those who are familiar with Mountain Man lore and jargon will know the use of the word *pilgrim* as a somewhat condescending term for those who observe, attempt or are novices but not proficient at Mountain Man ways of doing, thinking or surviving. Anyone who has seen the movie *Jeremiah Johnson* will hear actor Will Gere's use of *pilgrim* in this context.

In Biblical history, the Israelites were commanded by God to "appear before the LORD your God at the place he will choose" which ultimately became Jerusalem. That is to say, they were to make three *pilgrimages* per year to Jerusalem for the Feasts of Passover (*Pesach*), Pentecost (*Shavuot*), and Tabernacles (*Sukkot*). So, right off my Mountain Man had to get used to the word *pilgrim* in a more positive context than he had come to view it as a Mountain Man since we were undoubtedly on a spiritual *pilgrimage* in this *Journey To The Land*.

Various things caused us various delays over the years of dreaming about and preparing for this *Journey*. In the process we came to understand this verse from a Psalm in a significantly expanded way:

Delight yourself in the LORD and he will give you the desires of your heart.
– Psalm 37:4 (NIV)

The meaning of it to us that we share with you now is that Almighty God Himself is the author of our best desires and He puts those desires into our hearts. So, if we trust him enough to delight in Him and the desires He gives us in the first place, He will do whatever is necessary to bring those desires to pass! I even suggest to you now to re-read Psalm 37:4 above with that concept in mind and think about how He could apply it to any number of things in your own life. It's not about the desires we dream up but instead about the desires He gives because He knows they are the best for each of our lives.

Knowing this meaning made it significantly easier to wait with patience when disappointing delays happened and then with even more heightened anticipation until the day finally came to embark on our *Journey To The Land* which then – true to God's faithful form – was even better *because* of the delays. Imagine that!

So, we set our hearts on the *pilgrimage* I am about to describe:
Blessed are those whose strength is in you, who have set their hearts on pilgrimage.
– Psalm 84:5 (NIV)

Although many more than these adventures transpired during our *Journey To The Land* than there is room in this book to share with you, we were enormously blessed by trusting in the Lord who gave it to us and then by having the opportunity to travel on it.

We began dreaming about it in 1998 but never could figure out how to afford it. Then, one day in April of 2010, we were informed that someone had donated the funds for the entire six week trip to our church on our behalf – anonymously.

We were completely blind sided when we received this news – had never imagined the possibility that it could happen in such a miraculous way. To this day (over five years later) we still do not know who on Earth did that and we do not ever expect to know. What we do know is that Almighty God is the one who gave it because he had called us there and blessed someone out there with the means and the desire to give it to us for His purposes.

So in honor of the gift and in testimony to Him, we declare here that the Lord's very provision of our *Journey To The Land* is in itself a testimony to...
Delight yourself in the LORD and he will give you the desires of your heart.
– Psalm 37:4 (NIV)
which is why we now seek out every possible opportunity to share about the *Journey To The Land* and then anticipate the fruit that will be produced in the sharing.

With that purpose in mind and heart we have included some of our adventures on the *Journey To The Land* in this collection of stories as the ones which especially emphasize the things that most impacted my Mountain Man as he was transformed into a *pilgrim* in The Land and how watching and being a part of that transformation impacted me as his wife.

To begin, we became a *Mountain Man and Wife In Egypt.*

Mountain Man and Wife
in
Egypt

Oh My Goshen!

During the last week of January 2011 we were ticketed and packed ready to embark on our *Journey To The Land* which we had been planning for 13 years but with the specific dates selected for the past 10 months. Our scheduled departure date was February 16 – two and a half weeks away – connecting with a tour operator for a private day trip at first and then another tour operator after that for the first two weeks of the adventure. For a month after that we would rent a car in Israel.

We're not tour bus people and prefer to travel independently. Under the circumstances, a privately guided excursion for just the two of us as well as booked into a group for the first two weeks of our six week *Journey* were both definitely wise decisions and, as you'll soon discover, provided us with some choice *Journey* moments.

Cairo was to be our first stop. However...Egypt absolutely exploded into Revolution on January 25. After a few tense days of watching the news coverage and talking with our tour operators, the two week tour operator finally had no choice but to cancel the departure but we were allowed to postpone it without losing any money. We were enormously disappointed but quickly shifted into the notion that this was somehow going to make the experience even richer. That more positive way of grappling with our disappointment turned out to be one of the most prophetic perspectives regarding our *Journey To The Land*.

The two week tour operator had a most symbolic company name – *Pilgrim* Tours. Given the Mountain Man history regarding that particular word, *pilgrim*, is it any wonder that we entrusted this portion of our *Journey* itinerary to this company? Another reason we selected them was because they had so many departures that itinerary planning was much easier. That proved to be a most advantageous decision when we had to postpone the *Journey* for eight months.

We had originally picked our dates such that we would be in Jerusalem at the same time as the Jewish Feast of Purim. So, in dealing with the postponement, we decided to go in the Fall which meant picking dates that would put us in Jerusalem at the time of the Feast of Tabernacles (*Sukkot*).

Already this was a better plan because *Sukkot* was one of the three major *pilgrimages* ordained by God back in the day of Moses during the Exodus out of our first stop – Egypt.

Prior to connecting with the Pilgrim Tours group, we flew out of Denver and into Cairo a day early in order to go on our own private side trip to the Land of Goshen – really pronounced "GO-shin", not "GOSH-in" as I may have misled you with the title to this story. Goshen is about two hours north of Cairo where the Israelites lived for exactly, to the day, 430 years before The Exodus (Exodus 12:40-41). We had booked this private Goshen trip with a tour operator separately from our group trip so we had only expected one guy serving as both driver and guide.

What we wound up receiving was beyond our wildest imagination for this Land of Goshen excursion. Two men, an Egyptologist named Muhammed and a driver who didn't speak English, met us at our Cairo hotel and the four of us headed north in a minivan into the Nile Delta area toward some ruins in Tanis.

What happened next, the completely unanticipated way of HOW we got to Tanis, was an absolute display of God's protective covering over us.

Halfway to Tanis we pulled up to the curb in a little town for what Trapper and I thought was a stop to let the train in this photo pass.

We soon discovered that the train was not really why we had stopped. All of a sudden a very small blue car with blue lights on top and four men crammed inside showed up right behind our car.

We were told that those men were two military soldiers and two Tourism Police. We then headed out with that car in the lead flashing the blue rooftop lights and from time to time turning on and off the siren.

When we inquired what all the fuss was about, Muhammed informed us, "You're VIPs".

"Yeah – right," we laughed from the back seat.

Up to this point Muhammed had been quite affable and joking around. His face turned stone cold sober when he looked straight at us from the front seat and replied, "No. Really. You're VIPs. I have not taken anyone up to this area for over two years and we do not want ANYTHING to happen to you two." With the Revolution still in its early months, they were seriously concerned about the safety of the American *Mountain Man and Wife* in the back seat. We looked at each other, grasped the intensity of the moment and then nodded our understanding to Muhammed. Then he shifted back to his joking self and we sojourned northward, police escort and all.

After we arrived in Tanis, Trapper – a man who is enthralled with military readiness – thought this was all pretty cool and entered into conversation with these guys as much as language barriers allowed. And those guys, just like many in various places in Egypt, Jordan and Israel, found his brown beaver felt Mountain Man hat quite intriguing. It definitely made Trapper easy to spot in a Middle Eastern crowd throughout the entire *Journey*!

Muhammed took us around in the Tanis ruins of the Temple of Amun and taught us quite a bit of Egyptian history.

This was the day that I learned how hot the Middle Eastern sun can get. So, being my protector and being that this was the very first day of our *Journey*, Trapper gallantly loaned me his brown beaver felt Mountain Man hat. It looks significantly and proportionately better on his head rather than mine, don't ya think? For the rest of the *Journey* I made sure I carried a head covering with me when needed.

We had hoped for but really had not anticipated being able to see much in archaeological ruins in Goshen that would be credited to the Israelites. After all, they were not only asked to leave but given a lot of gold, silver and clothing because "the Lord made the Egyptians favorably disposed" to do that (Exodus 3). There were also the plagues sent by God on behalf of His Hebrew people – especially the last one – the night of the original Passover that happened because of the Pharaoh's delay of the Israelites' requested departure. It resulted in the death of the Pharaoh's eldest son. So, while at these ruins we could only speculate about a wall of bricks and other structures that MAYBE had been constructed by the Israelites.

Simply imagining that we were quite possibly standing on ground once walked on by the Israelites while in Egypt was well worth the trip to these ruins. Come to think of it, the trip there itself made the trip there worthwhile.

And then resumed our police escort back to Cairo.

Along the way we were handed off to another Tourism Police vehicle full of men and they stayed with us until our turn-off to the hotel in Cairo.

There Muhammed drew on the map where we had traveled that day. Then Trapper offered his handshake in farewell. Muhammed liked that hat too. We've wondered what has happened to Muhammed and our driver considering the continued uprisings in Egypt in 2013 and after that.

The day after going to the Land of Goshen we met up with our fellow Pilgrim Tours *pilgrims* to begin the next two weeks with them – a group consisting of 12 others including a family of five from South Africa plus others from Canada and various places in the United States.

Over the next few days in Egypt and Jordan and then over the next few weeks all over Israel – my Mountain Man and his Mountain Man brown beaver felt hat were a big hit – including when we got *Back In The Saddle Again.*

Back In The Saddle Again

For a variety of reasons, at the time Trapper had not been on a horse in awhile although he will probably always own a horse saddle. Prior to the *Journey* he spoke of missing his horseback riding days and often mentioned that he would like to get back into the saddle. He didn't expect his next saddle to be THIS saddle...

...on camel back at the Pyramids on the outskirts of Cairo.

What A Ride! that was. And then our little bus took us east of Cairo, under the Suez Canal and onto the Sinai Peninsula following one of the proposed routes of the Israelites in the Exodus from Egypt. We went down the western coast of the Sinai Peninsula with various stops along the way...

...including this one beneath the hill where it is said that Aaron and Hur held up the arms of Moses so that Joshua and the Israelites would prevail in battle against the Amalekites not long after the Exodus had begun (Exodus 17). I asked Trapper to raise his own arms. We didn't ask any fellow *pilgrims* to portray Aaron and Hur to help him out.

From there we traveled southward on down to Mount Sinai. Some say that the real Mount Sinai is in Saudi Arabia and we can definitely see basis for that theory – especially because it is said that chariot wheels have been discovered in a line under the water on the EASTERN side of the Sinai Peninsula. Also, there are Hebraic writings on rock formations plus other archaeological evidence in that area of Saudi Arabia.

But, since we were at the proposed site in Egypt, we decided to consider it the actual one for the moment and experience everything we could about it, which is how Trapper wound up as our *Modern Day Mountain Man Moses.*

Our new bunch of camels awaited our arrival at the base of Mount Sinai with a different, much smaller type of saddle on them which must have had something to do with the amount of uphill camel hoofing it we were about to do...

Ascending↗

Mount↗

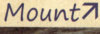

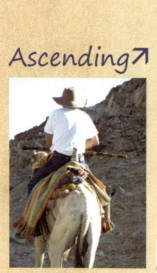

I was there in a camel saddle with those posts on both ends of the saddle (in front and in back) too – having a glorious time recording our Mountain Man Moses figure's ascent on camel back in front of me from the perspective of behind the ears of my camel named Rex. I'm in the red shirt at the front of this group and behind Trapper. My group was also in the shadows as you will see in a couple of pages. When I looked to my left and saw that image on the rocks and sand, the symbolism jumped out at me. I'm guessing it will to you too.

Modern Day
Mountain Man Moses

Sinai↗

According to the shopkeeper at the base of Mount Sinai, Trapper needed to prepare for this adventure with the proper head covering.

Nah. Even the shopkeeper agreed — Trapper needed his head covering identity back for his forthcoming *Modern Day Mountain Man Moses* trek.

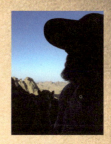

About half way up it was time for us to dismount our camels and hoof it on our own two feet up 750 steps.

We paused at times to take in what it must have been like for Moses to climb this place without the convenience of 750 pre-built steps. One of those moments was when Trapper climbed into a cleft in the rock...

Then Moses said, "Now show me your glory." And the LORD said, "I will cause all my goodness to pass in front of you, I will proclaim my name, the LORD, in your presence. ...But," he said, "you cannot see my face, for no one may see me and live." Then the LORD said, "There is a place near me where you may stand on a rock. When my glory passes by, I will put you in a cleft in the rock and cover you with my hand until I have passed by.
– Exodus 33:18-22 (NIV)

Another was my Mountain Man's joy in his brown beaver felt Mountain Man hat of reaching the summit of Mount Sinai and being our Moses figure at sundown there raising the staff he had purchased below instead of a new head covering.

But the Mountain Man hat respectfully came off to enter into a time of prayer at the top of Mount Sinai.

It was a four hour hike back down from the summit...no camels offered for the descent. The guide gave all of us flashlights to help us watch our steps down but my Mountain Man who knew how to travel the best way in the mountains suggested to me, "Turn off your flashlight and do this by moonlight." He was right! What we could see in the silhouettes once our eyes adjusted was an awe inspiring way to descend Mount Sinai. The treasured memory of it still whispers to me as I write this.

Thoroughly, blessedly exhausted that night we awakened the next morning with anticipation of becoming a *Mountain Man and Wife In Jordan*.

Mountain Man and Wife
in
Jordan

Back In A
More Familiar Saddle

The next day we ventured up the eastern coast of the Sinai Peninsula to the city of Aqaba where we were allowed time for lunch and to step into the water of the Red Sea of Israelite Exodus fame. Since Trapper and his brown beaver felt hat were such a big hit with the Egyptians, they found it great sport to engage him in various activities.

It would not have been good if Trapper had truly beaten up our bus driver in Aqaba. We have speculated if our last name of Davidson has perhaps been handed down from a Jewish ancestor (Son of David) in Trapper's lineage. And so was this squaring off near the shore of the Red Sea merely a comically symbolic continuation of the Egyptian enmity with the Israelites from so many centuries ago – and even more recent history? Nope. They really liked each other.

We then continued north parallel to the Jordanian/Israeli border toward the ruins of Petra. But along the way we stopped for a break at a roadside gift shop. After looking around the place myself I found Trapper enjoying a can of Coca Cola. He told me that while he waited in line with the other travelers

there who paid for their various refreshments with US Dollars, when he had offered him Jordanian Dinar for his Coke the guy at the counter was so happy to see someone with his local currency that he surprised Trapper by giving him the drink instead of allowing him to pay for it. That was something we had decided to do before we ever embarked on this *Journey*...pay with the local currency as a respectful thing to do. So we made sure to go to an ATM for cash as soon as we could upon arrival in each country.

Petra was an amazing place but we did not have nearly enough time to explore it properly. But we did find adventure there. These guys loved the Mountain Man brown beaver felt hat too.

If it looks familiar to you, this façade of The Treasury at Petra was used in the movie *Indiana Jones and The Last Crusade*. It was from this very spot at the end of the movie that Harrison Ford and Sean Connery took off on horseback to go out the passageway into the ruins at Petra – called the *siq* – to return to civilization.

Like I said before, that Mountain Man hat made it easy to spot Trapper in a crowd – whether a crowd of Middle Easterners or tourists.

To get in there we walked the mile-long *siq* and then walked most of the way out but decided to go for the short horseback ride the rest of the way out just to do it.

Trapper's back in the saddle AGAIN but more in his element on horseback instead of camel back.

We never imagined in 1993 that the horseback ride that led to our engagement (*What A Ride!*) and then marriage in 1994 would take us to a horseback ride outta Petra in Jordan in 2011! *What Ride!*...again.

After the stop at Petra we continued to Amman – the capital of Jordan. And then,

with great anticipation the next day we started making our way toward the border of The Land of Israel. But first we stopped for a mountaintop experience conceivably similar to that of Moses – a place where he and God and we took heart racing time for *Peering Into The Land.*

Peering
Into The Land

On the way to the Israeli border, we went to the top of Mount Nebo where God took Moses to show him the Promised Land. We considered the disappointment it must have been for Moses to NOT be allowed to go into The Land after the dramatic Exodus out of Egypt plus then at Sinai receiving The Torah and the Ten Commandments where he was also given the design for the Tabernacle, the instructions for the Feasts and the sacrificial system plus so much more that happened there. After all of that he then spent 40 years of desert travel with his people, The Children of Israel.

I didn't ask Trapper what he was feeling because, as I stood atop Mount Nebo myself, I was awed speechless by considering what I would have felt if God had said to us at that moment of being so close to the border of The Land of Israel and peering over into it from there, just like Moses did...that I could not go in now. My 13 years of anticipation was only about one third of the time of Moses' 40 years and much harder travel to get there.

What was Moses thinking when he too was standing right there on top of Mount Nebo? Was it disappointment at not being allowed to enter The Land or jubilation that his appointed mission of leading the Israelites to the border across from Jericho was accomplished and now the burden of leadership could be lifted from him and passed to Joshua. Moses quite literally rested in *shalom* (complete peace) near here. Scripture says that he died after God showed him The Land and then God Himself buried Moses at an unknown place near there (Deuteronomy 34).

So close and yet so far – for Moses.

Well, with great relief the next day we discovered that God did not ask for us to delay any longer and we were grateful to finally go into The Land as A *Mountain Man and Wife In Eretz Y'israel*.

Mountain Man and Wife
in
Eretz Y'israel
(The Land of Israel)

Into The Land

I tried my best to see the Jordan River as we crossed it and into The Land of Israel. But there were bushes in the way on the bridge so I only caught a mere glimpse of it at the time.

Thankfully, we would have multiple opportunities to see it and get into it over the coming weeks.

But, I know the very moment that we crossed the Jordan and it is thoroughly encased in my memory.

We were finally in The Land of Israel. Hallelujah! My heart was leaping for joy.

The first opportunity we had to take a more solid gander at the Jordan River up close was at the headwaters of it near Dan up in Northern Israel. Even though I couldn't record the first time across it, we do have a record of our first close look at it.

Our small little band of 12 was driven in taxis across the country (only an hour and a half drive) to Netanya where the next morning we met about 30 other people and a bigger bus.

Even though we're not really tour bus people, we were enjoying our small, close-knit group of 12 in Egypt and Jordan. But now it was time to explore our main destination – Israel.

We had planned it this way because it was best at the time to be escorted in Egypt and Jordan and so we selected this itinerary which provided our first week in Israel with a group.

That way we were able to pull out the map and get oriented to the lay of The Land while someone ELSE was driving that bus because we knew our month of driving around by ourselves was coming in the very near future...in just a few days.

You can be sure that I was also checking out the signs along the highway and getting familiar with which were the highway number signs and which were the speed limit signs – considering it extremely important to know which was which!

It wasn't long into our first full day in Israel before we found ourselves standing in front of *Most Excellent Festus' House.*

Most Excellent Festus' House

One of the first places our Israeli tour bus took us was to Caesarea on the Mediterranean Coast.

As our guide was telling us that Herod the Great had built the city and what historically had happened there, he mentioned the Roman governor Festus before whom Paul had been on trial right there in Caesarea. Well, of course, we knew all about that because of our red heeler of days gone by (*Most Excellent Festus* and *Farewell Most Excellent Festus*).

A few minutes later we were walking down the row of ruins parallel to the Mediterranean Sea there when the guide pointed out Festus' house. We were amazed that they knew which one actually was Festus' house.

Well of course a photo in front of Festus' house was in order. And look, Trapper is admitting to being a *pilgrim* with his Pilgrim Tours cap on again!

Our *pilgrimage* soon took us to the Dead Sea area and a whole bunch of other places in the Land that peaked the interest of my *Mountain Man On Military Maneuvers*.

Mountain Man On Military Maneuvers

Trapper was as impacted by The Land of Israel's more recent history as he was by the older Biblical history of each site – especialy regarding Israel's military history.

Being an independent sorta guy himself and also one who appreciates military training and discipline – typical of the Mountain Man persona – one place that struck Trapper the most was Masada. This was the place where Jewish families resisted the oppressive Roman rule and held out against them for several years until they were finally overrun at which time it was discovered that all of the rebels and their families had committed suicide rather than be captured by the Romans.

One of many things built by Herod the Great, this was a mountaintop palace overlooking the Dead Sea and the Negev Desert in southern Israel.

Mountain Fortress of Masada showing the massive earthen ramp constructed by the Roman army to breach the fortress' walls. Photo taken from north of the ramp looking south. ©Public Domain

Because of his interest in and knowledge of survival techniques, what fascinated Trapper the most about Masada was how long that many people were able to survive there – estimated at the end to be about seven years and just under 1000 Jewish men, women and children. Masada is a gigantic place perched atop that flat desert mesa and there surely were issues of food, water, community living and defense.

Use of Masada as a refuge was in about 66 to 73 AD which is also the same period of time that a half shekel you'll read about very soon was coined.

The view of the Dead Sea and the Negev Desert below from atop Masada is so huge it is hard to comprehend.

While there we were told that In contemporary times Masada has been used by the Israeli Defense Force (IDF) for a swearing in ceremony after completion of basic training.

We do not know if this is a current practice but the contemporary military significance still grabbed Trapper's attention.

Stout hearted souls can climb the long path to the top of Masada but we chose to ascend Masada by riding the huge cable car to the top and back.

Trapper was especially intrigued by this form of ammo there – catapult boulders – and asked me to stand in the middle of them. On to more sites...

At the base of the Gilboa Mountain Range we found the Spring of Harod where Gideon implemented God's instructions to him about how to reduce the size of Gideon's army against the Midians...

In order that Israel may not boast against me that her own strength has saved her...

So Gideon's army went from 32,000 to 10,000 men and then God said: *"There are still too many men. Take them down to the water, and I will sift them for you there." ...There the LORD told him, "Separate those who lap the water with their tongues like a dog from those who kneel down to drink." Three hundred men lapped with their hands to their mouths. All the rest got down on their knees to drink. The LORD said to Gideon, "With the three hundred men that lapped I will save you and give the Midianites into your hands.*
– Judges 7:2,4-7 (NIV)

Civilizations, nations and empires that have tried to destroy the Jewish People:

NATION	STATUS
Ancient Egypt	X - GONE
Philistines	X - GONE
Assyrian Empire	X - GONE
Babylonian Empire	X - GONE
Persian Empire	X - GONE
Greek Empire	X - GONE
Roman Empire	X - GONE
Byzantine Empire	X - GONE
Crusaders	X - GONE
Spanish Empire	X - GONE
Nazi Germany	X - GONE
Soviet Union	X - GONE
Iran	???

The Jewish People
The smallest of nations
but with a Friend
in the highest of places!

As a military minded man who understands tests of competency issued by commanding officers, when Trapper stepped down into the Spring of Harod to reenact this event he most assuredly did NOT kneel down to drink! Thankfully he had the advantage of knowing the story – unlike the original men of Gideon's army who most likely didn't know it was a test.

Speaking of military might, look what this says about Almighty God's military might. We saw this in a store somewhere in Israel.
The top line says
Civilizations, nations and empires that have tried to destroy the Jewish People:
The bottom lines says
The Jewish People
The smallest of nations
but with a Friend
in the highest of places!

At Susita we saw a lot of evidence and signage telling us of fighting there in the 1967 Six Day War. We found out that the IDF used Susita as a fortress to defend Israel's border with Syria during the 1967 Six Day War.

What a miraculous thing God did by giving Israel victory in those very few days. We do not know what the Hebrew letters on this sign say but if someone reading this story will tell us, we'll appreciate it. Under the Hebrew letters at the bottom of this sign it says: **1967**

This was a place at the entrance of Susita that was used as a bunker with openings to aim rifles through.

We went right up to both the Lebanese and Syrian borders several times in our travels around Israel – including one place near the ancient Biblical city of Dan, again north of Akko at Rosh HaNikra and also up on the Golan Heights at the top of Gilboa Ridge. We do not have photos of any of the border crossing gates or military installations because such photos are strictly forbidden.

At one place on the Syrian border there was a memorial that included a tank leftover from a battle during the 1973 Yom Kippur War where God miraculously intervened on behalf of Israel.

The ascent of our hearts all over The Land was immeasurable.

But when we went UP to Jerusalem we were truly in the clouds emotionally although at a lower physical altitude than at our Rocky Mountain home. After traveling The Land for several days, the time finally arrived for us to ascend to Jerusalem... *Up To The Mountain Of The Lord.*

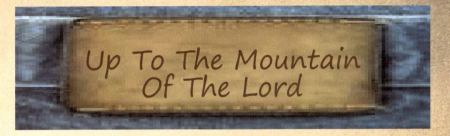

Up To The Mountain Of The Lord

In 2008 I studied the Psalms of Ascent (Psalms 120– 134) sung by Jewish pilgrims headed for Jerusalem to honor God's command to observe the Feasts there. But when we saw it – Yerushalayim – and then we were standing there, we understood the emotion of...

> *I rejoiced with those who said to me, "Let us go to the house of the LORD." Our feet are standing in your gates, O Jerusalem.*
> – Psalm 122:1-2 (A Psalm of Ascent) (NIV)

We had heard about Jerusalem being UP – a city on a hill – and it truly is. UP there on the Temple Mount is the rock of Mount Moriah on which it is believed that Abraham placed his son, Isaac, as a sacrifice. It was being used as a threshing floor when King David purchased it as the site of the Temple which he planned but was built by his son, Solomon. The rock is then believed to be where the Holy of Holies of the Temple was and so the place where the Ark of the Covenant was housed and visited only once a year on Yom Kippur (the Day of Atonement) by the Jewish High Priest. At the moment the Muslim gold Dome of the Rock structure so associated with the skyline of Jerusalem now sits there.

The Temple Mount, where the Temple was until the Romans destroyed it in 70 A.D., is one of many places where Yeshua taught and where He will one day return after first arriving on the Mount of Olives presumably somewhere near where I am standing here.

It is believed that He will then enter the Old City to return to the Temple Mount through that double gate down in the Old City to my right there (the East Gate or Golden Gate) which is the tallest part of the wall. It was walled up by the Ottoman Sultan Suleiman in 1541 – presumably to keep Yeshua out when that day comes... as if that would stop the Son of Almighty God!

> *Many peoples will come and say, "Come, let us go up to the mountain of the LORD, to the house of the God of Jacob. He will teach us his ways, so that we may walk in his paths." The law will go out from Zion, the word of the LORD from Jerusalem.*
> – Isaiah 2:3 (NIV)

225

Since this was the first day of our *pilgrimage* to Jerusalem, Trapper was still setting aside his brown beaver felt Mountain Man hat and enjoying being a *pilgrim* with a *Pilgrim* Tours cap on his head. It didn't take long for him to switch back to the Mountain Man hat which had already become his trademark with our fellow *pilgrims*.

Little did I know until we all received copies of our group photo taken just after the photo above, that my persona and trademark had become that brown *Journey Journal* in my hands there. I only realized it when I overheard a gal in the group say, "And look! Fae has her journal in the photo. Perfect!"

Up until that moment I hadn't realized anyone had noticed the journal at all. It has a gold embossed stamp on it that says *Fae's Journey To The Land*. Trapper also has one that says *Al's Journey To The Land* on the cover. "Trapper" caused his embossing to be too long so I had to request they put "Al" on it instead – darn. I ordered them knowing that we were going to be receiving so much information on this *Journey* that there would be no way to retain it all by memory. I have made extensive use of my brown leather *Journey Journal* in writing this *Journey To The Land* section of *Life as a Mountain Man's Wife*.

I'm the primary writer of this marriage team of *Mountain Man and Wife*...just in case you hadn't noticed that yet.

However, Trapper has a certain writing style all his own which you'll discover in a story coming up soon.

For many years we have felt such a closeness to The Land (Eretz Y'israel) that we figured there must be something more that connected us with it. A light bulb came on for us when we began the query into *What's In A Name*.

226

What's In A Name

Before going to Israel, Trapper had always thought of himself as being from Irish heritage and that had seemed logical to me. But in Jerusalem we went to Yad Vashem – in Hebrew meaning The Memorial of the Names – which is also known as the Holocaust Museum. It impacted us greatly.

After wandering through the many and powerful Yad Vashem displays, we came to a very large round room, *The Hall of Names*. The dome over the middle of it displays 600 photos of Holocaust victims. The binders around the walls of the room contain the Pages of Testimony which are as many as have so far been collected of short biographies of the six million victims. Walking into this room overwhelmed us both with the magnitude of the horror of the Holocaust and a conviction to be a part of standing firm for the overriding lesson of the Holocaust: ***NEVER AGAIN***.

In gaining permission by email from Yad Vashem to use this photo, they requested two copies of this book. We are delighted that these *Mountain Man and Wife* tales have been sent not only to Jerusalem but to this significant place in Jerusalem.

Hall of Names
Photo permission courtesy of Yad Vashem

227

As we were standing there in the middle of it and completely overwhelmed by the magnitude of the slaughter of these people, we spied a very small room in the back of it which turned out to be a computer room. I sat down at a computer and, at Trapper's suggestion, typed in my maiden name which I knew was German – Epting. We fully expected some names to come up but none did. I put in a few variations of the name and then some of those came up. But then Trapper asked me to type in Davidson and kaboom!...over 1000 names that were variations of the name Davidson immediately appeared on the screen. It stunned us both.

One thought that came to my mind took me back to a 1993 phone conversation just before we became engaged. I was telling my friend on the phone in Athens, Georgia, Kim Arnold, about this Mountain Man I was seeing. When she asked what his last name was, I replied, "Well, it's kinda boring – Davidson." I was accustomed to having an unusual last name so Davidson didn't seem that exciting to me. Her response was, "Davidson! Son of David! You can't do any better than that!"

Well, my whole perspective on the prospect of this becoming my new last name changed on the spot. Of course she was speaking of one of the names of *Yeshua HaMashiach* (*Jesus the Messiah*) who was born Jewish in His first appearance on Earth. And this was said by the gal who was faithful to let Him use her influence with me in 1992 to bring me into a deeper understanding of who He is and why being in relationship with Him is so essential.

But until sitting in front of that computer at Yad Vashem it had never occurred to us to find out if either of us has recent history Jewish heritage. We are in the process of researching that in both of our family lineages with DNA tests and other methods. Neither of us will be surprised if we discover such a near history Jewish connection because the Lord has given us such a heart connection with His Land and His Chosen People there so deeply already.

An aside about the Davidson name in Israel is that the Davidson Center is very close to the Western Wall of the Temple. It houses exhibits that give a true sense of the Old City of Jerusalem in days long ago.

You'll read a little more about the Davidson Center in an upcoming story called *Half A Shekel for Schaffer.*

The day came that our group left us in Jerusalem to return to their respective homes. So we were now *On The Road On Our Own In The Land*

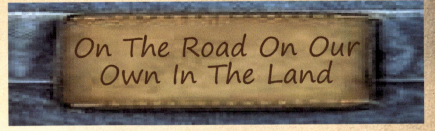

On The Road On Our Own In The Land

www.JerusalemHillsInn.com

We went to a nearby village called Abu Ghosh about 10 minutes from Jerusalem to check in at Jerusalem Hills Inn.

The Singerman family who owns and operates it were friends of friends of ours when we arrived but quickly they all became our own friends in this very special Land.

Some other guests there took us about 30 miles to Tel Aviv's Ben Gurion Airport to pick up our little rental car and thus began our month of self-propelled but definitely God-inspired adventures all over Israel.

A Jewish mother and daughter that we met at Jerusalem Hills Inn joined us on our first day of excursions out from there.

As we headed north on Highway 60 we discussed that the one place we needed to be sure we did NOT go into was Ramallah – the Palestinian headquarters. We couldn't find many highway signs around there to reconfirm to us whether we were on – or not on – the highway on which we wanted to be. We knew our destination was right beside the Arab territory of Ramallah so we were being as cautious as possible.

As hard as we tried to keep our wits about us as we were driving along, at one point I looked up, recognized the buildings that we had seen on the news for years as being where Yasser Arafat used to live and said, "Folks, THAT is Ramallah and we've got to turn around." Although there was a median in the road, we found a place to get our little car outta there. We were not in any danger not only because we paid attention but mostly because we had asked the Lord to order our steps...rather, our tires...as we set out on this escapade.

Someone at Jerusalem Hills Inn had given us directions to Ai (pronounced something close to "Yigh" as in "high") so we decided to go find it. We wound up going through the town of Psagot Ze'ev first and because the hand drawn map to Ai given to us was a bit difficult to match with reality on the road, we needed to ask for directions. Right in front of us was a synagogue and the two Jewish gals with us had the idea to go in there and ask for help. Well, out came a (what we called) Rabbi-In-Training who seemed about the same age as the daughter with us. Trapper is known for being an observer. And so, while we women were all looking at the map the young man was drawing for us, Trapper was watching him watch our young female travel companion. The young man kept saying and grinning, "Let me show you one more time" and "my map is BETTER!" We figured it was because he wanted to keep admiring her a little longer. It was a topic of conversation the rest of the day and the rest of our time in Abu Ghosh. Trapper teased her endlessly about it.

A few more stops and some Arab gates later we finally found Ai which was the city Joshua and the Israelites conquered after Jericho.

It was an incredible thing to read the scripture of what had happened there, including an ambush the Israelites perpetrated on the Canaanites behind a hill somewhere in the area – presumably the one right there in front of us. We also discovered that long before then, Abraham had twice pitched his tent just west of the ruins amongst which we were then standing – between Ai and Bethel.

From there we were successful at finding Shiloh (pronounced "SHEE-low" in Israel). This sacred place is where The Tabernacle sat for 369 years after it was built in the Sinai desert according to God's specifications given to Moses on Mount Sinai, carried around in the wilderness by the Israelites for 40 years, set up for 14 years at Gilgal just north of Jericho after the Israelites crossed into The Land and was eventually taken to Shiloh which established that place as the first capital of the Israelite people long before God told them He wanted His name established at The Temple in Jerusalem.

> The whole assembly of the Israelites gathered at Shiloh and set up the Tent of Meeting there.
> – Joshua 18:1

Trapper was seriously on duty as the protector of we three women throughout this day. At Shiloh we hiked up a trail to *The Tabernacle Plateau* – a flat place where the Tabernacle resided all of those years.

We stood in awe of being there. It was gratifying to us to know that we had done what God had suggested :

> *"Go now to the place in Shiloh where I first made a dwelling for my Name..."*
> -Jeremiah 7:12 (NIV)

Although this life-sized reconstruction of the Tabernacle is near Eilat at the southernmost tip of Israel, the terrain – at least in this photo – looks strikingly similar to that which we saw in Shiloh north of Jerusalem. This reconstruction of the Tabernacle is another place we plan to visit when we return to The Land of Israel.

Model of the tabernacle in Timna Park, Israel
©Creative Commons-licensed Image

231

Before going up the path we had received permission at the entrance to take pictures. We were very respectful about such things in The Land. But at the plateau there was a man moving rocks around at the far left end close to where the Holy of Holies would have housed the Ark of the Covenant. Trapper became nervously protective of me when the man started yelling something we couldn't understand at us. The only reason we could guess was for taking pictures so I snuck behind some rocks and took the photos I wanted to take. After all, we had sought out and obtained permission.

Since then I've read a book by a former mayor of Shiloh (*God, Israel and Shiloh*) and maybe we'll even look him up there whenever we go back to Israel – for we feel assured we'll go back.

After we returned home someone told us about this rock formation discovered through satellite images that appears to spell out God's name of Yahweh in Hebrew on the very same land where the Tabernacle stood at Shiloh. I have not researched to find out if this is true instead of photo shopped. Since it's more fascinating to believe this is true, I've included mention of it here. I welcome more information about this from any of you readers if you happen to know more about it. I believe it would be just like God to create such a rock formation.

Hebrew letters for Yahweh – Jehovah God YHWH

The next day Trapper remained on duty with two more women added to our traveling band. And so he was faithful to his calling as our protector and *Mountain Man Watchman.*

232

Mountain Man Watchman

The next day after the Ai/Shiloh adventures we set out again with two more gals from Jerusalem Hills Inn. This time we returned to Old City Jerusalem, went shofar shopping and a few other places. A shofar is a trumpet made from a ram's horn and is a very symbolically significant item in the history of Israel. We had waited for years to buy one while in Israel instead of just ordering one online. Hallelujah – we literally ran into a Shofar Sale at a shop in the Old City – there really was a sign saying "Shofar Sale" on the shelf.

Somehow we squeezed all six of us in that little rental car of ours...with the four gals in the back because the front had only bucket seats. Besides, since I needed to be the driver and it would have been inappropriate for anyone but me to sit on Trapper's lap, well, four in the back is how it had to be.

So now we had Trapper squiring FIVE women around Old City Jerusalem. That's the renowned Western Wall of the Temple behind us.

233

He took quite a shine to his role as pathfinder, protector and...herdsman. After all, his last name is Davidson. Who knows but possibly he is from the lineage of King David himself who started out life as a shepherd before he became a warrior and leader of Israel. I can honestly say that my Mountain Man would love to be able to trace his lineage to King David. For now, it's quite a treat to get to speculate about that, especially because Yeshua is of the same lineage. What an amazing possibility!

More than that, he was our Watchman who dutifully yet quite enjoyably did his protecting job throughout the day in the Old City of Jerusalem and then herded us all back, shofar bag with golden braid straps over his shoulder, to that little rental car parked just down the street from the Dung Gate.

From there we went to the *Temple Mount Sifting Project* just across the Kidron Valley from the Old City and at the base of the Mount of Olives. I had located this activity in a *Biblical Archaeology Review* magazine before leaving home. We were fascinated with the fact that the dirt at this place had been hauled over there from the actual Temple Mount where it had been unceremoniously dug up to make way for a new building without proper inspection beforehand and then dumped into the Kidron Valley. Thankfully some astute people were able to have it moved to the base of the Mount of Olives and came up with the idea of allowing *pilgrim* novices like us to come there to help out – with proper instruction and supervision. So, we were back to being close to the land again – that is, the DIRT of The Land.

That day all six of us enjoyed and action packed time of spraying dirt with water and sifting it. At times I looked our shoulders to see Old City Jerusalem across the Kidron Valley and thought, "Wow! Look where we are!"

We actually found a few pieces of bona fide artifacts there. During the orientation before starting our sifting they mentioned that someone had found an actual bead from some long ago time in the dirt that very morning.

So, there we were sifting away when, lo and behold, a purple bead appeared in front of me from our bucket of Temple Mount dirt. I was ecstatic and we called the expert over to take a look.

Darn. When he examined it...it was PLASTIC!...and utterly worthless – except for getting to laugh about it now. I wish I'd kept it as a memento of my awesome archaeological find at the Temple Mount Sifting Project. But alas, I let it go into the trash bin without thinking that through.

Since I took a photo of those four ladies with my Mountain Man there on the Mount of Olives overlooking where we'd sifted dirt below...

...one of them took a photo of me with my Mountain Man in the same spot before we made our merry way back to Jerusalem Hills Inn in Abu Ghosh.

The next day it was time for us to leave Abu Ghosh and set out on our own to wander around The Land of Israel with our list of friends of friends to meet.

It was kinda hard to leave the quickly found comfort of our little haven at Jerusalem Hills Inn but...adventures awaited us so off we went to find them.

But just before we left I walked out of the breakfast common area there and discovered Trapper with yet another young lady.

I ran and grabbed my camera to capture this precious moment of my Mountain Man there with this gorgeous child having an innocent moment together on the swing set.

We would meet many new friends in The Land and see things there that reminded us of home and our lives in Crested Butte – such as *Bassets In The Land.*

Bassets
In The Land

You've met our Basset Hounds in previous stories in this book. We discovered that Israel knows of Basset Hounds too.

We drove through Jerusalem and down to Jericho right after leaving Jerusalem Hills Inn – the reverse of the route close to the same road that Yeshua took from Jericho on his last trip to Jerusalem. I know I definitely thought about that as we drove that road. Trapper quite possibly did too. We went into the city of Jericho and even found the very tree proposed as the one that Zacchaeus climbed up into to see Yeshua pass below (Luke 19). It's a rather large tree now some 2000 plus years after that extraordinary day in the life of Zacchaeus.

After leaving Jericho we made an attempt to find Gilgal just north of there – the first place the Israelites camped after entering The Land. We were not successful so we continued north on Highway 90 toward Tiberius where we planned to spend the night. Suddenly I saw something ahead on the right-hand side of the road and, without informing Trapper what I was up to, yanked the steering wheel to pull us over there. I just had to stop and take a closer look. Ahhh – blessed spontaneity.

It was heavy – made out of we don't know what. But it was obviously not something we could ship home or carry on the airplane.

A man approached us and it appeared that he was loudly insisting that we buy the Basset. It briefly, very briefly, occurred to me to pull out Trapper's camera and show the man this first photo brought from home on it – Bridger sitting almost exactly the same way as this roadside Basset statue.

But my Mountain Man Watchman was reading the sign and doing his usual thing of being very aware of all that was going on around us and said, "I think we'd better get outta here." So I snapped the statue photo which was much more transportable than the statue itself, hopped into our little car and resumed our route on to Tiberius.

Our first indication that Basset Hounds are known in Israel was a wooden carving of one in a gift shop earlier in Caesarea back during our first day of excursions after arriving in The Land (see *Most Excellent Festus' House*).

So apparently Basset Hounds are there although we never did see a live one in the country. This wooden one was interesting but personally I am much fonder of the one we saw on the side of the road just north of Jericho. That one has a much more adventurous tale to go with it.

Many were our spontaneous adventures in The Land. The pullover on the highway north of Jericho was just the beginning day of the two of us making sudden stops to explore. At many of the locations we discovered that *Land Mines Would Ruin The Land's Ruins*.

Land Mines Would Ruin The Land's Ruins

Trapper was fascinated with these yellow signs like the one beside his elbow when he was standing beside our little car. We saw them at many of the ruins where often we were the only people there.

In Hebrew, Arabic and English it warns:
DANGER
MINES!

These yellow signs kept us on the straight and narrow – the paths in and out and around the ruins that warned us not to go off the path or into the nearby fields because of land mines potentially still live underground out there.

You are probably aware that Israel has had its share of wars – not only many centuries ago as described in the Bible but also in more contemporary times. We saw much evidence of that at these ruins of Susita.

At various places we saw signs telling us what had happened in the various ruins referring to the 1948 War of Independence, the 1967 Six Day War and the 1973 Yom Kippur War. So not only were we envisioning people like Yeshua, Abraham, Isaac, Jacob, Joshua, David, Saul, the Philistines, Nebuchadnezzar and more Biblical characters as having walked and fought battles all over these places long before we were there, but also 20th Century soldiers from Israel, Egypt, Jordan, Syria and other nearby countries fighting where we stood.

Knowing a fair amount of history as we stood on each site but also reading that history in the Bible while standing there, we were often overwhelmed with gratitude for the opportunity to be there.

Trapper expressed that in the ruins of a synagogue in Susita – one of the proposed sites where the pigs ran down the hill into the Kinneret (Sea of Galilee) below after Yeshua sent the evil spirits out of a man and into them. That's the Kinneret behind and below him.

Just a few feet from where we saw the 1973 Yom Kippur War Memorial in Northern Israel (see *Land Mines Would Ruin The Ruins In The Land* you've just read) we looked over the border into Syria at a road leading from Northern Israel to Damascus and imagined if that was the very same road that Paul took when Yeshua knocked him offa his horse and changed his whole life (Acts 9). I can relate on both a physical "ouch" level (see *They Call Me "Cookie"*) and a spiritual life-changing level (see *Way Up There*).

Our explorations in The Land took us down many paths and many steps of planning as well as walking them – some of which are now immortalized in *Trapper's "Steps"*.

Trapper's "Steps"

Throughout our *Journey To The Land* of six weeks we sent back 23 emails to share the adventures to just over 400 email addresses that had collected while we were planning the *Journey*. It was my job – rather joy – to send them out and the Lord gave me the stamina and creative ability to do that – mostly in the wee small hours at a variety of places – without taking time away from participation in as many adventures as we could possibly pack in.

But one night at the end of the day's adventures and in our room at a bed and breakfast in Poriya just above the Kinneret, Trapper piped up and said, "I want to dictate an email to send out. I want to call it..."Steps". Okay – so we did that and on the next page is the email he sent out.

To give you a visual before you read his email, here are the not cursed Kursi steps he referred to with the mosaic floored lookout at the top that HE saw but I didn't. Those infamous steps are on the mound on the lower right. There's Trapper on the left already most of the way down by the time it occurred to me to snap a photo of this place. At first I didn't want to immortalize the place where I wimped out. Now I'm glad I took the picture since he did the immortalizing a few days later.

Hi guys – this is from Trapper.

What a Journey it's been.

I'm entitling this story...STEPS.

First of all I just want to say Hi and I know for a fact that the Cardinals won the World Series, elk season is going on in Colorado and pine marten trapping will be starting for me in about two weeks.

The Middle East is full of steps.

Fae was the first one in our group to make it to the top of Mt. Sinai with all them...steps.

She was the last one to make it down with all them...steps.

Every archaeological dig has...steps.

Not just one step...lots of...steps.

I bet we've been up 10,000...steps – maybe more.

Going into the Old City of Jerusalem is full of, you guessed it...steps.

All the gates are full of...steps.

Lots and lots of...steps.

So far the most agonizing set of...steps...was going down into the cave where Jesus was born.

There were only 5 or 6...steps...but it seemed there were 5000 people trying to get through that little hole.

Since Fae and I have been out on our own we've stopped at a bunch of archaeological digs, etc. and they were all full of...steps.

Finally the other day, Fae reached her limit.

We had stopped at Kursi National Park on the other side of the Sea of Galilee in the Decapolis.

It's one of the possible sites where Jesus cast out Legion from the demon possessed Gadarene man and they ran into the pigs which then ran down the hill into the Sea of Galilee and drowned.

We were walking through the park heading toward a recently discovered mosaic at the top of a hill.

Do you know what stood between where we stood and the top of the hill?

Lots of...steps...approximately 100.

Fae came to a screeching halt. Her shoulders shrugged and she said, "More steps."

I've never heard my wife say a curse word and I still haven't.

But I'm expecting some of them went through her mind when she said, "I am not going to go up those steps."

Being the adventurous one, I had to do the 100 steps.

The mosaic wasn't much but the view of the Sea of Galilee was awesome.

See most of you in a couple of weeks.

My next installment will be...cats.

This country is full of cats...lots and lots of cats.

God bless, talk to ya later.

Trapper

Many were the emails back to us from our readers all over the United States and elsewhere. They loved Trapper's forthright style – just as a Mountain Man would say it – straight out.

Although his email was better left alone, I surely had to stick up for myself.

So in my next post I shared that in Kursi when I came to where I was standing in the bottom of the photo a couple of pages ago, I had reached the part of the path leading to that handful of steps and realized that Kursi was flat – a welcome change...

...but then I comprehended and was fully appreciating that going UP THERE would require an ascent to see it all after all.

At that moment the two white tennis shoes on my feet came to a screeching halt and slid forward together a few inches. I really did rally and was headed for the path that would lead to the bottom step when I noticed Trapper already coming down.

I passed on very, very few experiences on this *Journey* but, because the time for the site to close for the day was upon us, I decided to let this one go.

At least, that's what I told myself in the moment.

In doing that I had no idea I was fueling my Mountain Man's creative writing fire at the time, though.

There was much to see in that area around the Kinneret.

But twice we also spent some time floating ON it and were enthralled by *Dancing, Fishing, Faith & Gratitude on Kinneret.*

Dancing, Fishing, Faith & Gratitude on Kinneret

While in Israel we were blessed with two boat excursions on the Kinneret.

The first one was during the week in Israel with our tour group and during the day. That trip included a guy throwing fishing nets into the water just as Peter and the other fisherman disciples must have done plus group dancing to Jewish music ("Roni Roni Bat Zion" – which means "Rejoice, Rejoice, Daughter of Zion" in Hebrew). At one point they turned off the motor out in the middle of the Kinneret and suggested we have a silent time with God.

As I sat there I heard in my spirit, "Thank you for coming." I considered it a word from the Lord who, in His gentle way, thanked us for being obedient to not only the desire to come to His special Land that He gave us in the first place but then to be *faith*ful to that desire and persevere in planning it until He brought it to fruition which had resulted in us sitting on that boat out there in the middle of that extraordinary lake at that very moment. It brought tears to my eyes to think that He was thanking us when instead all I could think to do was to continually, throughout the *Journey*, thank HIM for getting us there.

The second Kinneret boat trip was in the works by email before we ever left Crested Butte with a fella named Daniel Carmel who operated a boat named *FAITH*. Can you imagine how much I loved that name?

With the 19th Anniversary of the night we had met in Crested Butte (October 31, 1992) happening while we were in Israel, we had pre-planned to take his boat on that night because he was known for singing worship songs on the excursion – on *Faith*. So we made our way back to the dock at Gennesaret north of Tiberius for that night's sunset ride.

At first we were the only ones there on *Faith*. And then a large French group piled on. It was a glorious evening of singing many worship songs familiar to us.

245

By the night of this second boat excursion we had been taken to or driven our little car around Kinneret to many of the sites within view – Golan Heights, Susita, Kursi, Capernaum, Chorizim, BeitShe'an, Tabgha and more. So we were much more familiar with what we were seeing along the coastline this time.

The sunset was so gorgeous and turned the water a purplish blue. But where we were sitting we couldn't see it very well because of a curtain on the front of the boat. So, while we were singing I slipped the safety loop of the video camera onto my wrist so I wouldn't drop it into the Kinneret, stuck my hand out over the water, pointed the camera toward the sunset and... hoped for the best. The result was a precious blending of English and French enthusiastically proclaiming in song *How Great Is Our God* with film of the sunset and the water of the Kinneret created by water of the Jordan River coming down from Mount Hermon in northern Israel which the Kinneret then releases out to send it to the Dead Sea in the south.

But there was another especially moving moment before I offered that camera out over the water. It remains one of the most precious videos of the entire *Journey*. During the first group chorus of *How Great Is Our God* I panned the deck of the boat with the video camera and filmed the French group singing with us until I came around immediately to my left – to my husband, Trapper, with his big brown beaver felt Mountain Man hat on his head. Trapper, bless him, just cannot carry a tune. But he can make a joyful NOISE unto the Lord just the same. With the camera close up on his face, totally out of tune and even out of sync with the French fellow singers, he belted out the line, "How Great Is Our God" for all the world – and our Lord – and all who ever see the video. I look for opportunities to share it because it is such a precious display of my husband's uncomplicatedly honest relationship with His Lord. That video makes me both laugh at Trapper and cry sentimental tears at the moving worshipfulness of it every time we see it.

Here's Fae-th kissing Trapper on *Faith* wearing the Jerusalem Skirt (see upcoming story called *Hebraic and Other Heritage Roots*).

Since Daniel Carmel was singing right beside us, we don't know if it was because he saw that honest worship, the Lord told him to do it or he knew it was one of our anniversaries but – when we went to pay him for the trip before disembarking, he waived us off and gave it to us as a gift. One of his crew took this photo of us with him:

But earlier in the day we had also celebrated our Anniversary through the joy of giving to someone else in a most unusual way – by *Painting With A Jewish Carpenter*.

Painting With A Jewish Carpenter

One of our stated goals in making this *Journey* was the notion of looking for opportunities to do service work during the independent part of the trip. Toward that goal we sent out several emails during the *Journey* planning stage before we left home and let it be known that we were available for such.

We actually had some takers who, by accepting our offer, gave to us as many blessings as we offered to them.

One of those days was the same day as our 19th Anniversary Kinneret boat ride. So, it was a perfect way to spend the day – in service to someone in Israel – and then the gift of the time on the Kinneret that the Lord gave to us that night.

We found our way to the home of an Orthodox Jewish Rabbi named Aaron (imagine that – given that Moses' brother, the first Jewish High Priest, was named Aaron) who was moving his family to a new house in a little town called Kfar Shamai. Unfortunately the previous tenants had left the place completely trashed. He had gone there wanting to paint the interior and get it ready for his family but what he had found was going to take him a lot more time than he had anticipated. When we arrived and surveyed the situation with him, we both offered whatever he wanted us to do.

It was then decided that I would clean up the trash all over both the interior and the exterior and Trapper would...

paint the ceiling which would give the rabbi time to invoke his woodworking skills to repair door moldings that the previous tenants had damaged.

The rabbi was skeptical of us at first. He knew we were believers in Yeshua and he surely wondered what we were doing there. We do not know for certain but we imagine that he imagined that we were there to try to convert him to belief in Yeshua. We knew that we were there only to help out with no ulterior motives and, if there was to be any conversion experience, that would be up to Yeshua Himself anyway.

Before

The inside was a quick cleanup because the bulk of the trash waiting for me was outside. That put The Rabbi and The Trapper alone inside for some amazing guy time.

I busied myself with filling up a large trash container with a lot of nasty stuff which included about 200 cigarette butts (yuk), wet socks and more that I have thankfully forgotten specifically.

After

After finishing our work, we headed back to Tiberius for our Kinneret Anniversary ride on *Faith*. On the way there Trapper told me what had transpired inside while I was outside:

Slowly the rabbi had realized that we were there only to help so he loosened up in his conversation with Trapper. At one point Trapper said, "When I get back to the states I'm going to tell people that I painted the home of a Jewish Rabbi." To this the Rabbi had replied, "No. Tell them you painted the home of a Jewish CARPENTER." We figure he knew exactly what he was saying – based on knowing that we believe in Yeshua who grew up as a carpenter in Nazareth. Here's my Mountain Man with the Jewish carpenter.

It was a moment of *shalom* – said here based on what we have come to understand that this Hebrew word really is – a peaceful wholeness and completeness. In this case it was a *shalom* moment of understanding between the two of them.

While I was outside at that house, this time in Kfar Shamai also provided me with one of our moments of sensing the *shalom* of Prolific Profound Protection In The Land.

Prolific Profound Protection In The Land

As mentioned during our story about police and military protection in Egypt, we felt an enormous sense of being protected by God while in The Land and in nearby countries. There are also several times mentioned elsewhere in these stories about how my Mountain Man fulfilled his God-given role as a protector in various situations.

A particular moment when I felt the Lord's covering was when I first sat down in the driver's seat of the little (very little) car we rented at the Tel Aviv airport about to embark on a month of maneuvering it around The Land.

I experienced an intense moment of terror as I put my hands on the wheel but didn't even have time to tell Trapper about it because an immediate sense of *shalom* came over me and the thought, "We've been given an amazing opportunity of driving this car around and exploring this country. Get over it!" I was fine with the driving before Trapper even hit the passenger seat and then from that moment on.

I admit that there were a few situations in the traffic here and there but even in those moments the Lord gave me determination and a sense of follow-through that even I could not explain. He also gave me some creative ways to handle some of those.

For example, fairly quickly we realized that the stop lights in Israel turn yellow in both directions. They would go green/yellow/red like here in the United States but then would also go red/yellow/green when you were stopped at one of them. At first I couldn't figure out why folks behind us were honking when the light went from red to yellow before turning green. But then – aha! I was given the idea to take my foot off the brake when it turned yellow and that put a stop to such horn honking from behind. All they needed to see was some action in the brake lights on the car in front of them when the yellow appeared and all was well. By that they could tell that the driver in front of them was paying attention. I tested it a few times by leaving my foot on the brake during the yellow lights and, sure enough, "HONK! HONK!" every time. Okay. I got the message and learned the etiquette of driving in The Land.

249

I've also compared that to how God perhaps views us. I wonder if sometimes He's just waiting for us to show some sort of action toward what He's called us to do and then He gives us a green light to move forward in that calling. Hmmm...

Here's how VERY little our little car was but we became quite attached to it as our means to wander in The Land much more expediently than the Israelites had done in getting there in the 1200s BC. What made this so funny is that when we first got to Tel Arbel in Northern Israel we were the first ones to park there that morning. We wonder if those who parked those vehicles around us enjoyed the comedy of it as much as we did. The close proximity of the smaller bus led us to figure that the driver of it got a big kick out of doing that.

In addition to the timing of the Revolution in Egypt, October 2011 was an especially active time of Hamas terrorists in Israel's Gaza Strip sending rockets into nearby Ashkelon and Ashdod to the north of them on the Mediterranean Coast of Israel, east of them into Beersheva and other areas of the Negev Desert plus also into the little town of S'derot about one mile northeast of Gaza Strip.

These were all areas we were planning to visit during the last week of our *Journey To The Land*. We were paying close attention to the news reports about it all. Although we felt protected by God generally while in The Land, we did not want to be irresponsible and then intentionally or unadvisedly put ourselves in harm's way.

When we were at the rabbi's house in Kfar Shamai doing our service work on October 31 I was outside most of the time. At one point I heard the sound of the IDF (Israeli Defense Force) jets flying overhead and assumed that they were flying protection missions over that area to the southwest. I looked up from the courtyard of the house I was cleaning and into the sunshine of the blue sky but of course I could not see them since they were already long gone at supersonic speed (the ability of which was made possible, incidentally, by the bravery of our previous acquaintance – Chuck Yeager (*I'll Be Darned*). I recall standing there pondering the wisdom of our pending travel down to that area in about a week.

The next day we left Tiberius for a powerful day of adventures – one of which took us along the top of the Gilboa Mountains on Gilboa Ridge Road (similar to Trail Ridge Road that runs along the top of the mountains in Rocky Mountain National Park from Estes Park to Granby, Colorado). It was on Mount Gilboa that both King Saul and his son, Jonathan, were killed by the Philistines on the same day that they stole the Ark of the Covenant from The Tabernacle in Shiloh and also Eli the High Priest died of a broken neck when he fell off his

For corrections
see inside back cover. 250

fd

chair in despair there in Shiloh after hearing the news of the Ark being stolen, the deaths of Saul and Jonathan and also the deaths of his two evil sons.

On Gilboa we stopped for lunch and climbed up to Mount Barkan Lookout at the top. As we stood there looking to the south we again heard the sound of IDF jets.

Again they were traveling at supersonic speed so we couldn't see them but the sound came from the Golan Heights to the northeast behind us and had flown over us to the southwest toward Gaza, Ashkelon, Ashdod, Beersheva and S'derot. During all of these times of hearing the IDF jets I recall thinking that it's one thing to hear a sound like that when it's just general airplane activity. It was a whole different feeling to know that those jets were headed to where bombs were coming out of and then into their country's land and people.

So, once more we both contemplated if it was prudent to be going to those areas and then just left the question hanging for the time being. It was November 1. We still had a few days before we needed to make a decision whether or not to tell the people we were going to see down there that we were still coming.

A couple of days after that we arrived in Akko on the Mediterranean Coast of northwestern Israel. While there on Friday night we went to *Katzir Asher* (Messianic Jewish congregation) for their Erev Shabbat service. Erev means evening and Shabbat means Sabbath which is from sundown Friday night to sundown Saturday night. The founder of *Tents of Mercy* in nearby Kiryat Yam, Eiton Shishkoff, gave the message that night – about none other than the fact that our security and safety are in the Lord and we can trust in Him to protect us. We looked at each other and said, "Maybe that's telling us to go south after all."

The next morning we went to the Shabbat service at Kiryat Yam, the original *Tents of Mercy* congregation near Haifa. We saw Eiton again but he did not give the message. Another gentleman did and...take one guess what HIS topic was: our security and safety are in the Lord and we can trust in Him to protect us. That did it! We made the decision then and there to go south and trust in the Lord's continued protection of us which resulted in a testimony of how he did it which you'll soon read. It was as if He literally wrote it in the sky for us with those jets and then with those two back-to-back messages.

So, we told our contact in S'derot that we were coming for certain. We spent a few more days in Akko which included time to go through the Akko prison where extraordinary things happened at the beginning of Israel's 1948 War of Independence. On November 9 we headed that little car to S'derot to the *Hands of Mercy* ministry where we helped pack emergency boxes for bombing victims in the town and did some other work to help out.

One of the things we saw in most houses and businesses all over Israel was what was called their Safe Room – essentially a bomb shelter cubicle. Many put their offices in their Safe Room which is where the *Hands of Mercy* office was. Our new friends there took us to the house two doors down where we would spend the next five nights. Lo and behold, the guest room of the house was its Safe Room – even equipped with a baby crib and stuffed animals. So, the Lord displayed his desire to protect us as we slept five of our six last nights in The Land. We also knew that at any moment during the night we could have a lot of company.

They had also warned us that incoming bombs from Gaza would prompt a loudspeaker announcement all over town: Tseva Edom (Code Red). That meant that we had 15 seconds to move into a Safe Room. Sure enough, on our last night there we heard the Tseva Edom announcement during dinner at *Hands of Mercy*. Everyone very matter-of-factly stepped into the office Safe Room. We followed along just as calmly where we all pretended we were scared for we absolutely were not frightened at all! It appears all there felt utterly protected by the Lord as we did.

While in S'derot, this was the closest we could get to Gaza Strip – about one mile.

Almost three years later in the summer of 2014 *Hands of Mercy* sent us a photo of the playground behind the Safe Room office where the above photos were taken. Sure enough, not far from the windows behind us in those photos, a bomb out of Gaza did actually land in that playground.

These camels on that playground are really bomb shelters for the children – as are several other critters there.

The experience of huddling in a bomb shelter together was a profound end to the profound day we had just spent with these new friends at *Hands of Mercy* by taking a day trip across the country (an hour and a half away) over to the Dead Sea area to explore Sodom, Gomorrah and Ein Gedi. It had been a glorious day that included *Sodom Shofar Sounding.*

Sodom Shofar Sounding

Even if you hadn't seen my Mountain Man's brown beaver felt hat in The Land already, this moment would still be a classic. We explored the ruins of one of the sites proposed to be Sodom where sulfur rained down to destroy it during the time of Abraham.

Armed with our shofars that we had purchased in Jerusalem, Trapper was clad in his Mountain Man fringed shirt and...that famous hat.

I was in my tasseled blouse from Jerusalem.

Accompanied by our S'derot friends from *Hands of Mercy*, we enthusiastically sounded our shofars in Sodom.

There are many spiritually significant reasons for sounding a shofar. One of them is for calling in God's presence to a place. We figured Sodom was a place where God and His commandments were ignored in days past so a good place to honor Him for our part.

WAAAAYYYY up above me and to the right at the top of the ridge is a structure.

We both hiked up to it.

But Trapper climbed up on it for a Shofar Sounding from the highest place at Sodom.

I was so intrigued by the terrain up there just below the structure that I stayed behind enough to capture Trapper's trek back down to the flats.

This terrain was spongy and flaky. It was such an experience to stand there and imagine the judgement that purportedly happened there in Abraham's day some 4000 years ago.

Your Own Shofar Sounding

This *Mountain Man and Wife* encourage you to mentally insert yourself into this photo and aspire to making a physical *Journey* to Israel. Whether you go there or not, you can spiritually embrace the significance of Israel to the world as God's extraordinarily appointed Land.

We loaned one of the shofars we had with us to our *Hands of Mercy* friend – Aaron from Brazil. He joined us in calling in God's presence, praising His sovereignty and celebrating many of the other meanings of sounding the shofar in this place.

From Sodom our caravan of three cars traveled north a few miles to En Gedi where we had a picnic and then walked the trail with *The Pathfinder's Pathfinder*.

256

The Pathfinder's Pathfinder

Mountain Men are pathfinders and trail blazers and sign finders of the first order. Many are the times that I have been with Trapper when he has shown me sign and figured out a whole history of what has transpired in a certain area which I never would have spotted before. So now I am even able to do some of that and share it with him. He has taught me well but he is still the expert in that area – and always will be.

Trapper was also an elk hunting guide for about 20 years – most of which were before we met. That is to say, the man knows how to read sign...yessiree.

So in The Land, it was with a delightful sense of amusement that we were adopted by an Ibex at Ein Gedi that decided we needed a pathfinder since he didn't know my Mountain Man's capabilities.

Trapper figured he could find that waterfall – being the pathfinder and sign reader he is.

A sign along the trail said, "Caution! Ibex may cause stones to roll down...Wait for the animals to pass before continuing along the trail." But our personal Ibex was not about waiting for him to pass.

This critter had unabashedly appointed himself to lead us to the waterfall we were seeking and he insisted upon accomplishing his task. As he walked, we followed. Do you think this is how God often wishes we would respond to His lead???

Sometimes we even stopped on the trail to see if he would continue with his persistence.

When we stopped, he stopped – every time – and looked at us as if to say, "C'mon already. Let's get going. Follow me." We did and he took us to...

Ein Gedi – a place that inspires worship

David hid out from Saul at Ein Gedi and there he even snuck up to him and cut off a corner of Saul's robe (1 Samuel 24). It appears to be a place that inspires mischief. It sure inspired Trapper, because at home and anywhere he can find – even in Israel – he is my *Mountain Man Who Kids The Kids.*

Mountain Man Who Kids The Kids

As much as Trapper is a Mountain MAN, he also has a KID-at- heart nature to him. That nature came out in a mountainous way in Israel.

At En Gedi he decided not to heed the cables and signs telling him not to go into the water below the waterfall. He wanted in and in he went.

But, just as his toes hit the water on the other side of the cable, a group of what appeared to be an Israeli version of the Boy Scouts showed up. They arrived as one big bundle of energy at just that moment. They figured that if the guy with the big brown hat on could go in that water, so could they and they piled in around him.

Their leader told the boys to get out of the water. Then he and Trapper had quite a conversation about the challenge of implementing some form of discipline while also letting boys be boys. He must have realized that he was talking to a big kid in Trapper.

Truth be told, Trapper was rather proud of himself for causing such a ruckus.

And then the man motioned for us to stand together — presumably so that we would have a photo of us there together there — or so we thought.

But his choice of a location for the photo is very telling. We thought his intention was to place us in front of the waterfall – which he truly did. But we have since wondered if he was also enjoying the moment of being careful to make sure the sign saying not to cross the cable into the water was his ulterior motive that he knew we would discover later – the context in which he would remember us. We think he may have taken one of these with his camera too.

After an energetic hike out with all those boys chattering enthusiastically in Hebrew the whole way, we enjoyed another funny visit with their leader. Trapper remained apologetic and we all parted company with fond memories galore and beyond the usual of Ein Gedi.

When a Jewish couple in Tel Adashim (near Nazareth) made arrangements for an Arab fella to take us around his nearby Arab village named Iksal, one of several places he showed us was a kindergarten. After those precious children sang for us as a class in English, it was time for them to go out to recess. So Trapper figured it was time for him to go out to recess with them! We call this Iksal kick ball:

Was it that brown beaver felt hat that kept these kids smiling or the fact that this gray-haired bearded adult wanted to go play with them? He was impressed with the fact that whenever they fell down, they just picked themselves up and got back in the game – no wimpy crying there!

We hope those children never forget the Mountain Man from America who played ball with them that day. We're certain we'll never forget them. We'll also never forget *Wildlife Management In The Land*.

Wildlife Management In The Land

Trapper's Mountain Man wildlife management profession did not stay at home. As you can gauge by the prolific use of the brown beaver felt Mountain Man hat, he took his persona and his name with him.

I wish (sorta) that I could tell you that he wrestled lions and bears like David did or that he dealt with a depredating jackal problem in The Land. Well, we saw some jackals run by here and there among various ruins. And Trapper Davidson really did handle some wildlife in Israel – wild...cats.

We had noticed that there are feral cats EVERYWHERE in The Land of Israel. We heard it was because long ago cats were brought in to handle the rodent problem. They did an excellent job too. We never saw one single rodent in The Land but we did see "lots and lots of cats" – as Trapper put it in his "Steps" email post...at every ruins site and even all over Old Town Jerusalem.

Hmmm. It just occurred to me that Trapper never did dictate a "Cats" email sequel as intended at the end of his "Steps" post. Too bad because he had plenty of material for it.

Just like all those other places in The Land, S'derot had a major feral cat over-population situation going on. So, when the folks at *Hands of Mercy* heard that a Trapper was on his way there to S'derot, within minutes, no kidding... really...minutes of our arrival they had him outfitted with a feral cat trap. We had told them before our arrival that we were available for service work so to please put us to work when we arrived. Well they sure did! We'd never seen a trap quite like this one before but that's what they had there waiting for us.

You can see that Trapper took his job very seriously during his morning coffee in S'derot. I helped...get the coffee.

It didn't take long to catch one...

...and another one

...and another one.

Yep - they were pretty darn easy to trap.

In case you're wondering, they were all released to a better local place for them to live.

When we were invited to a Torah study there in S'derot, we all enjoyed watching Trapper have a conversation with a domestic cat. No one was asking him to trap that one.

Also while in S'derot, we were blessed to have the opportunity to help pack survival boxes for bombing victims with folks from *Hands of Mercy*.

Speaking of local things, as you read earlier we were emphatic about using the local currency wherever we went so we were using Shekels all over Israel. There was one coin of which we experienced no shortage in The Land... the *Half A Shekel For Schaffer*.

Half A Shekel
For Schaffer

One of the best stories related to the entire *Journey To The Land* began just before we left in October 2011 and has continued to acquire additions since our return. In fact, it is quite possibly still gaining momentum while you are reading these pages.

On Sunday, October 2, 2011 we were three days out from departure on the *Journey To The Land* and were asked to stand before our church congregation to tell them a little about our upcoming trip and to also have the congregation pray for us and our travels.

Trapper and I pre-arranged it that he would speak first and then I would speak. He was wearing a cammo shirt and I was wearing my *Dream* slippers in order to make the point that I was "standing on a dream" to be making this trip and that I would be wearing these slippers on the airplanes.

And so Trapper began his part with a story which I knew absolutely nothing about until he was telling it in front of everyone that morning during the service.

This is when I found out that I had been dreaming in ways I knew not of until that moment. But sharing such things is when Trapper shines the best:

"Two things wake me up in a hurry. One is the sound of gunfire. The other is the sound of my wife slamming her hand on my pillow like she did last night [and he demonstrated by slamming his right hand down onto his left hand – WHAP!] and saying, 'Let's give Schaffer a half a shekel'. Then she did it again [again he demonstrated with his hands – WHAP!] and said, 'Let's give Schaffer a half a shekel'. She was about to do it again when I piped up with, 'I have an idea. Let's give Schaffer a half a shekel.' 'Okay', she said, put her head back down on her pillow and went back to sleep."

I stood there stunned and staring quizzically at my husband while he shared the tale. And then we all busted up laughing. Apparently I had really been asleep during this whole thing the night before because I had absolutely no memory of it. All I could figure was that I had been busy memorizing the currencies of the three countries we would be going to – Egypt, Jordan and Israel – in order to know the exchange rates in an attempt to avoid overpaying for anything.

I had thus logged in the New Israeli Shekel but honestly had no conscious recollection of logging in anything about a Half Shekel although we later discovered its great Biblical significance.

Hang on — I'll get to that in a minute. But we see it as even an enhancement to this story that we didn't recall consciously knowing about the Biblical significance of the Half Shekel yet because it has become a testimony of God's powerful design of our brains to be able to unconsciously retain things without our knowledge only to crop up at a later time as needed. Anytime something creates a laugh at the same time that it shows God's handiwork — well, I would say that it is needed in this world.

Also, at the time we could not recall knowing anyone with the last name of Schaffer.

So, with difficulty keeping on track in my comments, I got through whatever it was that I said to the congregation and we sat down...still laughing at Trapper's part in our brief presentation a few minutes before.

Three days later the *Journey To The Land* began in earnest as you have been reading about here.

A week into it, after visiting Egypt and Jordan, we were finally in Israel for our first day and on the tour bus sitting a few seats behind our Israeli guide, Micky. We had not had any time yet to go to an ATM and withdraw local currency as usual so we had not seen any coins in Israel yet.

Suddenly one of our fellow pilgrims came from behind us down the aisle of the bus with a gold colored round something in his hand and said, "Hey Micky. What is this coin with a one over a two on one side?"

"It's a Half Shekel," replied Micky.

We could not be contained.

We laughed so hard we were drawing inquiring smiles from many of the *pilgrims* on the bus with us.

In due time we explained that we had no idea such a coin as a Half Shekel had ever existed, why news of it had impacted us so comically and that we certainly had no idea it was spendable legal tender in today's Israel! As you can see it has 1/2 on one side and an image symbolic of David's harp on the other.

Turns out there's a lot about the Half Shekel in the Bible – Old and New Testament. We soon were told by others on the bus and also by Micky about those references. So we're guessing that at various points in my Biblical studies over the years I had read those and they were loaded into my brain. But I am certain that I had not consciously thought about them during my recent exchange rate studies or at any other time that I recall during our preparation study for this *Journey*.

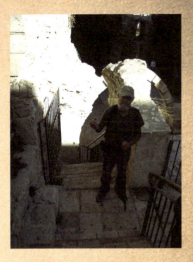

We learned that the Half Shekel was a Temple Tax that every Jewish male was required to pay each year.

There is the story of the coin that Yeshua instructed Peter to pull out of the mouth of the first fish he caught on a particular day and was to use it to pay the Temple Tax for both of them (Matthew 17). In some translations the Greek drachma is referenced but my understanding is that it is really referring to the same amount value as the Half Shekel. In the Davidson Center in Jerusalem, there was more info about the Half Shekel there. The low light made it impossible to get a clear photo in a hurry but here's what part of the panel in English explained:

The Half-Sheqel Tax

During the Second Temple period, the practice of collecting the Half-Sheqel Tax, earmarked for the maintenance of the Temple, was reinstituted. This was a uniform tax – half a Tyrian silver sheqel (equivalent to 130 perutot). The pilgrims required moneychangers to convert their own currencies into the half-sheqel coin. The New Testament relates that during a visit to the Temple Mount, Jesus overturned the tables of the moneychangers, accusing them of dishonesty and usury
– Matthew 21:12

With so much information coming at us so fast, I had good intentions at the time of researching Biblical references to the Half Shekel more after we returned home in November 2011 but then it just didn't happen until…

In early 2014 we received one of our occasional emails from the City of David – Ancient Jerusalem. We had signed up to receive their emails the day we did the Temple Mount Sifting Project in Jerusalem while there. This particular email mentioned a special offering of a necklace with a pendant made from a replica of a real Half Shekel coin actually found at the same place where we had sifted the Temple Mount dirt – one from the 66-67 AD period of the revolt against Roman rule.

After all of this about the Half Shekel how could we NOT order one? It was shipped straight from Jerusalem and it arrived at the Crested Butte post office a couple of weeks later. We considered that to be a quick trip under the circumstances.

Trapper put it on my neck for the first time on the first night of Passover – April 14, 2014. We then went out on our deck and took photos of each other sounding our shofar at the full moon – the night of the first Blood Moon of four in the coming year.

Then, just a few days after that, while selecting some of our *Journey* photos for this book, I ran across this photo that I took at the Temple Mount Sifting Project. By golly, right in the middle of the display were enlarged photos of the Half Shekel discovered there. I had not noticed the First Century Half Shekels in it before – the one the necklace I now wear is fashioned after.

During the same few days, while doing my reading for a study on The Tabernacle, I ran across this:

The Lord spoke to Moses, saying: When you take a census of the Israelite people, according to their enrollment, each shall pay the Lord a ransom for himself on being enrolled, that no plague may come upon them through their being enrolled. This is what everyone who is entered in the records shall pay: a half shekel...as an offering to the Lord. Everyone who is entered in the records, from the age of twenty ears up, shall give the Lord's offering: the rich shall not pay more and the poor shall not pay less than half a shekel when giving the Lord's offering as expiation for your persons. You shall take the expiation money from the Israelites and assign it to the service of the Tent of Meeting; it shall serve the Israelites as a reminder before the LORD as expiation for your persons.
– Exodus 30:11-16 (MJSHB)

Another version of the Old Testament puts the last part this way:

The rich are not to give more than a half shekel and the poor are not to give less when you make the offering to the LORD to atone for your lives. Receive the atonement money from the Israelites and use it for the service of the Tent of Meeting. It

will be a memorial for the Israelites before the LORD, making atonement for your lives."
– Exodus 30:15-16 (NIV)

The Tent of Meeting was the tent at the western end of The Tabernacle which housed the Holy Place which housed the Holy of Holies inside of which was the Ark of The Covenant. So now much has come together in one big picture for us about the Half Shekel and related things. Here's what we've learned so far but, knowing God, He's not done with this yet and we'll be finding out more for a long time to come:

We started the *Journey* with a Half Shekel story of our own so comically shared by my Mountain Man. Within a few days we went to Sinai where Moses received the instructions for The Tabernacle directly from God along with the Half Shekel offering instructions and then built The Tabernacle. We then discovered on our first day in Israel that there is a Half Shekel in use as currency today and saw a display about the Temple Tax history of it in the Davidson Center there. We then went to Shiloh where the same Tabernacle built in Sinai was placed a few years after the Israelites returned to The Land after the Exodus through Sinai and remained there for 369 years.

And then – as we shared this story with various folks we met all over The Land – we were given quite a number of Half Shekels which we dropped into Shabbat (Sabbath) service offering containers all over The Land hoping that somewhere out there someone named Schaffer would benefit from those symbolic offerings even though their value at the time was only about 10 cents each in US Dollars.

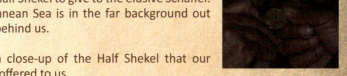

It developed that everyone we told the story to wanted to get in on the Half Shekel blessing. After discovering the original meaning of it in Exodus 30 – as Atonement or Ransom Money for our lives – now we understand even more why the Israelis who already knew that wanted to give them to us to give away.

Moshe and Tina Nagar own the bed and breakfast where we stayed for several nights in Akko. Moshe (Moses in Hebrew) was enthralled with our Half Shekel story and was one of those who insisted on giving us a Half Shekel to give to the elusive Schaffer. The Mediterranean Sea is in the far background out that window behind us.

Below is a close-up of the Half Shekel that our friend Moshe offered to us.

I found this gift from our Moshe so incredibly symbolic given the origin of the Half Shekel.

Tina took us on a very thorough private and spiritually focused excursion around Akko during our time there.

So, to summarize – because Yeshua died just before sundown began on that very extraordinary Passover and then was resurrected three days later, it is also a time of celebration of Yeshua's sacrifice as a ransom for our lives. On the first night of Passover 2014 my Mountain Man put a Half Shekel necklace of ransom money around my neck. The notion that I am now wearing something of such beyond-the-usual symbolism of the ransom Yeshua paid for our ransom is staggering to me.

For God is one, and there is but one Mediator between God and humanity, Yeshua the Messiah, himself human, who gave himself as a ransom on behalf of all, thus providing testimony to God's purpose at just the right time.
– 1 Timothy 2:5-6 (CJB)

But God was not done with this yet! A few days after Trapper gave me the Half Shekel necklace, on April 19, 2014 we saw a story on *Huckabee* about an organization called *Heroes To Heroes* (www.HeroesToHeroes.com) that sends American military veterans suffering from both physical and emotional war injuries over to Israel to spend time with folks in the IDF (Israeli Defense Force) to share their experiences and gain emotional support along with walking in The Land in order to feel closer to the God Who created them. We heard testimony of how this experience had saved some of their lives and how they had come to know the Lord through that time in The Land.

When Mike Huckabee introduced the founder of *Heroes To Heroes*, her name appeared right there in front of us on our TV screen…Judy SCHAFFER!!! Oh hallelujah (Hebrew for *Praise to God*) – we finally found our Schaffer to whom we needed to send Half Shekels (except we send them in U.S. Dollars).

As committed supporters of our troops and veterans, as passionate lovers of The Land of Israel and as the recipients of this Half Shekel story, we remain amazed at how the Lord continually weaves such things together so wonderfully – and creates the pieces of the puzzle of which we are often unaware until He reveals the whole picture. Only He knows if He has more to add to our Half Shekel experiences in the future.

In the meantime, we love the additional meaning of the equality in the Lord that the Half Shekel symbolizes – how in God's eyes we're all His children and all greatly loved by Him.

The rich are not to give more than a half shekel and the poor are not to give less when you make the offering to the LORD to atone for your lives.
– Exodus 30:15 (NIV)

We thank God for his comical as well as powerful symbolism of the Half Shekel's significance in our lives and the abundance of ways He continues to weave together revelation of our *Hebraic and Other Heritage Roots.*

Mountain Man and Wife
back into our Rocky Mountain Life

with greater insight

God's Words of special meaning in this
Life as a
Mountain Man's Wife

...I have presented you with life and death, the blessing and the curse. Therefore, choose life, so that you will live, you and your descendants, loving Adonai your God, paying attention to what he says and clinging to him – for that is the purpose of your life!
– Deuteronomy 30:19-20 (CJB)

...focusing on Yeshua, the initiator and perfector of faith.
– Hebrews 12:2 (MJSHB)

Delight yourself in the LORD and he will give you the desires of your heart.
– Psalm 37:4 (NIV)

For I know the plans I have for you," declares the LORD, "plans to prosper you and not to harm you, plans to give you hope and a future.
– Jeremiah 29:11 (NIV)

No temptation has seized you except what is common to man. And God is faithful; he will not let you be tempted beyond what you can bear. But when you are tempted, he will also provide a way out so that you can stand up under it.
– 1 Corinthians 10:13 (NIV)

Train up a child in the way he should go and when he is old he will not turn from it."
– Proverbs 22:6 (NIV)

Blessed are those whose strength is in you, who have set their hearts on pilgrimage.
– Psalm 84:5 (NIV)

I rejoiced with those who said to me, "Let us go to the house of the LORD." Our feet are standing in your gates, O Jerusalem.
– Psalm 122:1-2 (A Psalm of Ascent) (NIV)

Hebraic and Other
Heritage Roots

It is an honorable aspiration to know where you came from. We have discovered that knowing where you came from can be quite helpful in following the Lord's lead to where He wants you to go in life.

During the first day on our own in Israel we went shopping in Old City Jerusalem by ourselves. No group to follow around now or stay on schedule with – just the two of us picking our way through masses of people milling around in the narrow streets.

As we wandered by a T-shirt shop we saw a display of several with American college mascots and logos on them – something we considered odd considering we were in the Middle East. Trapper commented, "If we see one with the Georgia Bulldog on it we'll have to get it." He certainly knows where I came from.

Trapper then left me in a shop where I was busy picking out a beautiful multi-colored silk skirt. You've seen a photo of me wearing that skirt and kissing Trapper on *Faith* in a previous story. I call it my "Jerusalem Skirt". I wear at on various special occasions and whenever we share a presentation about Israel.

Well soon here came Trapper grinning from ear to ear under that brown beaver felt Mountain Man hat. He said, "You've got to see this."

I paid for my Jerusalem Skirt and followed him. Lo and behold he had found *Uga* – the University of Georgia bulldog mascot logo – on a T-shirt in that shop.

Of course we bought it!

I later put it on when we walked to the shore of the Mediterranean Sea near Akko.

You'll see a close-up of it in a couple of pages.

271

Three and a half years later and three months before the publication of this book, in March of 2015 we traveled to my hometown of Athens, Georgia for the wedding of one of our nephews plus all sorts of reunions and events that week with family and friends. And yes, I wore my Jerusalem Skirt to this special occasion of the wedding. As we were leaving the reception and in the parking lot across from the Methodist Church where I had been raised – the church roots of my faith in the Lord and where the wedding had been earlier that night – a gal we didn't know who was walking with a man to a car nearby called out to me, "Nice skirt!"

"Thanks," I responded over the parked cars. "It's from Jerusalem."

"Wow," came the response back. And then we all drove away in our respective vehicles.

We don't know who that couple was but maybe the Lord will use that moment to inspire them to go to Israel too. We hope He will use us to inspire that in lots of people for the rest of our lives. We offer a ministry outreach of encouraging travel to Israel and doing presentations about it. There's more in the *Afterwords* section about that. It is named in honor of Yeshua and as a play on our last name of Davidson----------------> **Son of David** *Sojourns*

Maybe this book will be used to get YOU there (if you haven't yet been), eh? We unabashedly declare that all need to discover, keep alive and revive our understanding of the importance of Israel in God's eyes and take our stand in support of Israel and the Jewish people. Anti-Semitism is absolutely unacceptable. Biblical and contemporary history teach us that.

Along those lines, in *What's In A Name* I mentioned that we are researching the possibility of Jewish heritage in each of our family lineages. We already have an understanding that Judaism is at the very root of our faith in Yeshua and that, as descendents of Abraham (which many of us are), we are counted as being of the house of Israel and are additionally grafted into the olive tree of this heritage through faith in Yeshua (Romans 11).

So, the Lord's timing of having someone call out to me right by THAT particular church in reference to The Land of His Chosen People, Israel, given the understanding He has now given me and my Mountain Man about the significance and importance of Israel and our Hebraic roots...well, He continues to amaze us daily. That couple could not have known the symbolism of that moment to us but God knew what He was up to with it in giving me an appreciation of the place where my roots in Him were established and that now we are grafting in a further understanding of the Hebraic roots of what belief in Yeshua is all about. On top of that, He arranged it so that my Mountain Man husband who represents my adult life after my childhood in that church in Athens, Georgia was there to tie it all together – past, present and future.

While there in Athens we also drove around the University of Georgia campus and I pointed out to Trapper the UGA Grady School of Journalism from which I had received my undergraduate degree in 1976 by walking onto the Sanford Stadium field to retrieve it.

We then walked on the bridge that overlooks Sanford Stadium and I reminisced about childhood, high school and college memories there on that field as well as the one time we have attended a UGA football game there together as an engagement gift from my cousin, Lee Epting, the weekend we became engaged which was also at the same time as my Dad's funeral (*Sir, I Promise I'll Do Her No Wrong*).

But before peering over the bridge we shared a precious time at the nearby University of Georgia Bookstore. Trapper had been to this bookstore once 22 years before. Two of my nephews took us there to outfit Trapper with a UGA T-shirt and ball cap in order to properly welcome him into the family just before the kickoff of that game we attended together there during our engagement in 1993.

But this time we took our Hebrew UGA logo T-shirt into the same bookstore in a Ziploc bag. We looked and looked but couldn't find what we were looking for. Finally I spotted a gal who seemed to be quite friendly thinking that she might get a kick out of what we had with us in that bag and could help us.

She was definitely the right gal! I laid out the Hebrew logo T-shirt..."Bet you don't have one of THESE!" We told her that we had been advised that it says "Georgia Dawgz" (yes a Z is intended here). She loved it, especially since UGA fans love to say "Go Dawgs", agreed that they didn't have any of those in stock and said, "I know what you're looking for. Follow me." She led us to the perfect shirt rack and there it was...the closest they had to – THE TRANSLATION!

After that, at Trapper's suggestion we drove over to Oconee Hill Cemetery, the entrance to which is on the back side of Sanford Stadium. While watching Georgia football games on TV I often watch to see if the coverage includes a glimpse of this cemetery back there. I had not been to our family plot in over 10 years so it was time for a visit to the graves of my parents and grandparents, a marker for my Dad's brother (Harry Epting) who died in The Battle of the Bulge in World War II (cousin Lee's father) plus some other markers.

273

True to the Lord's way of tying the past to the present and future, just as we pulled up to the grave side there our cell phone rang. We started not to answer it but, for some reason, Trapper answered it anyway. It was a gal in Crested Butte who had a live mouse in her toilet and had found our Yellow Pages listing under Pest Control. My practical Mountain Man Trapper replied, "Well, flush the toilet..." and then handed the phone to me.

I briefly shared the nature of the rodent control services of our business to her and then said, "But we're in Athens, Georgia right now. Could we call you when we get back there in a few days?" Of all the crazy things – of all the people who could have called at that particular moment, our caller enthusiastically replied, "My husband and I met there in Athens at Georgia and we have just moved to Crested Butte two months ago!" I couldn't help but tell her EXACTLY where we were. I figured she knew the campus and nearby Athens layout and could probably appreciate the gravity (pun intended) of the moment.

We took care of their mouse issue as soon as we returned to Colorado.

What a way to kick off a customer relationship! – another pun intended considering the football stadium and game references and the touchdown T-shirt photo in the story here. That call could not have been timed any better.

So what a way to tie together the roots of past, present and future although we have found ways to do that at other times in our marriage. For example, when Trapper arranged it for Bridger to watch the current live mascot, *Uga*, on TV during a football game broadcast.

In 2002 we went to Athens for my 30th High School Reunion. Trapper had to do some identification adjustment this time by wearing a name tag with my high school senior portrait on it. He got a big kick out of telling some folks how long it'd been since he'd seen them when in truth he'd never met them in his life. My aunt in Athens put him up to that and he had much fun with it.

Full Circles that take us back to our roots have greatly blessed our marriage. We fully believe this phenomenon will continue *The Whole Time*.

The Whole Time

As mentioned in a previous story, whenever Trapper is asked how long we've been married, he is fond of replying, "The whole time."

He says that gives him a chance to add up the number of years while the inquirer is still laughing.

Such is the nature of walking life on Earth with not only my Mountain Man but especially with our very creative Almighty God who astonishingly put us together as a team for...*The Whole Time.*

He chose me as the writer to chronicle the antics and character of my Mountain Man who provides the material inspired by Almighty God – the Him in the opening story title, the Him who loves historic significance partly because He was and is and is to come (Revelation 4:8) and because He is the same Him who loves to create meaningful symbolism and creative irony in the lives of His people. What a privilege it is to be loved so much by Him that He takes great joy in creating such moments in our lives.

We offer these stories to give abundant credit where the credit is due and to offer glory to Him with His purpose in mind as the purpose in the telling of them.

We thank Him for giving me the gift of sharing with Trapper, and now with you, this *Life as a Mountain Man's Wife.*

And so we celebrate in these stories the often comical, sometimes confounding or preciously sentimental but never boring life He has given us by saying...

which is Hebrew for

L'Chaim - To Life!

275

We purchased this *Mountain Man* statue
two days into our marriage during the Ouray, Colorado
part of our honeymoon in honor of our
Life to come *as a Mountain Man and Wife*
– whatever that *Life* had in store for us.

Life
as a

Mountain
Man's
Wife

Afterwords

Encouragement To Tell The Tales

My Mountain Man husband, Trapper or Al Davidson, has been an on-going source of encouragement once we both recognized that the writing skills God gave me were meant for writing narrative – not just for use as a handy tool in various endeavors.

There was the day in 1999 that we both received a word from the Lord that I needed to be writing. We received it separately but simultaneously. When we were back together that afternoon, Trapper said to me, "I need to share with you what the Lord said to me today...you need to be writing." I was astounded because I too had received that same word while doing some other work. While working that day I had begun feeling so out of sync and came to a place of sitting down in a chair and crying because I knew I was not doing what I was supposed to be doing – writing. So, when Trapper came home and said what he did, we knew it was most assuredly a calling to be heeded. This book has been in the works ever since – along with many other publications that have come about since then.

The Lord gave to me and my Mountain Man the extraordinary blessing of friendship with another true character in nearby Gunnison, Colorado – Phoebe Cranor. Early on in our friendship when Phoebe would introduce me to folks she would say, "When I first met Fae and her husband I thought, 'If I were God I would not have put those two together.' But the more we've gotten to know each other the more I understand that He really knew what He was doing." She knew we were very different from each other and that the Lord had a plan that would make amazing use of those differences. No kidding! You've just been reading about the predicaments those differences have caused in our lives together as *Mountain Man and Wife* and the various ways we've learned to sort those out.

In 1996 and 1998 Phoebe and I published two books together, _High Altitude Ranch LIfe_ and _More High Altitude Ranch Life_. It was because of these two books that we founded Davidson Publishing in the first place. These were both collections of her stories that she had been placing in a local newspaper, _Gunnison Country Times_, for several years. For both books Phoebe sat on the other side of my computer and fed the original paper manuscripts into a scanner in the same chronological order that she had submitted them to the newspaper while I punched the buttons on the computer keyboard when they came up on the screen.

One day while working on the first book, Phoebe (age 72 at the time) and I got to giggling like little girls about a way we had figured out to treat some photos and Trapper called upstairs to us, "What are you two DOING up there?" We were simply enjoying the process of putting those funny stories together. Another day during that time Phoebe said to me, "Fae, one day you'll write trapper's wife stories like I write ranch wife stories." We both knew that I had as much training to be a trapper's wife as she had had to be a rancher's wife... which was absolutely nothing in both of our cases. We both discovered that the Lord was at work in both of our lives prior to meeting our husbands such that preparation had occurred but we just didn't either one know it at those earlier times in our lives.

Well, that day of which Phoebe prophesied has arrived in the form of this collection of stories that you have just read. Phoebe went to be with the Lord in 2010 - five years ago at the time of the original publication of this book. My last conversation with her was just as precious as our friendship:
"Phoebe, I'd like to ask you something."
"You can ask me anything, Fae. You know that."
Yep, I surely did know that.
"When you get there, what's the very first thing you're gonna do?"
She'd obviously been pondering that.
"I don't know if I'm going to hug His neck or fall at His feet."

It was one of the most delightful conversations of my life because we didn't have to play any games of wondering if we should talk about death, wonder if the person knew the time was nigh or wonder about anything other than the childlike wonder of what it was going to be like. She knew where she was going, couldn't wait to get there and it was great fun to have that moment to talk with her so honestly about it just before it happened. I am sincerely grateful to the Lord – to whom Phoebe would want the credit to go anyway – for her encouragement in the writing and her example as God's gloriously gregarious Gunnison Gal.

There are many more of you out there who have encouraged the writing of these stories. Thank you for cheering me on and looking forward with us for the day this book would finally be a reality.

The Adventure of Simple Patience

by Trapper Davidson

Instant gratification. Sure seems to be the way of the world these days, doesn't it?

Some folks get impatient when the microwave takes more than a minute and some expect things shipped from anywhere to arrive the next day.

A little phone in our pocket can reach us wherever we go – with few exceptions – unless we have the presence of mind to turn it off.

Thankfully there are some havens of sanity provided through *The Adventure of Simple Patience.*

One of them is the art of trapping. And, since the name most folks know me by is Trapper, simple patience is both a constant adventure in my life and my livelihood.

Most men need a sense of accomplishment in what they do. Women do too but it's an especially common trait in men. I suppose that's because God created us to be hunters and gathers back there in the garden.

But, it ain't always easy – which makes for a much greater sense of accomplishment when we reach our goal. Too much too soon can make us unappreciative and ungrateful.

Not so with trapping.

I know when I put out a set that I am going to need to check it, tend to it, make sure it is well set and baited, expect to see it triggered and the bait or lure gone with nothing in it and more. I expect a certain amount of disappointment when nothing is in it but then that is just part of the deal.

And then, after all of that, when my goal is accomplished and my targeted critter is there I appreciate it all the more.

Many times when I've taken others out with me I listen to their expectations and see the fur market dollar signs in their eyes. I quietly keep my thoughts to myself and think, "That won't last long." More often than not, after a couple of days of coming up empty, they lose interest and move on to something with...you guessed it...instant gratification.

With trapping there is no such thing as a microwave and only occasionally is there overnight delivery. You can attempt to call animals in but you may or may not connect with them immediately like we do on our cell phones.

Speaking of cell phones, one time I was patiently moving toward an animal in a trap and was talking to him to keep him calm. The scene was quite serene and he was curled up unafraid when *The Lone Ranger* rang out in my pocket...
"Da-da-dum, da-da-dum, da-da-dum-dum-dum;
Da-da-dum, da-da-dum, da-da-dum-dum-dum..."

Darn. I had forgotten to turn off my cell phone. On top of that, to my utter dismay it was a call to the wrong number! I fought off the urge to shoot the phone so instead turned the darned thing off, turned back to the matter at hand and patiently began the process with the animal all over again. Cell phones are important to have on hand as a safety precaution and communication tool but the off button is equally important to a trapper.

I patiently got revenge on that particular cell phone. Sometime later I was tilling ground for a garden and at some point noticed my cell phone was no longer in my shirt pocket. My wife, Fae, went into the house and called the number. We found it where the ground started singing *The Lone Ranger* tune. Since it wasn't six feet under, but should've been, it amazingly survived to travel with me on many more adventures.

Nowadays my cell phone sounds like a train whistle which more than once has given me a fright while on a ladder doing exclusion work to keep bats out of a house or for some other reason. Such are the trappings of modern-day wildlife management services. It just might be Fae calling to inform me of an emergency service call needed to capture a live skunk in someone's crawl space, a porcupine in a tree on someone's deck or an owl in someone's glass-enclosed fireplace! All of those have happened, as you have just read.

Patience is also a valuable attribute when it comes to preparing pelts for market or tanning. A hurried or harried hand with a knife can make for a disaster in pelt preparation. Even the slightest slip can ruin the market value of any critter's covering. After I methodically skin and flesh out the animals I stretch and dry them which takes several days to accomplish. From time to time trappers are asked to charge a lower fee on the service of the trapping itself because the trapper will receive the pelt to sell. However, that request does not take into account the separate work and various costs involved with preparing and sending pelts either to the fur market or to a tannery. It truly is a whole separate aspect of this profession – but a rewarding one if approached with...patience.

Speaking of the fur market, it goes up and down like the stock market and depends greatly on world situations. Sometimes the market's good and sometimes it's down and the slightest event can change it in a moment... instantaneously...which does not lead to instant gratification either. So it goes. It takes patience to ride that out too. We send many pelts to market through a fur auction house in Canada that attracts worldwide buyers four times per year. But sometimes not all of the pelts sell. So then they hold onto them for us and we have to patiently wait for the next auction. Sometime later we will receive a check for whatever price at which they eventually sell.

We also send a lot of pelts to a tannery all year long and practice even more patience while we wait for the several months that process takes. Sometimes our customers want the pelts of the animals captured on their property and other times we sell them to the public. For anyone we can also coordinate the making of a hat, coat, throw, bedspread, stuffed animal or more items from the tanned pelts. It is my firm belief that no part of an animal be wasted if at all possible to find a way to make use of it. For example, many creative craft projects are made from teeth, claws, quills and more in addition to the fur. No matter the use, the preparation of whatever critter part takes time, patience and an understanding of the value of each animal which has been entrusted to the trapper.

All said and done, not much about trapping involves instant gratification – with the occasional exception of the homeowner who is ecstatic that the pack rat giving them fits and smelling up their home, the porcupine that is killing their pine trees or the beaver that is causing flooding of their pasture (plus other critter situations) is captured the first night the traps are out. That is always a joyful thing to be of such valued and immediate help. It is a boost to the spirit to have those times but certainly never something to be counted on as a regular event. If that's the goal – another profession is advisable. However I highly recommend the character development that trapping – and all hunting activities – give us hunters and gatherers.

Faithful Friend At My Feet

Hello – Fae-th again here. Bridger has faithfully overseen this whole project as the stories were being written and the layouts were being formatted in the computer.

He's sitting at my feet as I write this right now. He makes us laugh and we hope you have laughed with us.

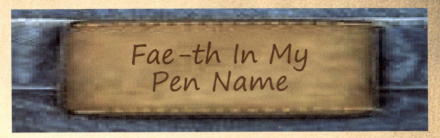

Fae-th In My Pen Name

From birth in Athens, Georgia in 1954 I was called Sissy by family and friends alike until at 10 years old I chose the name of Fae selected from my full name – Helen Fae – "because it's spelled funny" as I said to my parents, Gene and Frances Epting, at the time of making this decision. Although they raised me and my siblings in a devotedly Christian home, I mentally ran away from my church-raised roots from the age of 18 until I was 38. During those 20 years various people I met along the way would try to clarify what they had heard as my name when I was introduced to them by saying, "Is your name Faith?" My flippant response was often, "Nope but I need some."

After an astounding and unexpected revelation which brought me to *true faith* in the Lord in 1992, I realized that those quips must've been prayers for *faith* because when I did agree for God to bring me around, He generously gifted me with a gigantic portion of *faith* and I learned what a joy it is that He delights so in the giving of it:

> For by grace you have been saved through faith. And this is not from yourselves – it is the gift of God. It is not based on deeds, so that no one may boast. For we are His workmanship – created in Messiah Yeshua for good deeds, which God prepared beforehand so we might walk in them.
> – Ephesians 2:8-10 (MJSHB)

And so this book is something that I, under the pen name of *Fae-th*, *faithfully* believe that God prepared beforehand for me to write. He has been instrumental in each and every one of these stories in one way or another. They would not be the same and not even worth telling without sharing His creation of them, His outright involvement in them and the blessed perspectives He has given us as each one has happened. I offer all on these pages in *faith* that the *Shekinah* glory of God and His Son, *Yeshua*, by the power of their Holy Spirit as our three-in-one God will shine through to bless all who read them.

With an abundance of joy during our *Journey To The Land* in 2011, the owner of our bed and breakfast in Abu Ghosh, Israel found me one glorious  morning in the most extraordinary place in which I have EVER enjoyed writing so far – not only in Israel but in their courtyard *sukkah* which they had erected in observance of *Sukkot* (Feast of Tabernacles). "Fae, that's perfect!" she exclaimed with childlike delight. "You're writing in the *sukkah* you've been writing about!" So now this photo of writing there is my official Author's Photo for this journal.

Fae-th Davidson

Learned Lessons & Literary License

As I warned you could happen in the first story, there's some mangled grammar in our stories – incomplete sentences, made-up words, prepositions at the ends of sentences or thoughts, repetition of the same word or phrase, conversational style and more. I hope you were able to sit back and enjoy it all with us and did your best to avoid letting some literary license concern you.

Nope – it's surely not proper grammar in those places. The Lord blessed me with two excellent High School English teachers in Athens, Georgia in 1970-1972 who taught us well on the use of proper sentence structure, vocabulary and spelling. Then, through a degree from the Henry W. Grady School of Journalism at the University of Georgia right there in Athens, I learned about writing styles, content, continuity of thought, flow of the narrative and much more. Therefore, I would not be faithful to the excellent training gained from their lessons which I happily retained if I did not acknowledge that I KNOW BETTER than some of this writing. But, it's done here for effect, definitely on purpose and not because I forgot their fine teaching.

Junior English Teacher: To my knowledge I have never produced a written comma splice and that sacrilege is one thing my readers will absolutely NOT find in here as that would be taking literary license to an impossible place for me – for heaven's sake. A comma splice is when two complete stand-alone sentences are joined together with only a comma between them instead of a conjunction or a semicolon. I learned that lesson well from this teacher on the very first day of High School Junior English class that the one time an editor chopped up a sentence I had written and converted it to a comma splice I cried when I read it in the magazine. I then immediately and adamantly contacted him about it. When he didn't see the problem it was an easy decision to advise him that I would not be submitting any more articles for his publication in the future. Period. How could he?!

Senior English Teacher: Many have benefitted from my High School Senior English teacher's lessons of vocabulary and spelling as I have been known as the walking spell checker in many settings during my life – thanks to her persistent and excellent instruction. There was the time in our Adult Sunday School class a few years ago when the fella teaching the class wrote "Davine Calling" on the board. I saw it but restrained myself from saying anything until he saw it himself, turned to me as the speller in the room and said, "Is that right?" to which I blurted out, "Well, I just thought you meant 'I am da vine and you are da branches.' " It's a tough job but somebody has to...well, not everyone wants to do it or can do it but the Lord and my teacher gave me the know-how to do it.

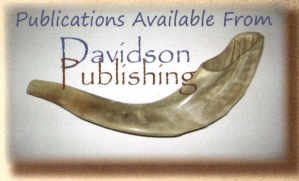

Publications Available From
Davidson Publishing

(as of June 2015)

Life as a Mountain Man's Wife
by Fae-th Davidson

A collection of tales gathered to celebrate God's gift of often comical, sometimes confounding, sometimes sentimental but never boring *Life* to this *Mountain Man and Wife.*

High Altitude Ranch Life
by Phoebe Cranor

Both of these books are comical accounts of Phoebe's life on a ranch in Gunnison, Colorado with no prior knowledge of how to do it. These stories are just as funny today as they were when they first appeared in the *Gunnison Country Times* starting in 1995 and are in the same order as when published by the newspaper.

More High Altitude Ranch Life
by Phoebe Cranor

Speaking Engagements

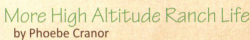

Trapper and Fae Davidson are available for speaking engagements regarding...

Life as a Mountain Man's Wife

– encouragement to answer God's call on your life
– encouragement to enjoy and find symbolic meaning in life's surprising, confounding, comical and sentimental moments even when they make no sense at first

Son of David *Sojourns*

– encouragement to travel to Israel
– encouragement to stand firm in support of Israel
– emphasis on Scriptural and geographic topics related to Israel

To schedule a presentation or ask publication information and current prices:

Website: www.Davidson-Publishing.com

Email: info@Davidson-Publishing.com

The Tales & Tails Continue

When it comes to *Life as a Mountain Man's Wife*, these things appear to be a given:

My Mountain Man will continue to provide story material for the rest of our lives together and we plan to stay together for the rest of our lives.

We are going to keep recalling stories that have happened in years past which are not in this volume for some reason or another.

Other folks are going to recall some stories we have forgotten – or perhaps have conveniently ignored for some reason or another.

Thanks to all of these resources, the moments continue and the tales keep piling up to the point that there just may be a need to compile another one of these collections of them at some future date. Time and tales will tell. If that happens then here's a very likely title for it because –

Life Goes On as a Mountain Man's Wife

Should we later decide to make that additional journey journal and you come along with us, you will undoubtedly need to heed what our highway signs warn...

because where there's a Mountain Man there is sure to be wildlife.

As you've read in this collection of *Life as a Mountain Man's Wife*, not only do we encounter wildlife and livestock in the Rocky Mountains but...

A Cattle Crossing above the Kinneret (Sea of Galilee)

A Camel Crossing in the Negev Desert

...we also discovered intriguing signs of such in Israel.

We are all the recipients of stories more intricately woven together by God than any tall tale a Mountain Man could conjure up – whether we're aware of them or not.

My Mountain Man and I both hope that these stories will serve as encouragement to you to look for the Lord's hand in the stories of your own life for the whole rest of your life – *The Whole Time.*

As you have just read in the *Mountain Man and Wife in Israel* section of this book and because we have so heartily embraced The Land of Israel along with the Hebraic roots of our faith in Yeshua, we again offer this toast in Hebrew to you and yours as we head on down the trail toward more critter tales...

L'Chaim! To Life!

from

this

Mountain Man and Wife

plus all of the characters – both critter and human – that have been such creative additions to this entertaining Life.